Turning the Tune

DANCE AND PERFORMANCE STUDIES

General Editors:

Helena Wulff, *Stockholm University* and **Jonathan Skinner**, *Queen's University Belfast*

Advisory Board:

Alexandra Carter, Marion Kant, Tim Scholl

In all cultures, and across time, people have danced. Mesmerizing performers and spectators alike, dance creates spaces for meaningful expressions that are held back in daily life. Grounded in ethnography, this series explores dance and bodily movement in cultural contexts at the juncture of history, ritual and performance, including musical, in an interconnected world.

Turning the Tune

Traditional Music, Tourism, and Social Change in an Irish Village

Adam R. Kaul

Berghahn Books
New York • Oxford

Published in 2009 by
Berghahn Books

www.berghahnbooks.com

©2009, 2013 Adam R. Kaul
First paperback edition published in 2013

Library of Congress Cataloging-in-Publication Data

Kaul, Adam R.
   Turning the tune : traditional music, tourism, and social change in an Irish village
/ Adam R. Kaul.
      p. cm.
   Includes bibliographical references and index.
   ISBN 978-1-84545-623-8 (hbk) -- 978-0-85745-808-7 (pbk)
      1. Tourism—Social aspects—Ireland—Doolin. 2. Tourism—Ireland—
Doolin. 3. Folk music—Ireland—Doolin. 4. Music and tourism—Ireland—
Doolin. 5. Music and anthropology—Ireland—Doolin. 6. Doolin (Ireland)—
Economic conditions. 7. Doolin (Ireland)—Social life and customs.
G155.I7 K38 2009
306.4/819094193--dc22

                                                        2009047662

British Library Cataloguing in Publication Data

A catalogue record for this book is available from the British Library
Printed in the United States on acid-free paper.

ISBN: 978-1-84545-623-8 (hardback)
ISBN: 978-1-84545-961-1 (institutional ebook)
ISBN: 978-0-85745-808-7 (paperback)
ISBN: 978-0-85745-832-2 (retail ebook)

Contents

List of Illustrations

Preface to the Paperback Edition

Ethnographies differ from other genres of non-fiction: memoirs, travelogues, or historical accounts both celebratory and academic. They are meant to be *analytical,* but also *positioned.* In that sense, they purposefully occupy a liminal space between a subjective personal account and an objective scientific analysis. While we attempt to provide an accurate depiction of what a particular culture is like—to "say something of something," as Clifford Geertz once wrote—we recognize that everything we write is filtered through our own personal experiences of the culture during and after fieldwork. This is what is meant by positionality. For the bulk of the history of anthropology, this paradoxical space was papered over rather than exposed. As a result, a fundamental contradiction developed in the genre. The key anthropological method called participant observation has at its core the assumption that experiencing a culture firsthand, actually participating in it, gives us a unique perspective about what the society is "really like" even though we remain outsiders. At the same time, generations of ethnographers tended to present rather dry, aloof, academic texts that sublimated their own participation in the lived experience of the culture. Many older ethnographies read like formulaic recipes. Over the past few decades, however, anthropologists began to criticize this writing style because it created a false sense of clinical objectivity. As a result, in more recent decades, it has become commonplace to very consciously straddle the span between the subjective and the objective. Not only is this simply more honest, but we now realize, perhaps ironically, that a truer objectivity can be achieved if we wholly embrace the fact that ethnographic writing is always in the first instance derived from the subjective experiences of the ethnographer. This book, like most current ethnographies, is both analytical and positioned. The most fundamental aspect of my positionality is the fact that I am an outsider; I was not raised in Ireland and have no kinship ties to the community I describe. However, I have spent a good deal of time there over the past decade and feel that I know the place well. Though I will always be an outsider, I have been graciously welcomed into peoples' home and into their lives. The positionality in this book is also temporal. Ethnographies are based on a particular period of fieldwork, typically a year, but a single year cannot capture all of the nuances of peoples' lived experiences in that one place *over time.* All cultures are dynamic just as all individuals are, and if we fail to acknowledge their development, we run the risk of presenting them as static and unchanging. I make this clear in this book, but it is worth pointing out again.

I have been reflecting on these issues because it is exactly ten years ago that my wife and I first drove into the village of Doolin to begin the fourteen months of fieldwork upon which this book is based, and a lot has changed since then. In some respects, the village that is described in the following pages no longer exists. Some people have moved on or passed away, and new people have settled in the area. Babies have been born and children have grown into adults. Other things have changed as well. A huge amount of tourist development has occurred over the past decade; in fact, the built environment of the village has expanded by about a third. This has changed some of the local economic relationships, resulting in a rerouting of tourist expenditures to new businesses, for example. Another dramatic development occurred more recently. Starting in 2008, the Irish economy began to collapse under the weight of massive property inflation, bank scandals, and corruption. The Celtic Tiger, which had begun to look a little weakened during the period described in this book, is well and truly dead today. The European Union and the International Monetary Fund eventually stepped in to bail the country out, but in doing so it put huge financial stress on individual citizens as taxes went up, austerity measures were implemented, and property prices plummeted. The immigration described in this book quickly turned into emigration once again. At one point, thousands of people were streaming out of Ireland every week. The nation's immigrant population left in droves, returning to their home countries or finding new economic opportunities elsewhere, and then the Irish-born youth began to leave as well to find work in places like Britain and Australia. I cannot speak for the whole of Ireland, but for at least one recent graduating class from Doolin, a very old pattern of emigration re-emerged: young people who expected to inherit a farm or a family business stayed, but most everyone else left. Modern communication technology makes this generation's emigration experience much easier on families (gone are the days of American Wakes in which young people were ritually mourned as if they were about to die when they emigrated), but still, this is a pattern of emigration that goes back well over a hundred years. This book, however, describes the kinds of social changes that were taking place during an era of economic prosperity, social exuberance, and immigration. It is in that sense that it is positioned in time.

As a result of these changes over the last decade, the music has changed in Doolin as well. Once again, the tune continues to turn. As I describe in the following pages, a decade ago, a relatively small number of the traditional musicians in the village were born and raised within the parish boundaries ("true locals" in the strictest definition of that term), and maybe half were from other parts of Ireland. The rest were musicians from South Africa, France, Britain, the United States, and elsewhere. To say the least, this was a very cosmopolitan group of people. But today, while some of these "blow-in" musicians have remained, others have moved on to other locales or to other countries, leaving a larger proportion of Irish-born musicians. There is another change that is important to note: some international blow-in musicians in County Clare have described an atmosphere that feels a bit more exclusive than it used to. Low-level tension between Irish and non-Irish musicians has been described by other authors in other contexts, but a decade ago in Doolin it was something that was notably absent. It is difficult to know if the cross-cultural inclusivity described in *Turning the Tune* is the more typical pattern or not. One might argue the case either way. Perhaps inclusivity is more the norm but recent economic pressures in Ireland brought cultural boundaries more to the fore, or conversely, perhaps the Celtic Tiger era was so ebullient that people could afford to be more inclusive. Finally, the economic downturn, combined with a smoking ban in pubs, tighter enforcement of drunk driving laws, increased living costs, decreased wages, and a significant decrease in tourist numbers from abroad have depressed the atmosphere in the pubs these days. Today, the pubs are far less populated at night, and people go home early. Places with historically strong tourist economies like Doolin have fared the economic storm far better than other towns and villages, but the *craic* is not as "mighty" in Ireland as it was when the Celtic Tiger was in full swing. Taking the long view, the following ethnography might have captured an anomalous rather than typical moment in Irish history. I hope prosperity will return to Ireland, but time will tell. Having said all of that, there is still plenty of great music to be heard in the pubs around northwest County Clare. Unlike a generation ago, there does not seem to be any doubt that the traditional Irish music in Doolin and the surrounding area is alive and well. Tourism, globalization, and immigration have changed many things about the tradition, but they have also ensured its long-term survival.

Even before the first edition of this book went to press in 2009, I showed the manuscript to almost everyone who was interviewed and got their approval. I also had it vetted by the village book club (which was frankly a more nerve-wracking experience than my Ph.D. dissertation defense). Since then, I've had some interesting reactions to the book. One of the highest compliments that I received was from one Doolin resident who told me that I describe the development of relationships between locals and blow-ins in a way that he'd been experiencing day-to-day his entire life but had never fully recognized before. Now, he told me, he understood some of his own relationships in the village better. This, to me, is the strength of the etic perspective: outsiders can sometimes see things that are too close to those who live them on a daily basis. Others have told me that the description of sessions, something that is notoriously difficult to explain, does a good job of capturing the experience. Not everyone in the village likes the book, however, or completely agrees with my analyses. That is to be expected. One musician was clearly hoping the book would be a celebratory history of the village musicians and was disappointed with the analytical, ethnographic tone and also the focus on tourism and blow-ins. Last year, another Doolin musician and I had a very long conversation over a few pints about positionality and how, had I interviewed different musicians, different blow-ins, different locals, etc., I would have written an entirely different book. It took him awhile to make his point. I think he thought I would be offended by this "critique" and he seemed a little surprised when I told him I could not agree with him more. It is simply true. It was a great conversation, and I was struck by the fact that he came to the same conclusion after reading one ethnography that the whole discipline of anthropology took over a hundred years to figure out!

In the end, I hope this book can shed some light on some of the complexities of tourist settings, the development of cultural traditions, and the social reality of a cosmopolitan community. One of the major points I want to make in *Turning the Tune* is that we need to avoid the simplistic conclusion that the economic and social impacts of tourism are black-and-white. In reality, things are far more nuanced (and far more interesting) than the easy binary oppositions that are too often set up between the fake and the folk, the authentic and the inauthentic, the tourist commodity and the "real thing." Likewise, the awkward relationship between money-making and music-making is a particularly contentious one for artists in many parts of the world. It seems obvious to me, however, that artists ought to be paid for their craft and that getting paid does not necessarily reduce the intrinsic quality or value of the art-form. The real danger emerges when musicians and artists lose control over the production of their art. I also hope this book makes a contribution to the understanding of immigration in Ireland, which still seems to be an understudied topic. As I write in the acknowledgements, I hope this book can act as a small piece of local history for my friends in Doolin. Finally, I want to thank, once again, everyone who has generously supported my research over the years. It would be impossible to thank everyone in Doolin by name, but I do want to extend a special thanks to the people whose frequent appearance in the following pages reflects their particular generosity: Christy Barry, Gus O'Connor, Peter Curtin, Tim Shannon, Seamus MacMahon, Stephane, and Adam Shapiro.

Acknowledgements

First and last, I thank all the people of Doolin. You have given me a great deal, and in return I hope this book can serve as a small document of local history. It is my imperfect gift to you. Inaccuracies, omissions, mistakes, and poorly phrased descriptions are all mine. The good stuff is all yours. I only hope these pages are "good enough altogether" in your eyes.

Second, I thank my wife, Becca Rice. You helped and encouraged me at every stage, starting in 1996 when, as recent college graduates with overstuffed backpacks slung across our shoulders, we first stepped off the P&O ferry onto Irish soil. Your presence during fieldwork in Doolin (where your singing is still talked about), and your own anthropological insight since then have been invaluable. You are always my first audience and the critic whose opinions matter most.

Thanks also to Tamara Kohn, my Ph.D. advisor at the University of Durham, a great friend, and a remarkable anthropologist. Your thinking has shaped mine in more fundamental ways than you probably know, and for that I cannot thank you enough.

Sean Williams and Robert Layton provided many thoughtful comments. Thank you. Sean first mentioned that I ought to go visit Doolin as a potential fieldsite, and your own insight into traditional Irish music has been invaluable over the years, so Sean: many, many thanks.

In what has been called the "reciprocal ethnographic method," the Doolin Book Club read, commented on, and critiqued an early draft of the book manuscript. Their thoughtful suggestions and careful corrections have been included within these pages. Thank you all so much, in particular Mary Jo and Cindy, for organizing that event. Thanks to everyone else in Doolin who took the time to look over the manuscript during that trip as well, including Mícheál Shannon, Stephane, Tim, Mattie and Carmel, Christy and Shiela, Orla and Skip.

Special thanks to Helena Wulff (who I first met in Ennistymon, County Clare at the end of my fieldwork), Jonathan Skinner, and Marion Berghahn for taking a second (and third) look at this project. Many thanks also to Mark Stanton and Noa Vasquez at Berghahn Books, Jim Henderson, and Caroline Richards. Many thanks go out to the anonymous reviewers whose insightful comments made the book far stronger.

Many others need naming whose support has been invaluable over the years, including Dan and Karen Edwards, Mike Michlovic, Mike Hughey, Ann Brunton,

Ron Provencher, Mark Merher, Judy Ledgerwood, Andrea Molnar, Sue Russell, Matt and Jessica Davis, Scott Smith, Julie Mauchenheimer, Sveta Yamin, Nick Ellig, and Polly Fassinger. Thanks to all the guys at the shop. Thanks to my many former professors, colleagues, and friends at Durham including Michael Carrithers, Peter Collins, Simon Coleman, Iain Edgar, Steve Lyon, Russell Hill, Catherine Panter-Brick, Paul Sant Cassia, Paul Sillitoe, Bob Simpson, Dorothy, Una, Anselma, Sal Buckler, Trudi Buck, Lisa Dikomitis, Erik Willems, Nick and Beccy, and Les Jessop. Thanks so much Sophie and Sylvan for everything! Thank you Jerry Erion, Ethan Paquin, Seana Logsdon, Daniel Kotzin, and everyone else at Medaille College. Thanks to my current colleagues at Augustana, especially Carolyn Hough, Peter Kivisto, Marsha Smith, Vicki Sommer, Paul Croll, the unstoppable Jean Sottos, Molly Todd, Jason Mahn, Kelly Daniels, Margaret Morse and Mike Batz, Margaret Farrar, Tim Bloser, Steve Warren and Kristy Nabhan-Warren, Jeff Abernathy, Mike Green, Anne Earel, and everyone at the Faculty Research Forum. My students always challenge and inspire me. Thanks in particular to those who, through their own talents, have pushed me to be a better teacher, including Sinead Devane, Ashlee Peed, Nick Kasprzak, Ian Fletcher, Ashley Stange, and Sarah Cermak. Many thanks to Sean Murphy and Jen Burnam for turning my cartoonish maps into cartographic marvels. Special thanks to Danielle Suits and Amy Howard for being my research assistants during the final stages of the manuscript's preparation, and for looking up those obscure sources for me. My family deserves thanks as well for supporting Rebecca and me over the years as we pursued what must have seemed a little crazy at times. Thanks Bob and Maryann, Leonard and Norma, Wayne and Carol, Jim and Neil, Rich and Monica, Sarah, Miriam and Randy, Isaac, Indigo, Salinger and Rowan. Thanks to Chuck and Carol, Arlene and Dotty, Rachel and JP, Ruth and Rowan.

The research for this book was financially and intellectually supported in various stages throughout the years. My Ph.D. was generously supported by an Overseas Research Studentship from the Committee of Vice Chancellors, and by a Radcliffe-Brown Trust Award from the Association of Social Anthropologists and the Royal Anthropological Institute. The Clare Local Studies Project and the County Clare Libraries at Ennis and Ennistymon provided invaluable resources for my research. Many thanks to the staff at these institutions. Institutional grants and faculty development monies were generously provided by the Department of Anthropology at the University of Durham, Medaille College, and Augustana College. The "Anthropology in Development" and "Public Cultures in Theory and Practice" research groups in the Department of Anthropology at the University of Durham provided much intellectual stimulation and support over the years, while a student, a lecturer, and as an honorary research associate there. The Faculty Research Forum at Augustana College has been similarly supportive.

Lastly, (I did say first and last after all), thanks again to the people of Doolin, to whom this book is dedicated.

Chapter 1

Introduction

There is an older way of talking about instrumental styles of traditional Irish dance music that has perhaps begun to fade in recent years. A typical traditional Irish tune is divided into two 16–bar parts which are often simply called the A part and the B part. But in that older language these parts are called "the tune" and "the turn." Playing music is even called "turning a tune." "In this way," Micheál Ó Súilleabháin wrote, "'turning' has a wider meaning which could be taken as synonymous with the creative process itself" (1990: 119). It is a notion that emphasizes the playing of music (and playing with music) rather than focusing solely on its structure. In one sense, this book is about the creative process of "turning," writ large. It is about diverse actors in one particular place who adapt to, play with, and play within changing structures—musical structures as well as social.

To be more specific, this book is an ethnographic description of a small village called Doolin on the west coast of Ireland, which is undergoing rapid social change as a result of globalization, tourism, and immigration. It pays particular attention to the complicated, contested, and multivalent spaces, conceived both literally and figuratively, between tourism and public performances of traditional Irish music. Diverse categories of people interact in these spaces pushing along the social change that occurs there including—to give names to just a few—locals, tourists, incomers (who are sometimes called "blow-ins" in Ireland), and musicians.

Doolin's popularity among tourists is due not only to the beautiful natural landscape that surrounds the village, but also because it has an international reputation for traditional Irish music "sessions". Sessions are not concerts. They are more casual gatherings of musicians who generally share a common repertoire of traditional music from the Irish and Scottish instrumental traditions. Sessions are social events as much as they are musical events. A great deal of chatting, joking, and general interaction occurs. Unlike a concert, the boundaries between the session and the surrounding environment are porous, and the musical performance becomes one aspect of a larger social milieu.

At the very height of the summer tourist season, going to experience one of the nightly sessions in one of Doolin's three pubs can be a bit of a task. Even though the coastal village is home to less than six hundred permanent residents, well over a thousand tourists can pass through each day during the busiest weeks. In the daytime tourists commonly walk the country lanes, hike through the stony landscape called the Burren, take daytrips to the Aran Islands, lounge around at the seaside, or drive up to the Cliffs of Moher which can be seen from the shore at Doolin. At night they flock into the pubs for a meal, for drinks, and to hear a session. In a village this small, with few venues for public social interaction besides the diminutive grocery store, the pubs act as the hub of the local social world, a place to meet with friends and neighbors after the days' work. So before even getting in close proximity to the table where the musicians have their sessions, one must first contend with the crowds of tourists and locals.

When you pull open the pub door, a blast of noise, cigarette smoke[1], and body heat engulfs you and pulls you in. The collective low rumble of human voices is punctuated by the sharp sound of clinking glasses and small explosions of laughter. Even on a sunny summer day, the light is dim enough indoors to force you to wait for your eyes to adjust before delving any further. The locals cluster in the section of the pub furthest away from the musicians' table so that they can hear themselves talk. Usually, this gathering point for locals is nearest the main entrance, and it is this crowd that you must first squeeze through. In order to get anywhere, you must sidle closely past people dearly clutching pints of lager and stout beer. People are gathered more thickly along the bar. When you catch the barman's eye you shout your order and a pint is pulled. Once purchased, you lift your drink gingerly over the tops of the heads of people seated at the bar. Off in the next room, tourists mill around, waiting intently for the music to start. Even though it is close to 9:30 in the evening, some people are still finishing up meals. The bar staff rush around trying to keep up. Every table is occupied, and every stool, chair and bench is filled. People also stand in packs along the wood-paneled walls. On particularly busy nights, there is barely any standing room either. The crowd, predominantly consisting of tourists, creates a carefree and expectant atmosphere.

When the musicians arrive, the designated table (with the "reserved for musicians" sign fixed onto the wall behind it) is cleared. The current occupants are asked to find somewhere else to sit. The crowd stirs a little as the musicians sit down, pull their instruments from their cases, and tune up. One of the musicians orders a round of drinks. Cigarettes are passed around and smoked. Eventually, someone behind the bar flips a switch and the small microphones that dangle inconspicuously over the musicians' table crackle to life. One of the musicians starts to play a tune and the rest chime in after a few seconds. The crowd moves in closer. On particularly busy nights, it is nearly impossible to see the musicians because they play behind a semi-circular wall of humanity. In order to see what is going on, you must find an opening and move in quickly before someone standing next to you does. The pace of the jigs and reels is clipped, with a steady rhythm. Feet tap and heads bob slightly as the musicians tear through the instrumental pieces. The tunes are catchy and exciting, but they are so fast that, to the untrained ear, it is sometimes difficult to pin down a distinct melody, which is complicated by rhythmic flourishes and grace notes. Several tunes are strung together into a "set" without a pause in between, and the set of tunes lasts ten minutes or so.[2] Cameras flash in the dim smoky light as people take pictures of the musicians. When the first set of tunes ends there is a roar of applause. The musicians pay little heed to the audience though, almost ignoring the fact that all these people are showering them with so much attention. If anything, they seem slightly sheepish about it all. They fine-tune their instruments and then settle back in their seats to talk amongst themselves. Several minutes might pass before they begin a new set of tunes, and it seems that the audience, so keen to hear this music, is a secondary concern. For the rest of the evening, the music and the periods of chatting in between are like partners taking turns, and hand in hand this goes on for hours. More musicians come in to sit around the table, others get up to leave, and they all face inwards towards each other rather than out towards the audience. There is no sign of a score or a piece of sheet music, but everyone seems to know the same tunes.

As the evening progresses, the energy in the pub ebbs and flows. There are moments when the excitement of the music seems to compel audience members to get up and dance, or to "whoop" suddenly. There are other moments, when a local singer might join the musicians for an unaccompanied *sean nós* (literally, "old style") ballad, and the room goes quiet. A tangible tension permeates the air as the singer relays some inevitably sad story in a slow, somber style. The applause afterwards is explosive. Locals cheer, "Good man yourself!" or "Lovely!" When it dies down, the musicians launch once again into another set of instrumental tunes.

Even to a novice who has possibly only read a few sentences about what a session is in a tourist guidebook, it is immediately clear that this is a very different experience from a formal concert. The musicians do not sit on a stage. Instead, they sit in a circle with their backs to the audience. There is also a lot of talking in between the sets of tunes, unlike a concert where the noise and the pauses between pieces of music are kept to a minimum. Often, tourists draw a quick analogy to something they are more familiar with—a "jam session"; however, the musicians themselves would immediately repudiate the use of this term because it implies that the music is being improvised when nothing could be further from the truth.

Just as clearly, there is a great deal more to it than a few local musicians casually looking to play a few old traditional tunes with each other down at the pub, as sessions are often portrayed in the tourist literature and popular culture. There are microphones and huge crowds. There is something premeditated about it all. This would be confirmed at the end of the evening if one happened to notice several of the musicians being paid by a bartender, or if one realized after listening to them speak that not all of them were in fact Irish. Some speak with English, American, South African, Australian, French, or German accents. The session experience appears to be a very "traditional" musical practice, but just below the surface is a multilayered and ironic complexity: here is a cosmopolitan group of musicians, playing a local style of traditional Irish music, to an audience that consists mostly of international tourists.

Many tourists do not seem to dwell much on these things, or even notice them, but for those who do, it tends to raise a series of questions. What *is* going on here? Has tourism undermined traditional Irish music somehow? Are these musicians being exploited? Or is it the reverse: are they exploiting the tourists somehow? And since they do not all seem to be Irish musicians, who are they anyway? If they are getting paid, is it all just "commercialized" now or is it still "traditional"? What does any of it mean, or maybe better put, does it mean anything anymore? Tourists tend not to ask these specific questions though. Instead, they often sum it all up into one concise but highly loaded question: "Now, tell me, is this the real, authentic Irish music?"

These are common immediate reactions of tourists to the complicated encounter with a session in Doolin at the height of the tourist season. They are a touchstone for a wealth of issues, some of which I hope to shed light on in the following pages. To paint a preliminary brushstroke and to paint it broadly, some of these issues include the economic and social change caused by the tourism industry, the tensions between music-making and commercialization, cosmopolitanism and the integration of immigrants in Ireland, changing notions of "Irishness," the appropriation of culture, and the trope of authenticity. Throughout, all of these issues are approached through the lens of ethnographic descriptions of this one particular place. In other words, this book does not construct a theoretical scaffold upon which the ethnography is hung. Instead, the ethnography itself forms the core of what follows. Theoretical implications and cross-cultural comparisons are drawn out from it.

Conceptual Orientation

Having said that, it might be useful at this early stage to briefly position myself within some of the relevant current debates. I want to avoid the standard propensity of presenting a "literature review" though; rather, my intention here is to simply (and only in sketch form) orient the reader to my approach to the study of traditional Irish music, tourism, and social change in Doolin, and to give the reader a sense of what I hope to contribute to those subjects. Firstly, while my particular perspective is that of an anthropologist, the issues discussed herein have led me to draw upon several adjacent areas of inquiry, such as ethnomusicology, tourism studies, and Irish studies. In that sense, the following book might be considered interdisciplinary, to invoke that increasingly esteemed but seemingly little understood term. Interdisciplinarity recognizes that reality is far more nuanced, complicated, and contradictory than can be thoroughly explained by means of only one discipline's set of models, theories, or methods. When successful, an interdisciplinary study contributes more to each area of knowledge than it takes. Difficult though this may be, the unfortunate compulsion in academia to subdivide areas of knowledge, sometimes to the point of meaninglessness, while simultaneously celebrating it as "expertise" leads me to feel that broadening my scope rather than narrowing it is worth the effort. While it is hoped that the following ethnography uses an interdisciplinary approach to contribute something more than it took from these other disciplinary perspectives, I also recognize that it no doubt has a decidedly anthropological tone.

What's more, the following book is decidedly ethnographic. Recently, in their excellent overview of the social scientific study of Ireland over the past century, Wilson and Donnan (2006) argue that Ireland must continue to be studied "from below" (as Curtin and Wilson put it in the title of their seminal 1989 volume *Ireland from Below*), "from the terra firma of locality, from the perspective of those who live and work in the marshland of the bog, on the shop floor, in the government office, and at the IT workstation" (2006: 167). I agree. Throughout, I have made every attempt to bear down on the complexity of lived experience and social relations of one locality, grounding the theory in careful ethnography. In another context, Paul Sillitoe has called this method "ethnographic determinism" (2003: 3), the idea that the ethnographic data determines the theoretical model rather than the other way around. This, it seems to me, is simply good thinking and I heartily subscribe to it.

I have also been careful to pay attention to varying points of view, including the fact that my own subjective experience of Doolin is a factor in the way the following analysis unfolds. Anthropologists used to contend that our discipline was, if not an objective science, than at least one that strived to be so. We are no longer under any such illusion. There is no need to dwell on the nuances of the "postmodern turn" in anthropology, but needless to say, one result of the debate has been a more thorough recognition of subjectivity in qualitative analyses. Indeed, we have found a renewed depth and vigor from the inclusion of the self and the ethnographer's own voice in recent decades. This certainly does not mean that anthropologists have given up on seeking out facts and data, or to tell an accurate story. To the contrary, the goal is to present as true a depiction as possible. This approach, my approach, which requires us to be far more attentive to the dialogic nature of complex social milieus and to recognize that the ethnographer's own perception cannot be overlooked while at the same time recognizing that these dialogic narratives are built upon a consistent and shared extant reality, might simply be called constructivism.

Likewise, anthropologists have become more attentive to issues of scale. In other words, we are far more careful to not see the world in a grain of sand (or all of Balinese society in a single cockfight) as often as we used to do. Proper scalar contextualization is important in any ethnographic case study, but in Ireland this has been a particular pitfall. Sloppy contextualization of Ireland has, "quasi 'created' many different Irelands" (Kockel and Ruane 1992: 7). Anthropologists are not the only ones who have perhaps "invented Ireland," to use Declan Kiberd's phrase (1995). I am also not alone in finding it difficult to even circumscribe exactly what is meant by "Ireland." Is it the Republic of Ireland, the isle of Ireland, or the "Irish people"—however that might be defined (e.g., do we include the recent influx of African and Polish immigrants? What about the Irish Diaspora?). Roy F. Foster, in his book *The Irish Story* (2001), similarly contends that there has never been a singular Irish history, but rather a multiplicity of histories. "Irish history," he writes, "has inspired such a broad and compelling range of narratives, reiterated in every generation, that scope must be restricted" (2001: 2). I take these critiques about the complexity of the Irish context quite seriously and do not presume to make sweeping claims about an Irish Story per se. This ethnography is clearly set in one locale in Ireland, but it is also not simply a "community study" in the outmoded structural-functionalist sense, one in which a supposedly static unchanging community is cohesively integrated via its ancient traditions, kinship networks, mythological hegemony, and isolation from other cultures.[3] Quite the opposite: this is an ethnography about radical social change, shifting traditions and meanings, and cosmopolitan reorientations caused by constant intercultural interaction. At the same time, I do not want to take this too far. Despite recent critiques about the notion of "community" and other classic anthropological concepts, one of the major points I hope to make in this book is to demonstrate exactly how community relationships aggregate around varying notions like locality, the musical experience, and sociality.

This book is also about traditional Irish music. I make no universal claims about the music, although I think what is described here might be recognizable elsewhere. In this regard, this book attempts to fill a gap that Harry White recognized a decade ago in *The Keeper's Recital* (1998), which is that music—and more specifically in the case of this book, traditional Irish music—has generally been left out of the discourse about Irish cultural history. Here, an analysis of Irish music forms one of the central threads in the narrative. There are two major areas that I focus on. First, the book tracks how traditional Irish music changed in the latter half of the twentieth century as a result of its revival, and later, the symbiotic relationship that developed between music performances and tourism in Doolin. For example, Irish music is not the only European traditional music to have become "professionalized" (Bohlman 1988: 85–86) in recent decades, and this book adds to the literature on that topic (cf. Lortat-Jacob 1981, Buchanan 1995, Kaul 2007b). Second, especially towards the end of the book, I pay particular attention to how the music is experienced and understood in the present. This is complex, having to do with subtleties in emotive and cultural meaning that very diverse actors give to performances, the change in the performance space through time, and how traditional Irish musicians are able to maintain what Charles Keil would call "participatory discrepancy" or "creative tension" (1994b: 96–99) even in a heavily touristed and commercializing context.

This is also a book about tourism in Ireland. Tourism is a particularly powerful force for economic and social change, rife with ironies, inequalities, and essentializations. It may be the case that in historical studies "Irish tourism is an under-researched story, too often retailed simply as institutional history" (Foster, 2008: 155). However, there has been some excellent work done on Irish tourism in the social sciences (for a start, see the 1993 and 2003 volumes edited by Michael Cronin and Barbara O'Connor). It is my hope that this book will contribute to that growing literature. The touristic consumption of traditional Irish music sessions in Doolin is a classic case of what is typically called "cultural tourism" in which part of the point of the holiday is to experience local culture. But the brief international encounters that cultural tourism affords may in fact only reinscribe stereotypes about other people instead of creating a sense of cosmopolitan openness as is sometimes assumed. The idea "that tourism facilitates international understanding", Urry writes, "seems very dubious" (2004: 436). As we will see, tourists bring their own narratives about Ireland with them, something Bruner has called the "tourist tale" (2005: 19–20), and these are hugely influential on the development of local places, the consumption of local performances, and occasionally, the stories that locals begin to tell themselves. It is worth noting here at the start, however, that this book is not primarily an analysis of cultural tourism. The main focus of my attention is on the way that tourism creates intense culture contact and cultural disjuncture, intensifies the process of commercialization, and impacts the locale's changing social structure, economy, and expressive culture.

Finally, this book tells the story of resident incomers ("blow-ins") in Doolin, and how they negotiate belonging. Given the huge influx of immigrants into Ireland in recent years, and the return of Irish émigrés (sometimes now called "blow-backs"), this is an area that is in dire need of more research. Given the longstanding tradition of categorizing resident incomers as "blow-ins" (a term which has Gaelic roots in the phrase *séid isteach*s), and also given the obsession in the anthropology of Ireland with notions of "community" (Wilson 1984) and boundary-making, it has always surprised me that more has not been made of this. I make no claim to tell the whole story of recent immigration in Ireland of course. Its modern form is complex. However, it is hoped that the analysis in this book might contribute to the nascent study of immigration(s) into Ireland (cf. Shandy and Power 2007, and Lele 2008).

One of the main theoretical contentions that I make is that globalization and cosmopolitanism are not new to Ireland or "the Irish" (however we define these terms). While a local/global dialectic is frequently invoked in anthropology and related disciplines, all too often it is not fully articulated with fine-grained ethnography. Vered Amit (2002) and Anna Tsing (2008) among others have correctly critiqued the current obsession with all things global for the way it disconnects globalizing processes from real lives. Amit writes that "[t]he result can be ... a distortion of how people actually experience and engage with mobility and social fragmentation" (2002: 25). Furthermore, Tsing rightly challenges us to "stop making a distinction between 'global' *forces* and 'local' *places*" (2008: 90), as if globalization somehow does not occur in some local place or other, or affect local lives. Instead, while our ethnographic investigations may ultimately lead us to the analysis of larger patterns of social change in the modern world, we must embed our studies in ethnographic specificity, in (to perhaps completely reinterpret Tsing's terminology) a particular "global situation."

In the past two decades, the discourse surrounding globalization has become so dominant that other perspectives are only recently beginning to emerge. One useful approach is to ask how non-local practices, people, commodities, etc. become "domesticated" and localized (cf. Caldwell 2004). Another rich vein to mine is the study of "cosmopolitans," individuals who have a particularly global orientation that seeks to transcend geographic boundaries and cultural difference (Werbner 2008: 2). In particular, the case study presented in this book is a good example of what has been called "vernacular cosmopolitanism" which "pose[s] the question whether local, parochial, rooted and culturally specific loyalties may coexist with translocal, transnational, transcendent ... and modernist ones" (ibid.: 14). The answer that Doolin provides is strongly in the affirmative. It is also an interesting example of how a "tradition" (often characterized as the very essence of the local and parochial)—in this case traditional Irish music—has become a vehicle for cosmopolitanism. Moreover, given its historical global reach, it might even be considered a "cosmopolitan tradition." This type of analysis helps to liberate us from the heavily laden identity politics about "Irishness," nationalism(s), and the Catholic/Protestant divide, so common in much of the Irish Story of the past. It is not as though these blunt categories and divisions mean nothing, but they no longer seem to mean everything.

For many reasons, Doolin presents us with a particularly interesting "global situation," one in which locals, incomers, and tourists interact, live, work, and play together. Ireland has become a premier European holiday destination, especially over the last several decades, and Doolin has long been one of the "must see" places on the tourist map. What is it about this small coastal village that attracts people from all over the world? There are several reasons why places like Doolin seem to have a gravitational pull and heavily evoke notions of "Irishness" for tourists and academics alike. The west coast of Ireland is often popularly romanticized as some sort of cultural wellspring of Irishness. It is in the western counties that most of the remaining Gaelic speakers dwell (although the area around Doolin itself is no longer Gaelic-speaking). It was the west that attracted poets, playwrights, and artists like Yeats, Synge, Dylan Thomas, and Augustus John (the latter two even spent time in Doolin). Folklorists were attracted to communities in the west as well because they found what they considered to be "survivals" of older traditions: storytelling, dance, and music. Seamus Delargy spent significant time in Doolin collecting stories.

Anthropologists followed. In fact, although his primary fieldsite was the town of Ennis, Conrad Arensberg spent a significant part of his fieldwork in the early 1930s in "Lough," an area within reach and certainly within the same social world as Doolin. Arensberg and Solon Kimball, his research partner, later published *Family and Community in Ireland* (1968[1940]), which "set the standard by which much of the anthropology of Ireland was judged up to the 1980s" (Wilson and Donnan 2006: 17). Another anthropologist, John Messenger, studied nearby as well. The island he calls "Inish Beag" is Inisheer, just seven miles off the coast from Doolin. Other influential anthropologists were attracted to "the west" as well, including Hugh Brody (1973) and Scheper-Hughes (1979) among others. No doubt, literary and academic attention on the western counties helped solidify the popular romance about the region.

The gravitational pull to places like Doolin intensified in a different way following the revival of traditional Irish music in the late 1960s and early 1970s. As we will encounter in detail in Chapter 3, since Doolin was home to a large number of highly talented musical families, it was one of a small number of places that acted as a crucible for that revival. What began as a kind of musical pilgrimage to Doolin slowly evolved into mass tourism. Today, the result is that Doolin is perceived to exude Irish "traditionalism" while at the same time being incredibly cosmopolitan due to the sheer number of international visitors who visit annually and the relatively large number of incomers who have settled there permanently. By searching for something "traditional" and local, mass tourists and incomers have helped to internationalize Doolin. This only forefronts questions about "Irishness" further by constantly calling it into question.

Conceptual Organization

The intertwined relationship between tourism and traditional Irish music, and the complex social changes that this relationship has spurred on, runs like a series of threads through the following chapters. At first, they are largely distinct, but at various points in time each thread radically influences the others until they become indistinguishable. The first thread has to do with the music, its development over the last century, changes in its meaning and performance, and its changing relationship to other domains of life such as economics. The second thread has to do with the development of tourism in the region. Over time, the music and the tourism became inseparable entities entering into what Moya Kneafsey has called "a kind of symbiosis" (2002: 358). The third thread has to do with changes in the local social structure.

Parts One and Two of the book carefully document how these once unrelated entities became interwoven into the same fabric in the present. Part One focuses on the past, or more precisely, on the way the history of the locale is remembered and depicted in the present. The nature of the local tourism industry and the changes in the local social structure are such that they deserve special attention. To that end, Part Two of the book looks at the impacts of tourism on, and the integration of non-locals into, the village. Chapter 4 is devoted solely to tourism in Doolin. Instead of ignoring the music though, the goal here is to pay adequate attention to tourism's complexity. In fact, while it would be easy to assume that modern mass tourism has invaded northwest Clare only recently, changing this old, "pure" tradition of folk music, the truth is that tourism and traditional Irish music have been deeply interconnected for nearly fifty years now. It is such a prominent aspect of local musical and social life today, driving most of the change, that it would be a mistake to treat it lightly or pretend that it is not integral to everything else. Chapter 5 takes a closer look at the permanent residents of the village, and in particular those who have moved there from elsewhere, the blow-ins. They are a categorical grey area between those who are often called "hosts" and "guests" in tourism studies (cf. Smith 1989[1977]). Blow-ins helped reshape the social and physical landscape of Doolin. However, inclusion into village life is not without conflict and negotiation.

All three threads—music, tourism, and social change—are interwoven throughout the rest of the book. Part Three and the concluding chapter deal with how all of these changes affect the traditional Irish music as it is played and perceived by various actors in northwest Clare including tourists, musicians, and permanent residents. Chapter 6 takes a closer look at how globalizing processes in general, and tourism in particular, have "consolidated" and diffused traditional Irish music over time. Chapter 7 looks at how the blow-in population has all but totally appropriated the traditional Irish music scene in Doolin. Perhaps surprisingly this has passed with very little conflict or cognitive dissonance. In Chapter 8, I conclude with a broader theoretical analysis of some of the more resonant issues: the appropriation of tradition by cosmopolitan incomers, the relations between the local and global, agency and structure, the nexus of commercialism and expressive culture, and the trope of "authenticity."

Meanwhile, this book is organized in three conceptual dimensions, which are sometimes dealt with in order and sometimes simultaneously. The first dimension is chronological. The book starts with a broadly painted backdrop and finishes in the present. In Part One, I begin with the "remembered history" of local people. For me, the maxim that we cannot understand the present unless we know the past is not merely good advice; I take it quite literally. The past is lived in the present in two very real ways. First, the meanings that people ascribe to events in the present are always couched in the understanding that they have of notions of tradition and of past events. This is true for local people, but since the local remembered history is often sought out and learned by incomers as well, modern events evoke the local past for them too. As Bruner wrote, "Life consists of retellings" (1986: 12). This quickly became clear to me in the field as stories were told and people dipped back into the remembered past. Certain events, specific characters, and particular "eras" began to form a sequential pattern of remembered history. Secondly, historical precedent shapes modern social structures, expressive culture, and political policy in very real ways. In order to understand the Doolin of the present, it is necessary to understand the "Doolins" of the past.

Three historical periods are particularly important in people's retellings of local history, and the titles of Chapters 2, 3, and 4 are phrases that people often use to label these periods. The Old Days is a phrase locals often used when I asked them about the era before the 1960s, before the music was "revived," and before visitors began to come in droves to the area. Chapter 3, The Revival, deals with an era from the late 1960s to the mid-to-late 1980s, when traditional Irish music was revitalized. The 1960s ushered in a worldwide musical Folk Revival that rode on a larger wave of social change. The "hippy generation" shed earlier traditional values, viewing them as antiquated. Ironically, in Doolin traditional music became part of a social casting-off of tradition, and this was not cognitively dissonant. Doolin was one of a handful of localities in Ireland where the revival really took off. It was during this intense era that the music and the tourism became inextricably linked. Chapter 4, The Celtic Tiger, brings us into the most recent decade and a half and deals with another dramatic historical change: the emergent Celtic Tiger economy and, more specifically, the onset of mass tourism. This is an era in Doolin's history characterized by explosive development and prosperity, a prosperity that has been called into question more recently. Indeed, Ireland has clearly entered a post-Celtic Tiger era, but that is a subject beyond the scope of the present book.

The second organizational dimension of the book is an erratic narrowing of scope from history to individual narratives, from structure to agency, from the global to the local scale, and from the lifeworld to phenomenological experience. While the focus of my attention in the following pages narrows and widens and narrows again, the scope of analysis increasingly closes in on the session experience as it is expressed and understood in the present. It is no longer possible to neatly describe local places without addressing their messy, paradoxical, and dissonant relationship to larger processes. History is broad. Economic and political developments might have national and international origins, but cannot be ignored if we truly want to understand their local impact.[4]

By moving from the past to the present, and by closing in on the intimate experiential interactions surrounding the sessions in Doolin, the analysis that follows passes through various interrelated domains in the lifeworld of the village, particularly economics, politics, social structure, and expressive culture. This is the third organizational dimension of the book, and it is key to understanding the interdigitation between the local and the global, and how individual agents interact with and influence social structure.

It is important that the people we work with in the field are given a voice in our writing. Timothy Rice calls this a "subject-centered" approach (2003: 156) and in part, that is what I am after here. Our informants give us an account of their lives in interviews, and while we may couple these stories with quantitative methods, participant-observation, archival research, and comparative literature, without their input our interpretations would approach meaninglessness. Throughout the book, I attempt to let the people I talked to in Doolin tell their own story. In this regard, the folklorist Henry Glassie, who argues that we need to begin with the words of the people we study, heavily influences my writing (1995[1982]: 14), and his presentation of people's "voices," making "them look like they sound. To that end the most important device is leaving white space on the page to signal silence" (1995[1982]: 40). I present my informants' words as they said them to me, and whenever possible, I include the hedges, the spaces, and the repetition of phrases in order to allow the reader to "hear" their inflections and phrasing. Some of my informants are fast speakers whose words and thoughts flow in almost perfect sentence-paragraph formation. Some speakers use hedges to a greater or lesser degree. My Irish informants often punctuate their statements with "d'y'know" and attach "like" to the last word at the end of a phrase to emphasize a point. Some particularly skilled storytellers utilize pauses to a greater degree, and in the transcribed quotes herein, I try to be faithful to the way people speak.

There are characters that the reader will meet throughout the book, some of whom march in and out of the pages with no further appearances. Others have more to say, and the reader will have the benefit of getting to know them a little. Naturally, some of my informants were nervous about being identified, and I have given them pseudonyms. Others expressly requested that their real names be used. I have respected both requests, but I have not indicated which names have been changed.[5]

In summary, my intention is to present a particular kind of ethnography, one that is about a traditional Irish music scene in a particular place which is seasonally affected by a strong tourist economy. Today, the interaction between the tourism and the music in Doolin has resulted in complex social change, a re-structuring of identity and meaning, and the build up of new commercial relationships. To do justice to that complexity, we must delve into the past. But first, let us begin with initial impressions.

Doolin

In April of 2002, my wife Rebecca and I traveled around County Clare in an attempt to find a place to carry out the fieldwork that led to the material presented here.

I knew that Clare was famous for its strong tradition of Irish music, and I knew that most villages or towns along the west coast of Ireland would provide a good opportunity to look at an interaction between tourism and local life. We visited three sites that are particularly well known for traditional music. Each site had its merits, and we knew that to some extent the final decision would simply be serendipitous. (Before the trip, I had even relayed the story to Rebecca about an anthropologist who famously chose his fieldsite because that was the first place where someone bought him a drink). Our first choice was the city of Ennis, the county's economic and political seat. We also visited a small town called Miltown Malbay, close to the coast, where every summer a massive festival and school of Irish music and dance is held. Then on the advice of Sean Williams, the American ethnomusicologist, we made a short trip of less than twenty-four hours to the coastal village of Doolin.

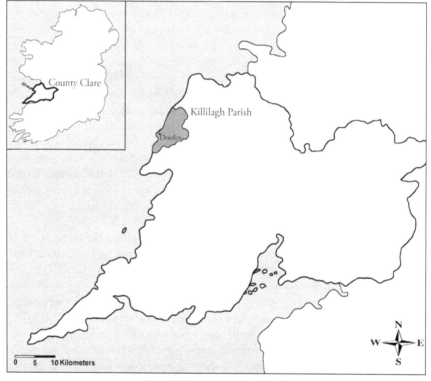

Figure 1.1 Doolin, County Clare, Ireland

On the wet and foggy afternoon when we first arrived in Doolin by bus, we dropped our bags off at our B&B and headed into the first pub we saw. In fact, the fog was so thick that the pub was quite literally the only other thing besides the B&B that we were able to see. We sat and drank coffee at a table close to the bar. There were only a handful of customers, and since we were seated so close, we could not help but to overhear an interesting conversation unfold between the young woman behind the bar and two Irish men who we guessed were locals. She told them about how the previous day they had been "slammed by four coaches." By her accent alone, we could not tell if she was Irish or American, and we wondered what her story was. The two "locals" then asked about the previous evening's session. She replied, "There was loads of music, but no *craic*."[6] It was only the briefest of conversations and the two men left shortly afterwards. But I was fascinated. That night, we attended a session in the same pub. Three musicians sat around a table in the corner in a room and played sets of jigs and reels. Doolin's worldwide reputation for traditional Irish music was clearly not hyperbolized. The musicianship was amazing. At the same time, the musicians used microphones and they sold CDs. I saw this as a sign of some level of commercialization, perhaps as a direct result of tourism. All around us, we could hear tourists speaking in several different languages. Heading back through the fog to our B&B that evening after the session, I knew this would be a good setting to conduct my study.

The next day, we woke to find that the fog had lifted. The sun shone across a cloudless sky. It was dry and bright, what the Irish call a "hard day." On the advice of our B&B proprietress, we made our way down to what she said was "the other section of the village" to ask in another pub about getting part-time work and accommodation.[7] Amazingly, within ten minutes of entering O'Connor's pub on Fisherstreet, we had assurances from the publican that he could find work for us if we decided to come back, and we had secured accommodation from one of his friends. To top it all off, the publican bought us cups of coffee. My wife and I exchanged secret smiles because it was the first drink anyone had bought us on our trip. We left on the bus an hour later. That was our first impression of Doolin, and many of the initial questions that we had about the place were not dissimilar to the ones tourists sometimes ask. We came to know it better after spending fourteen months there between June of 2002 and August of 2003.

Doolin is a small, coastal village in northwest County Clare with fewer than six hundred permanent residents. Around eighty children attend the local school. Beyond this, like many amorphous things there, the issue of what exactly is meant by the word "Doolin" is a somewhat confused one because it is a village that is scattered throughout the parish rather than one central concentration of buildings. It is generally described in guidebooks as a village that "stretches for several kilometers along the road" (Callan et al. 2002: 447). This road lies in a valley created by the Cliffs of Moher to the south, which rise dramatically to over 200 meters in the space of a few miles, and the gentler rise of the limestone landscape of the Burren to the north. To the east lie rolling green hills, and to the west is the Atlantic Ocean. The Cliffs can be seen off to the south from Doolin's pier. In stark contrast, the Burren rises out of the sea in grey, mountainous, lumps on the northern horizon. Off the coast, in Galway Bay, the Aran Islands can be seen from Doolin's pier lying low in the sea in a single line, one behind the other like three washed out sandcastles. On a clear day, you can see the mountains of the Connemara ("the Twelve Pins") across Galway Bay. From the height of the shale mountain that creates the Cliffs of Moher, you can look northward across the sweeping valley, and down on the scattered village of Doolin within it. From that height, the village looks like a confetti of buildings caught in a network of stone walls which gives the impression that some ancient mythological giant threw up a fishing net to dry and forgot it there. The crosshatching of dry stone walls was built by hand over many generations simply by carefully balancing one rock on the other. Tension and gravity hold it all together. All of this landscape is dotted with cattle and the crumbling ruins of centuries-old cottages.

Figure 1.2 Doolin

In the past, the village itself was divided into two main concentrations of buildings: Roadford, which is about a mile from the sea, and Fisherstreet about half a mile away. In between, along the road that runs between Roadford and Fisherstreet, more recent development has created a third concentration colloquially known as "Fitz's Cross." This is where another road meanders uphill and inland to meet the "main road." Another concentration of development has sprung up at this juncture as well in recent years called "Garrihy's Cross."

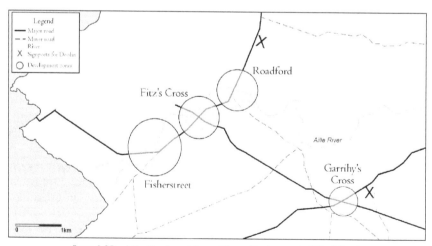

Figure 1.3 Population Density and Areas of Recent Development in Killilagh Parish

The main road runs along the coast to the south before climbing up to the top of the Cliffs of Moher, passing the new visitor center (now the single most visited sight in Ireland) on its way to the towns of Liscannor and Lahinch. In the other direction from Garrihy's Cross, the road winds inland towards the town of Lisdoonvarna. The concentrations of buildings, what we might call hamlets (although no one uses that term in Doolin), should not create a scene in the reader's mind of distinct clusters like one might see on a postcard. Doolin exhibits what is known as "ribbon development," which is to say that wide tracts of green space separate the buildings. In fact, unless someone points them out to a visitor, only one of these hamlets is clearly discernable. This vagary is such that there is sometimes even local disagreement about how many hamlets exist in Doolin. There is one exception. Fisherstreet is a much-photographed single row of attached buildings that arches along a parallel curve of the Aillee River, flowing just in front of it.

Figure 1.4 Fisherstreet

All of these hamlets together are what most people consider to be the village of Doolin or the place they refer to when they discuss the Doolin people, but "locality" is not constricted to within these parameters. The parish boundaries are the primary means by which Doolin residents determine who is a "local" and who is not. The parish that Doolin is situated in is a large one called Killilagh.

Parishes also include smaller named areas called "townlands." In Doolin, some of these townland names, like *Lough*[8] or *Carnaun*, are commonly used in conversation because they too have a higher concentration of inhabitants, but not enough for them to be considered hamlets. Other townlands consist mostly of pastureland with few residents and are rarely used in the local discourse about "place."

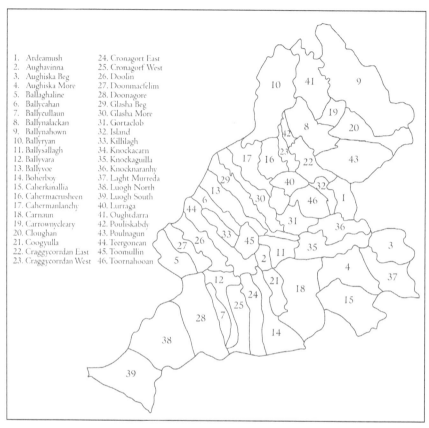

1. Ardeamush	24. Cronagort East
2. Aughavinna	25. Cronagorf West
3. Aughiska Beg	26. Doolin
4. Aughiska More	27. Doonmacfelim
5. Ballaghaline	28. Doonagore
6. Ballycahan	29. Glasha Beg
7. Ballycullaun	30. Glasha More
8. Ballynalackan	31. Gortaclob
9. Ballynahown	32. Island
10. Ballyryan	33. Killilagh
11. Ballysallagh	34. Knockacarn
12. Ballyvara	35. Knockaguilla
13. Ballyvoe	36. Knocknaranhy
14. Boherboy	37. Laght Murreda
15. Caherkinallia	38. Luogh North
16. Cahermacrusheen	39. Luogh South
17. Cahermanlanchy	40. Lurraga
18. Carnaun	41. Oughtdarra
19. Carrownycleary	42. Pouliskabdy
20. Cloughan	43. Poulnagun
21. Coogyulla	44. Teergonean
22. Craggycorrdan East	45. Toomullin
23. Craggycorrdan West	46. Toornahooan

Figure 1.5 Killilagh Parish Townlands

Due to the multiplicity of conceptualizations of the place of Doolin, I discuss it in various ways, generally calling it Doolin or "the village," but specifying Killilagh or "the parish" when necessary. Tourism, driven originally by the strength of the local traditional Irish music scene, has in fact essentialized the notion of "Doolin" out of a more multilayered complexity.

Today, the regional economy largely depends on summertime tourism, and tourism has literally reshaped Doolin. Around fifty B&Bs dot the parish. Four hostels and three campsites within the village also cater to tourists. The main section of Fisherstreet has been completely transformed since the 1970s. Now, every building along this streetscape functions at least in part as a business geared towards tourism, including O'Connor's pub, five gift and craft shops, a B&B and a restaurant. The original three pubs in the village[9] have expanded significantly over the last few decades to make room for the burgeoning tourist crowds that come to hear sessions. More recently, Ireland's blanket smoking ban forced further expansions of roofed patio areas to accommodate the now-shunned smokers.

While the parish's primary source of income is from tourism, in fact, it is a mixed economy. Although not dealt with to any great extent in this book, farming remains an important part of local economics, and an important part of the local culture. Many residents who run tourist-oriented businesses are also farmers and even those who in no way depend on agriculture sometimes keep a few cows "because it's nice." While tourism is highly profitable, it is also highly seasonal, and maintaining a farm becomes one way to secure one's household income. Even those farmers who do not have tourist oriented businesses are smallholders due primarily to the rough and rocky terrain of the parish. Beef cattle are the main farming resource and pastureland blankets all parts of the parish, including even the most heavily touristed areas. Less commonly, some residents keep sheep, and many farmers have horses. Donkeys and goats are kept as well, but only in very small numbers. In the summertime, manure is spread over the pastures, silage is made, and hay is "saved," bundled into large, black plastic-wrapped bales for winter feed. Cultivation occurs only at the subsistence level in the form of gardens where potatoes, onions, carrots, and cabbages are grown. Most farming today is heavily mechanized, but some smallholders still rake hay into "haycocks," move their cattle by foot from one field to another, and tend subsistence gardens.

The agricultural nature of the parish is one of its predominant features, in terms of both the landscape and the sensibilities of many of the people who live there. It communicates itself to the visitor through every sense.[10] The smell of manure-spreading in the early summer and the smell of freshly cut hay later on permanently perfumes the air. As various fields mature in the summertime and the hay is saved and baled, the parish begins to resemble a patchwork quilt. Some fields remain bright green while the cut fields turn golden. Tractors rumble back and forth down all of the roads that run through the parish, trailing a cloud of dust on dry days and streaks of mud on wet days. Even the main roads get choked with agricultural activity. Cattle are moved from one field to another along these roads, and it is common for all cars, buses, and coach-tours to have to wait in traffic for a herd of cattle to make their way to a new pasture, prodded along by a patient farmer in Wellington boots wielding a walking stick. Cattle low complainingly in bad weather and fill the air with their noise. After the sounds of tourism (coaches, crowds, and varying accents), the sound of cattle and horses was one of the first major sensory impressions I had of Doolin. Indeed, there seemed to be a stark, dichotomous contrast between the sounds of tourism along the main part of Fisherstreet and Roadford, and the sounds of agriculture and ocean everywhere else in the parish.

Unsurprisingly, fishing used to be the main economic resource of the residents of Fisherstreet, but today only a small few fishermen still launch boats from Doolin. Like other parts of the parish, the pier at the sea has now been largely appropriated by the tourist economy. There, the ferry companies run tourists back and forth from the Aran Islands in huge numbers during the summer months. As a result of EU and Irish policies, fishing has become a much more regulated and difficult occupation in Ireland in general in the last few decades. The fishermen who operate out of Doolin do so out of handmade motor-powered fishing boats called *currachs*. These fishermen run small commercial operations, and in the face of much more profitable incomes in other sectors fishing has declined significantly in recent times. Competing with the huge trawlers that occasionally pass through Galway Bay make it even more difficult. However, like farming, fishing remains an important symbolic identifier, and Doolin is often described as "a small fishing village."

Peat turf and coal are commonly used as heating fuel in the wintertime and there are several productive peat bogs in the area. Peat *riks*, stacks of peat "bricks" carefully laid into watertight piles, stand to the side of people's houses. While peat-cutting is mechanized today, families that use peat often still go to the bog themselves in June and July to "turn" it and "foot" it (in order to let the sun and wind dry it out), and then haul it home themselves at the end of the summer.

Ireland in general has changed quite a lot in recent times. It used to be a very impoverished place, one that could be described as a third world country at the periphery of Europe. Doolin was no better off and perhaps even poorer than many places in Ireland—but no longer. The Celtic Tiger economy that began to take off in earnest in the early- to mid-1990s left real and observable impacts. Allen puts a precise date on its arrival, stating that it was "baptised in 1994" (2000: 9). Of course, its roots lay much further back. Two important developments, initiated decades earlier, led to the explosion of recent economic prosperity in Ireland. First, through a series of grants and tax shelters, and by allowing companies to repatriate all of their profits without investing in Ireland, the government lured multinational corporations to set up shop in Ireland (Gottheil 2003: 725). The singular motivation behind the new strategy was to create employment. A secondary development was Ireland's entry into the European Economic Community (later called the European Union or EU) in 1973. Ireland was required to dismantle all protective tariffs with other EEC countries, which it completed by 1977 (ibid.: 727). The immediate economic effects of this early globalizing economic policy were mostly negative; however, Ireland was also able to draw on huge amounts of EU money. By 1993, over 3 percent of Ireland's gross national product was drawn from EU coffers (ibid.: 728). By the mid-1990s, these processes reached a kind of critical mass. Most of the multinational companies that moved to Ireland were based in the United States, and a "cluster effect" occurred whereby rival companies in the same industry (Internet companies clustering in Dublin for example) set up shop in Ireland in order to be competitive in the EU market (ibid.:731). Importantly, tourism was another major source of fuel for the explosion of the Celtic Tiger. Amazingly, by 2002, a United Nations report was able to conclude that Ireland was, per capita, the fourth richest nation in the world (O'Toole 2002: 12).

As I discuss in Chapter 4 though, the wealth has not been equally distributed. The result of the Celtic Tiger on the lifeworld of northwest Clare is a stark mixture of "traditional" Ireland and the "new" Ireland. Some people are wealthy, drive expensive cars, and live in big new suburban-American style homes, while next door others live without central heating in old stone cottages. It is not uncommon for the ones who live in the new suburban-style homes to be the grandchildren of the ones who live next door in the stone cottages. Signs of the "old days" are everywhere, but this is no longer (if it ever really was) an Ireland "on the decline" as Hugh Brody described in 1973. This change has been so fast that it has created a generation of young people who arguably live in a different social world from that of their grandparents. The tension between the old and the new, between modernity and tradition, and between the local and global scales are manifest in the landscape, the architecture, the language, and the music.

This is Doolin's complicated present, but to fully understand that present, we have to dip into the remembered history about the past.

Notes

1. The Irish smoking ban put into place in the spring of 2004 has changed this scenario. The primary fieldwork that forms the basis for this book was carried out over fourteen months between 2002 and 2003. While some of the material presented herein has been updated, it is primarily set in that time period.

2. Technical ethnomusicological analyses of traditional Irish dance music have been done (cf. Ó Súilleabháin 1990 for an excellent and succinct description), but some explanatory comments are appropriate here. Most tunes are structured with an A part and a B part, each consisting of two 8–bar subdivisions. Each part is repeated once, sometimes with a slight melodic variation, before moving onto the second part. In other words, a typical tune is structured like this: part A (8 bars), part A repeated with a possible variant (8 bars), part B (8 bars), and part B repeated with a possible variant (8 bars). Each tune is typically repeated three or four times before moving immediately into another tune. Three or more tunes are strung together into what is called a "set." "Ornaments" or "decorations" are grace notes or more commonly, rhythmic techniques, that enhance the basic notes of a tune. For example, a "cut" is essentially when one emphasizes a note by starting off on a harmonic note. "Cutting" the note D involves playing an A first but only by "tapping" it. On a tin whistle for instance, one merely taps the hole which would produce the A while holding onto the holes that would produce the D (Cotter 1989[1983]: 23). The most common types of tunes are jigs, which are played in 3/4 time at tempos as slow as 80, and reels, which are played in 4/4 time at consistently faster tempos of around 110–120. It is the combination of the fast speed, the repetition, and the decorative nature of the music that makes it great for dancing on the one hand, but on the other, can sometimes sonically overwhelm the first-time listener.

3. Again, anthropologists in and of Ireland began to break from this framework in the late 1980s with Curtin and Wilson's 1989 volume *Ireland from Below*. For a detailed discussion of this shift and of the many new directions anthropology has taken in Irish ethnography, see Wilson and Donnan's *The Anthropology of Ireland* (2006).

4. See A.J. Racy's recent book Making Music in the Arab World (2003) for a similar method in which the analysis telescopes in from the broader context to the narrower spaces of music-making.

5. On this issue, I feel that we must ask ourselves who we protect with pseudonyms: our informants or ourselves? A few of my informants in particular (and in fact the name "Doolin" itself) are well-known and have been written about many times in the popular literature on Irish music as well as in tourist guidebooks. Giving them all pseudonyms would only protect myself, and further, it would be condescending to bury their words in a fake name that most anyone could uncover. For these reasons, I have chosen to take a mixed approach to the issue of pseudonyms. But my choices at every stage were to follow

the requests of my informants first, then to ask myself who I was protecting from whom, and when in doubt, to change the name.

6. This is typically translated to mean "fun" or "entertainment". See Chapter 7 for an extensive discussion of this concept.

7. For a discussion about the challenges and benefits of being employed in the field, see Kaul 2004 "At Work in the Field: Problems and Opportunities Associated with Employment During Fieldwork". *Anthropology Matters*. Vol. 6 #2. (www.anthropologymatters.com/journal/20042/kaul_2004_at.htm)

8. *Lough*, a townland along the main road in the southwest corner of the parish, is where Conrad Arensberg spent part of his time doing fieldwork in the 1930s. The folklorist Seamus Delargy had recently been there collecting stories and songs from the locals (Arensberg 1959: 20), which suited Arensberg's desire to "find something of the old tradition still alive" (ibid.: 22). This academic gaze has no doubt had an effect on the area and its self-image, but its extent is difficult to gauge.

9. At the time of my fieldwork, there were three pubs in Doolin, two in Roadford (McGann's and McDermott's) and one in Fisherstreet (O'Connor's). In 2006 though, a new hotel was built at Fitz's Cross complete with another pub, but this new development does not feature in the present analysis.

10. For an interesting discussion on the multisensory nature of fieldwork, see Kohn 1994.

PART I

Remembered History

Chapter 2

The Old Days

[T]he past is most fully experienced through everyday life in the present.
—Joanne Rappaport (1988: 718)

[T]he tendency has been to make history less of an art and more of a
pseudo-science, and hence for everyone in the profession to know 'more
and more about less and less'.
—Norman Davies (1999: xxv)

Ethnography, History, and Memory

Put simply, ethnography is the act of making a written account that contextualizes the data and experiences from anthropological fieldwork. Often this means that ethnographies like this one begin with history. Unlike reading written histories though, doing fieldwork is like "reading" a kind of backwards history. Events in the past form patterns that shape today's social structures. When we enter the field, we observe, we participate, and we ask questions about what relationships are important and why. In order to understand those relationships, we find ourselves searching for chronological causality. We ask questions of the friends we make and we receive stories that allow us to dip into a pool of remembered events, which we piece together and come to understand sequentially.

Living in the ethnographic present means that we live with the experience of the past as it was lived by others. Their experiences, once existential, meandering, and contingent, become factual and structured into narratives. Stories become histories. Histories are contested and reinterpreted in the present, and it is through collective interpretation of received narratives about the past that history becomes real. Through storytelling and hermeneutics, the past and the present collide and collude. Very broadly, this is how I understand the process that Bourdieu calls the habitus, living dispositions created by the "structuring structures"(2000[1977]: 72) of history and culture. On one hand, the pace of social change in Doolin extends beyond a simple "restructuring" of social "dispositions," but on the other, this concept is useful in this context because it recognizes the important interaction between individual actors and the structure that they inherit. History, in other words, is lifeless if it is separated from the people who lived it and from the people who live with it in the observable present.[1]

So, this ethnography begins with a living, remembered history. This is necessary. Without it, the story of the present that follows will be unframed, uncontextualized, and misunderstood. In particular, it begins with an historical period I have labeled "the old days."[2] In Doolin, depending on the context of a conversation and the speaker who uses it, "the old days" is a phrase that can refer to many different eras of local history, but I use it here to label a time before the mid-1960s when a very different way of life existed in northwest Clare: mass-tourists had not arrived yet, the Catholic Church dominated daily life, emigration and poverty still haunted rural Ireland, and Irish customs and traditions, including traditional Irish music, were often seen as reminders of poverty and insularity. This view of Ireland was darkly represented in works like John Messenger's *Inis Beag* (1969), Hugh Brody's *Irishkillane: Change & Decline in the West of Ireland* (1973), and Nancy Scheper-Hughes' *Saints, Scholars and Schizophrenics* (1979). People were poor. The depression was economic and emotional. A cultural and religious conservatism created an oppressive hegemony that carefully policed individual behavior. Other researchers such as Arensberg and Kimball in *Family and Community in Ireland* (1968[1940]) depicted life differently, and saw integrated, functioning communities. Northwest Clare had largely maintained local traditions and the Gaelic language in spite of this poverty and hegemony—or perhaps because of it—and a subsistence economy persisted that allowed people to live mostly without hard cash. A system of generalized reciprocity and a strong sense of community endured.

Of course, in retrospect, we can see the theoretical and conceptual shortcomings that these authors made about Ireland. In a ground breaking piece, Wilson demonstrated how all of these works utilized similar conceptions of "community" and "kinship" to either bolster a structural-functionalist argument or to tear it down (1984: 1). This is our own shortcoming though. For local people, things were always more complex. Life during "the old days" was described to me by the people who lived through it in terms that Arensberg, Kimball, Brody, Messenger, and Schepher-Hughes would all agree on: it was lovely. It was harsh. It was worse. It was better. There was a strong sense of community. Society was falling apart at the seams. All true to the people who lived life then and remember it now.

Subsistence and Seasonality

Gus O'Connor described to me what life was like in the old days as we sat at his kitchen table one day, shortly before he passed away in the spring of 2003. He was born in the village and eventually took over his family's pub. Seventy-eight years old, he had only retired and sold the pub a few years previously. He told me what it was like when he was growing up:

Everyone had their own produce, their own firing peat. So they were self-sufficient. When I was a young fellow, we never had to buy a vegetable. We had the turf for heating and all kinds of potatoes and veg and cabbage.

I suggested,

So people didn't make a lot of money, but they didn't need a lot of money.

He agreed with me:

They didn't need a lot of money, you know. No. Probably your clothes would be the most expensive. Your clothes and shoes … . Even in the bad times, Doolin [people] were well-off, most of them. They had very good land around, the farmers. They produced cattle. And the old people, they made their own butter, their own turf, their own potatoes, their own veg. They were almost self-sufficient. Except you had to pay "rates" to the council. And whatever other incidentals might be needed. Like shoes and clothes. But other than that, there was no "poor" person that I knew of. No. None whatsoever.

As Gus O'Connor describes, cattle were important to the local economy. Cattle became a central agricultural resource in this region after the Great Famine in the mid-nineteenth century, as farming became more extensive and less intensive (Byrne et al. 2001: VI). The ground in northwest county Clare is too stony for much cultivation anyway. In fact, this part of Ireland is dominated by the Burren, a mountainous exposed-limestone landscape.[3] To strangers, the Burren looks completely barren, stripped of all plant-life and fertility. In reality the opposite is true. The rich grasses that grow between the limestone "pavements" that cover the mountains are fantastic for cattle grazing, and according to locals, Burren cattle are prized throughout Ireland. Killilagh parish, on the southern borders of the Burren, is grassier than the land just to the north, but still only commercially suitable for cattle grazing. A quick glance through the 1901 Census of County Clare reveals that roughly half of the working population in the Killilagh parish listed farming under the category "occupation"[4]. The farms around northwest Clare are predominantly what Arensberg and Kimball would call "small farms" —family run affairs with relatively low acreage and a concentration on subsistence rather than profits (1968[1940]: 3–4). Essentially, though, this was a "peasant" economy in the sense that people lived relatively self-sufficiently, satisfying most of their own needs. So as Gus put it, even though they had very little money, they weren't necessarily poor.

Argonauts of the Eastern Atlantic
The Fisherstreet section of Doolin was appropriately named. It was a single street of houses where many of the fishing families lived in the old days. The 1901 Census shows that almost exactly half of the working population of Fisherstreet defined their

occupation as either "fisherman" or "fish dealer". It is a well-chosen, sheltered spot that still largely protects inhabitants from the worst that the Atlantic offers up. At the same time it is close to the seashore. Doolin's fishing fleet was never as big as other Clare fishing villages, but fishing was always an important economic activity locally. An imposing eighty-four year-old local named Seamus MacMahon, who was once endearingly described to me as "Doolin's grandfather," told me about fishing in Doolin in the 1930s:

> The fishermen that was down below, they made a fair-good living by the sea that time. There was about eight or nine people fishing there, out of Doolin when I was a young fella. And in the summertime, they'd make a fair bit of money out of mackerel fishing. And then they had the spring fishing, and the harvest fishing.

Figure 2.1 Mural in O'Connor's Pub portraying Fisherstreet in the "Old Days"

Because of their fishing fleet and their proximity, the Doolin people also maintained a close personal and economic relationship with the Aran Islanders. My friend Tim – heavily bearded and always accompanied by his dog Oscar – is a local fisherman who, when he's not out on the sea in his hand-made *currach*, can often be found marching along the seashore or through the parish's back fields. One rainy day as we sat in his cottage he told me about his grandparents' relationship with the Aran Islanders. He said,

> This house here, it was all Gaelic that was spoken, because my grandfather-like, he would be spending a lot of time with *Aranochs*. *Aranochs* is the Irish for "islander", the people from the Islands—the Aran Islands: Inisheer, Inishmaan and Inishmor … .

I used to go with my grandfather and my uncles and that, and my own father-like when they'd be going off gettin' *poteen* and stuff like that ... . He used to have *bonards*, young pigs, small pigs, and he used to bring them across to the Islands.

And he used to sell the pigs on the Islands.

And he used to row across by *currach*, a small little *currach* across. Which is what? Six, seven miles. And then he'd sell off the pigs there and then head off again the next morning.

And he'd go away across from there to the Connemara, which was thirty miles straight across the bay. And he'd pick up *poteen*.

We had relations in Connemara.

He'd pick up the *poteen* in Connemara, and then he would turn around—of course, after he'd stayed there a night or two, said "hello" to the lot of them and drank enough for two because he was fond of the drink himself—and then he'd come back to the Islands, and deliver off some *poteen* at the Islands on the way back. And then bring the rest of the *poteen* back here. And sell it off here as well.

"And start all over?", I asked. He replied,

And start all over again. Well, he was fishing [in] between as well.

Seamus MacMahon also traded with the islanders in this manner. Seamus was not only known locally as the bearer of a wealth of traditional songs and stories, but also as a lifelong entrepreneur, who, as a younger man, would trade hay and potatoes with the Aran Islanders. In those days, economic relationships were also personal ones. These relationships between the Islanders and the Doolin people continue today, although they continue for very different reasons, tourism taking precedence over the trade of pigs, hay, fish, and *poteen*. The summer ferry services that run from Doolin to the Aran Islands ensure that an economic relationship is maintained. Indeed, the fact that Doolin is the nearest ferry port to Inisheer strengthens the relationship between the people of Inisheer and Doolin over other communities in northwest Clare, especially today when the professional ferry services act as the major means of transportation, not the *currachs* of the old days.

Personal relationships like this continue as well, relationships of friendship, responsibility, and obligation. On one trip to Inisheer, an Islander, after finding out that we lived in Doolin, bottled up some water from a holy well for us to deliver to a Doolin couple whose families are close. Another time, Tim took me out to Inisheer in his *currach*. He was greeted by by name every other person we passed, and after we settled into Tigh Ned's pub, he gave me money to go up to the bar to order "his round" of drinks. This was very much against the elaborate protocol of Irish drinking customs and I asked why he was suddenly breaking this rule. He told me that if he approached the bar, two or three drinks would be bought for him by his islander friends, and he would not be allowed to protest. This would result in a "serious round" of drinks and we would never get back to the mainland until the next day.

Seasonality

When there was no farming or fishing to be done, other jobs were taken up. Seamus told me what else they did when he was a young man.

> In the wintertime, they'd be breaking stones for the roads. And they be getting so much for every ton of stones they break.

> Now when the month of April and May come, those fishermen'd be putting up *kelp*. You know what *kelp* is? They'd be putting up the seaweed. And they'd burn it … And they'd export it from Liscannor in the boat. That boat might've come in with a cargo of coal into Liscannor — which is only a couple 5 or 6 miles down the *road*. There was a couple of merchants in Ennistymon that'd take the whole cargo of coal. And she wouldn't be going back empty. She'd maybe be goin' back with a load of *kelp* maybe. Or maybe she'd bring a load of flags[stones] from the Moher and Doonagore Quarries. See.

I asked for clarification,

> So even the fishermen at that time had to supplement their fishing with all kinds of work in the wintertime?

He replied,

> Oh they had. Definitely. Definitely. They might have no land. They might have the place of one cow. And that's the very most they had.

Supplementing ones' income in this manner was common due to the seasonality of available work.

Despite the recent shift from a farming economy then to a tourist economy today, as in the old days, seasonality still underlies all aspects of life in northwest Clare. The mixed economy follows a very similar calendrical cycle that Brody describes (1973: 18–44). The farming calendar still begins on St. Bridget's Day (February 1st) when crops are planted and fields are prepared for cattle pasturage. Farmers are particularly occupied with lambing and calving in February and March, and this season can extend into June. Sales of cattle occur in Ennistymon, Kilfenora, and Miltown Malbay in May and June as well. Around the same time, whenever the bogs dry out from the winter rains, turf is cut. The turf used to be cut with a specialized *sleán* (pronounced "schlon") shovel by hand. Today it is machine-cut. But as in the past, after cutting the turf "sticks," they are laid out to dry in the sun. Later they are turned by hand, stacked (or "footed" in local terminology), and then hauled home. Fishing for crab, lobster, and salmon begins when the weather becomes suitable in May or June and continues until September or October when the seas get too rough. In May, silage is cut, and in the summer months that follow, hay is cut and raked into haycocks (or today, mostly baled and wrapped in black plastic by machine). Cattle are herded from pasture to pasture by prodding, whooping farmers. In September, the crops from the gardens are harvested and stored. In August and September in the old days, pigs were killed, salted, smoked, and hung from the rafters. Today, the local butchers or the national grocery chains supply the pork, but it remains a staple. Winter preparations are made then in October and November. Cattle are brought in, and the ditches and dykes around the pastures are cleaned out. Generally, the regular working season ends for farmers and fishermen in November, and all is idle and fallow again until St. Bridget's Day. During the winter in the old days, supplementary work in the stone quarries around Doolin helped sustain the local people. In 1901, census records document a large number of quarrymen who cut limestone "flags" from what the locals call "the mountain" that rises up on the southern edge of the parish. (The Atlantic has sheared off the western edge of this mountain, forming the Cliffs of Moher). Other occupations included publican, postman, blacksmith, shepherd, herdsman, domestic servant, general laborer, nurse, beggar, tailor, and teacher, amongst others. What is abundantly clear from the 1901 Census is that tourism was in no way an important part of the economy of the parish yet. Unusually for this era though, tourism was essential in neighboring parishes.

Tourism in Clare after 1859: On the Origin of a New Species

Although the first recorded tourist came to County Clare in 1749, very few people traveled there at all—for holiday or for business—before the mid-1800s. Clare is surrounded on three sides by water, and extremely poor roads disallowed the use of wheeled carriages. As Brian Ó Dálaigh wrote, "Most visitors avoided the county altogether" (1998: v). For all intents and purposes, tourism began in Clare in 1859 when a railroad line opened up from Limerick to Ennis. The line was both inexpensive and (relatively) fast. A few years later, a steam-ship from Galway began a service to Ballyvaughan in the north of the county, and from there travelers often visited Lisdoonvarna. Eventually, three major travel routes developed through County Clare. One followed the railroad line through the center of the county from Limerick up to Ennis and then further north to Gort. A second commonly used corridor roughly followed the Shannon River as it made its way along the eastern and southern borders of the county from Scariff to Killaloe and down to Limerick. The third corridor that developed, and the one that concerns us most here, followed the western coastline from Kilrush and Kilkee in the south up to Miltown Malbay, Lahinch, the Cliffs of Moher, and north to Ballyvaughan (Byrne et al. 2001: v-vii) in the north of the county.

The nature of tourism from 1859 through the end of the Second World War was very different from the tourism that followed. Holiday-making in the late 1800s and early 1900s was largely undertaken by the upper classes, people who were "able to afford the costly time-consuming and bone-aching journeys to the coast for long periods in the summer season" (Walvin 1978: 70). Class differentiation was a key characteristic of Victorian tourism, a characteristic that distinguishes it from the more democratic mass-tourism that followed the Second World War.

Three locales in County Clare figured on the holiday map for early Victorian tourists. Kilkee is situated in the southern part of the county, but given the modes of transport and the poor quality of roads in Clare, Kilkee's Victorian tourist industry would not have had much influence on Doolin. Lisdoonvarna and Lahinch, however, were in the north of the county, and very close to Doolin. Like Kilkee, Lahinch attracted tourists because if its wide, sandy beach (Ó Dálaigh 1998: 279). The establishment of the West Clare Railway line made traveling here even more popular and accessible. In 1892, a golf course was established at Lahinch making its tourist "industry" two-pronged overnight (www.lahinchgolf.com). Lisdoonvarna lies several miles inland, and became known for its sulphur springs. A Lisdoonvarna publican, Peter Curtin, told me,

> You're looking at very up-market, very uppity, landed gentry-type people [coming] to Lisdoonvarna to "sample the waters". Very luxurious hotels out in the sticks, as it were. The common people, the ordinary folks, were merely servants.

The development of Lisdoonvarna—also known colloquially as "The Spa" or "Lisdoon"—as a tourist attraction was central in Doolin's own history because of its proximity, only a few kilometers inland. Tourism played an important role in Lisdoonvarna's historical development and is still important to its modern economy. Doolin people would have encountered these early Victorian tourists in the old days because they often traveled through the parish on their way to the Cliffs of Moher or to the seaside near Fisherstreet. However, it was not until much later that tourists took anything more than (literally) a passing interest in Doolin itself.

In 1944, the commercial use of an airport on the County Clare side of the Shannon River halfway between Limerick City and Ennis opened the door for a new era in tourism, not only for County Clare, but for all of the west of Ireland. The United States of America signed an amazing accord with Ireland, agreeing that all commercial flights entering Irish airspace would stop at Shannon. The first flight passed through in 1945, and the concept of "Duty Free Shopping" was invented there in 1947 (Deegan and Dineen 1997: 13–14). Up to 1958 Shannon was used as a stop-over by almost one half of all trans-Atlantic fights (Ó Gráda 1997: 183). By 1959 though, trans-Atlantic flights began from other European destinations, and "Shannon Airport was, strictly speaking, already obsolescent" (ibid.). Still, the airport quickly transformed the potential for tourism in the west of Ireland and made an important early impact. One traveler, writing in 1948, already noticed the tremendous impact that the airport was having on the region.

> From being a quiet little hamlet, Ennis has become the most prosperous place in all Ireland … . The inhabitants of Ennis benefit in many ways from

their unique position. Every room in the little town was taken, and sixty new houses were being built … the local shops were doing a roaring trade in Irish tweeds, Irish shirts, Irish ties, and Irish souvenirs of every description. The bars were doing a roaring trade too … . The American aircrews certainly had a wonderful time at Ennis. They wore very colourful clothes, usually red plaid shirts over their trousers. They were very fond of saying: "Top o' the morning to ye!" and "Begorra!"—expressions only used by stage Irishmen. (Charles Graves as quoted by Ó Dálaigh 1998: 343–344).

Suddenly, tourism officials considered County Clare a "top-flight destination" (Deegan and Dineen 1997: 17). This was certainly a far cry from the type of tourism that Clare had become used to during the previous century. Here was the beginning of mass-tourism, more accessible to all classes. From Ennis, it was common for travelers to make their way to Lahinch (Ó Dálaigh 1998: 343–344) or other destinations even closer to Doolin like the Cliffs of Moher. This tourist activity that began skirting around Doolin in the old days was, like everything else in northwest Clare, seasonal. The disreputable Irish weather always dictated the seasonality of tourism, and this remains true to this day.

It would not be for at least another decade that tourists finally started having a direct impact on Doolin itself. However, locals would have felt the peripheral effects of Lisdoonvarna's popularity. "When they came to Lisdoonvarna", Peter Curtin told me,

> they used to go to the Cliffs of Moher on coach trips … and around [to] different sight-seeing tours.

The main road that leads from Lisdoonvarna to the Cliffs of Moher passes directly through Killilagh parish. Conrad Arensberg lived along a section of that road overlooking Doolin when he did his fieldwork there in 1933. He wrote that it was common to see "Pleasure-bent motorists from the cities driv[ing] through along [to] the cliffs" (1959[1937]: 21). Seamus Ennis records that as early as 1945, people were traveling from Lisdoonvarna to bathe in the sea at Doolin Point: "We were sitting in a canvas *currach* in the bay …," he wrote, "watching the swimmers from Lisdoonvarna in case of a drowning accident—twenty sidecars came out to Miss Murphy's[5] for tea, with four people each, and most of them went swimming" (quoted in Bourke 1986: 54). In other words, as Peter told me, as far as its own tourist industry, "Doolin didn't feature on the map at all." But later on, long after the upper-class tourism had faded, a small domestic flow of local visitors began to create what Peter called the "absolute embryonic stage" of tourism in Doolin:

> In the sixties, there was public transport … . Buses would do three runs a day, return to Doolin from Lisdoonvarna. For two old pence—a return trip for adults, and a penny for kids … . We're talking about cheap, cheap fares. So people went down on the bus. They went to the shore on fine days. They

swam. They walked around, and bits and pieces … . But. Particularly on Sundays, some of the older guys would go out. They wouldn't bother with the sunshine. And in between the notion of taking the bus out and the last bus in, they'd sit around and have a few pints. And this was in the sixties. And at the same time, some Americans started to return, some of the Irish Diaspora coming back to Ireland and going round and around … .

So, the pub, instead of being empty, had customers in it … . And that was the core that allowed the beginnings as it were.

The pub that Peter refers to is O'Connor's Pub on Fisherstreet in Doolin. It was established in 1832 by the Shannon family and was appropriately called Shannon's. But as was the tradition, when Gus O'Connor's father, Jack, married into the Shannon family and took it over in 1923 from his great aunt, Noreen, the pub took on the new owner's name. Thereafter it was called J. O'Connor's Pub. Gus and his wife Doll took it over in 1960, and the name changed again to Gus O'Connor's Pub.

In the old days, when Gus and Doll first owned the place, O'Connor's Pub was a very small venture. Gus told me that,

it was only a small bar. Half of it was grocery, and there was very little money around in them days. But we made a living—a *kind* of living.

When he and Doll took it over, they even had to supplement the pub trade by traveling around in a van selling groceries around northwest Clare. But importantly, the pub did attract a regular, albeit small, local crowd from Doolin and Lisdoonvarna. The Aran Islanders would also occasionally come into the pub when they came ashore at Doolin to conduct business on the mainland. The Islanders knew Gus O'Connor personally because he spent summers as a boy out on Inisheer learning to speak Gaelic. As Peter said, a few visiting Americans of Irish descent were also stopping through. "Instead of nobody being there," he said, "there were some people there," which created a bit of an atmosphere that other less frequented pubs could not guarantee.

But tourism was almost non-existent up to the late 1960s. Economic activity in general was fairly lacking. "Ah sure," Seamus MacMahon told me, "it wasn't long ago that things were bad. Things were very bad fifty years ago—very bad forty years ago." Michael Coady, an early traveler to Doolin and a long-time friend of its inhabitants, wrote that, "when I first knew Doolin at the beginning of the 1960s it was without question a dying community in economic and social terms" (1996: 27). Michael Coady and some of his friends are still remembered as some of the first "tourists" (even though they were just from the next county over) who came to Doolin specifically to hear the music. They were followed by many more. Seamus told me,

an awful lot of people started coming then in the '60s because they heard about the music you know. And the music was the big attraction and that's what *made* Doolin.

It was a refrain I heard over and over during fieldwork. The next chapter deals with those who came to Doolin for the music beginning in the late 1960s, and how their arrival began to change everything. But for the rest of this chapter, it is worth spending some time discussing the music itself.

The Traditional Music of the "Old Days"

One of the more dramatic changes to traditional Irish music over the last forty years or so is that it used to be a single element in a larger contextual milieu of interdependent social entertainments amongst consociate relations: dancing, gambling, chatting, and courting. According to Hall, "Music-making and dancing too, conformed to the complex rules of role and status that governed all aspects of social and economic life" (1999: 77). As social and economic life has changed, so too has the way in which the music is performed and understood. More often than not, the music is now listened to on its own in Doolin in the context of pub sessions. In modern concert settings or in spectacles like *Riverdance* or similar touring stage-shows, the music has even been rarefied out of a folk tradition into a "high art." In the old days, while the music was greatly appreciated and loved in and of itself, it was not often played outside of the larger context of the *céilí*, the crossroads dance, the country house dance, or the dance hall. These contexts intimately tied the music to dancing, chatting, gambling, and socializing.[6]

The Céilí and the Crossroads Dance

Music used to be played regularly in houses when neighbors would get together in the evenings to socialize. Glassie calls this a *céilí* (1995[1982]: 41), but locals around northwest Clare would use the terms "party," "soiree," or "hoolie" just as often. According to Arensberg and Kimball, the old terminology for it in northwest Clare was a *cuaird*.[7] They found that men especially would gather in the evenings at particular houses to play cards, sing songs, play a few tunes, tell stories, and talk (1968[1940]: 173). My own experience of what is usually referred to as "small talk" elsewhere revealed that talk is in no way small in Ireland. The structure of conversation is in itself important. A bit of gossip can even be structured into a "tale," or it can be a game. Sides are taken on an issue, and the conversants parry and debate. Or, a story might begin with facts that are then spun into "tall tales." The structure makes normal talk entertaining. When gossip or conversation skillfully employs the performative structure of the tale or debate, it becomes "great *craic*" and rises above small talk. Likewise, music can be great *craic*, and in the context of the *cuaird* or *céilí*, music and chat occupy similarly lofty places.

Parties where traditional music is played still happen today, but compared to the old days, they are no longer the primary context for performances. Firstly, they are not the regular events that they once were. The television and the pub have somewhat reduced the primacy of the "visit" as a form of entertainment. Secondly, possibly due to their irregularity today, they are not the structured events that they used to be.[8] In the old days, *cuairds* were organized by generation. Young men would rarely assemble at the older men's *céilí* house and vice versa. Similarly, the *cuaird* was a collection of consociate relations with exclusive boundaries. Some even gave themselves official, though jocular, names like *The Dail*, a reference to the Irish parliamentary assembly (Arensberg and Kimball 1968[1940]: 173). By contrast, the "soirees" that I experienced were rare, and were more or less accidental gatherings of close and not-so-close friends. They did not resemble the structured and intimate environment described by Glassie or Arensberg and Kimball.

Christy Barry, an energetic flute and whistle player with a sharp sense of humor, grew up in the midst of Doolin's older generation. He told me what it was like to grow up in a "*céilí*-house":

> Ah. All I remember in our house was music. Music, dance, socializing. All the neighbors came in. Everybody just came in … . Even though it was a very small, little house … . That's where I got my love for music I suppose. D'y'know? Young and old came in and they played games or whatever they had to do. There was no television, no nothing like that … . We were just the main event for entertainment … even though it was a small, little house.

> They'd start by talking about their problems and the hardships of life, and they'd cry, and they'd share their problems: the awful amount of kids they had, and some of their kids would be sick, and—. It was all done at those events. That was where it was all done.

"So I suppose it was a group of friends, then," I said. "Fairly close people."

"Yeah", he said,

> Close people who loved the music. Music was loved. It was loved for the reason that it was nourishment. It was all they had. It was their upkeep in life. It was their spirit. It kept them alive. It kept their minds right, and it kept them going … .

> They seemed to be very faithful and loyal to each other. And so it did do a lot for them. D'y'know? And that's where it was used mostly: in the houses … . They'd all assemble at somebody's house—some farmhouse, some—. Different people would have it in different areas, different houses. D'y'know? And they'd stay at it all night until morning—like. They'd live it out until morning. D'y'know. That was the main purpose it, of music … . The ladies got together. The men got together. And they talked about their working problems. The women talked about their children, their families, their hardships, the whole thing. Sometimes tears were shed. Sometimes there was hugging going on. All this stuff happened at a musical event. And the music was the—at the end of all that—they'd let free and they'd dance and they'd sweat. And, let's say, after the stories being told, that's where they got their healing to go on the next day. And that's really what music was about in Ireland.

In the summertime, music might be played outdoors in a level field, or more commonly, at a crossroads where dancers would have enough room to move about. "The road in front of us—," Christy told me,

> the 'cross' near us in the road just near Ennistymon a couple of miles—the crossroads going onto the main road, every evening would be, like, full of young people, sitting on the walls, either dancing, singing, or playing sports … .

The days were long and there was plenty of time in 'em.

Music was a skilled craft with a purpose like any other rather than an art-form set aside from the rest of one's workaday life. People still use the term "musicianers" instead of "musicians" which describes the musician in action, contributing to a larger social environment, one who *does* something, not one who is passive. Like other skilled crafts, music tended to run in some families and not in others. Often, those who can play are the granddaughters or the nephews or the sons of some well-known musician, and often, their brothers and sisters are good players as well. Still, tunes have to be learned, and some "just don't have music" while others "have it." In the old days, musicians would learn tunes from locally renowned players. Christy Barry's mother was one such local teacher. He told me how people would come to the house, they'd have a chat over tea and biscuits, and maybe then she would teach them a few tunes. The lesson was the purpose of the visit but again, it had to be included into a larger social setting of visiting, gossiping, and taking some tea.

The Country House Dance

House dances were more formal events than the habitual but casual gathering of neighbors at a *céilí*. I went to ask John Killhoury about the country house dances one day because he and his brother used to play for them, and occasionally host them. John, who has since passed away, was just past ninety years old when I spoke to him. He was always renowned as a fixer of clocks as well as a "musicianer" so a chorus of wall-clocks surrounded us and paced the rhythm of his narrative as we sat in the dim light of his kitchen. He closed his eyes and told me in his booming voice,

> Well, in my young days, I was going around to all of the house dances. Myself and my two brothers used to go, playing music to 'em. We'd have 'em every week, maybe sometimes twice a week, the house dances. They were great, you see.

> A crowd might come into this house, you see. And they'd be dancing there, you see, until, maybe three or four o'clock in the morning, maybe … . Or maybe five, and even six, maybe, in the morning.

> Well, they might be charged—a little charge put on 'em for coming in, you see. A majority of the houses, they charged a tariff at the door—about a

shilling ... there were turkeys for gamblin', you see. There'd be Gambles then inside. Maybe down in the room, a-gamblin, along with the dance, d'you see. 'Twould be about two shillings, maybe. One-and-six [pence] or about two shillings, a fee, to go into the dances. 'Twould be.

We used to travel far and near, and we had no transport in them days, only the bicycles. And walking along. D'y'see? Walking! We used to go over to the Cliffs of Moher for the dances. That direction, you know. Not exactly into the Cliffs, but in the direction of Moher. And ol' Moymore. And we'd go down then to Ennistymon and up to Moy in Miltown Malbay maybe. And Doolin, in Carnaune above, up near Lisdoonvarna. Kilshanny. Maybe occasionally in the Kilfenora direction, to the dances.

Boys and girls would collect in, you see. You had to invite the girls who knew how to dance, of course. You had to go around to the houses, to fifteen or sixteen or twenty houses maybe, and ask the girls, the ladies to come. And they'd come then, you see. They'd come.

Oh, it'd be great enjoyment. A great big open fire down, a big fire, and you'd have seats up in by the walls for 'em to sit down in, all along. You'd have two, three, four, maybe five musicians up on a stage on a table. And chairs up on the table. About three together'd be playing. Or maybe four.

So, that was the carry-on.

Of course, House Dances were great *craic*, but they were also highly profitable. Often, a host would organize one simply to raise money. Seamus MacMahon told me about how lucrative the gambling could be.

There might be a prize going of a couple of geese or a couple of turkeys or something like that. And maybe you could play anything—maybe a pig or a few *bonards*. And it'd be a shilling to a guy. And I'd often see thirty or thirty-five teams of four.

The hosts could make a very respectable profit from two turkeys or geese that they most likely raised themselves, and could host a night of great fun for the whole community.

The country house dance, then, was a rather different context from the *céilí*. They were bigger. They were wilder. They were public. They were organized to make money. But in one significant way, they were very similar to the *céilí*. The music that was played at a country house dance was, again, part of a larger social context of entertainments among neighbors. The music and the dancing were symbiotic species. The one could barely exist without the other.

Locals in Doolin recall that on Sundays set-dancing also used to take place at Miss Murphy's, a shop that sold sweets, cigarettes, and tea down by the seaside. "She had a nice dancing stage made in the back of her little shop," Gus O'Connor told me.

> And it was an attraction, you see, because she'd be selling some of her stuff .... The lads'd be there every Sunday and they'd be dancing and playing the music, d'y'know. An awful lot of musicianers used to come there .... .

> Every Sunday, a few sets. And they were good. The girls got great practice back that time, you know. The girls that was down there on Fisherstreet, they were great dancers.

It was at this tea shop that the famous "collector" of tunes, Seamus Ennis, made his first acquaintance with Doolin and its musicianers (Bourke 1986: 54).

Ironically, the country house dances were made illegal in 1935, an era in which the newly independent government was trying to promote Irish "Cultural Nationalism" (Curran 1999: 57). Under the Dance Halls Act, dances required a license, and had to be supervised. Ostensibly, the Act was aimed at the commercial dance halls that were mushrooming around the nation, but it also covered country house dances and even the more informal crossroads dances (ibid.). Parish priests would often use the pulpit to claim that sexual depravities were associated with dancing (ibid.; Ó hAllmhuráin 1998: 101–102), and in fact it was the Catholic Church that pressured the government to pass the Act. Armed with the new legal backing and occasionally accompanied by the police, black cassocked priests began tramping along country lanes looking (and listening) for dances to thwart. But despite this outwardly moral crusade, it was obvious that the priests simply coveted the profits that their parishioners were earning from the dances, because after the passing of the Act most of the licenses went to the parish priests themselves (Curran 1999: 57).

The Dance Halls Act effectively eradicated country house dances in most places in Ireland (ibid.; Curtis 1994: 14), but in more rural pockets like northwest Clare the practice was altogether more difficult to immobilize. John Killhoury told me about the last country house dance that he could remember in the area, one that he happened to host himself many years after the passage of the Dance Halls Act.

> It came in then at the end that you'd have to have a license for the dance. A license. D'y'see. A license! And if you didn't have a suitable premises, you wouldn't get the license. If it weren't like a dance-hall—the house, d'y'see.

> And ah, I had a dance here. I think it wound-up all of the dances that were around the place, the last dance that I had in this house. That would have to be over forty years ago. Let me see. It would be, I'd say, over forty years ago since I had this dance.

And the Guards[9] raided me, at my house. And I got a summons and I were brought into court. I were brought to court ... .

So that put an end to the dances.

The Dance Halls and The Céilí *Bands*

But something else had also begun to keep people away from the country house dances. Jazz and big band music had been growing in popularity well before the Dance Hall Act was passed. A musical fusion had been created between the big band music and traditional Irish music, and in the dance halls of the towns and cities, this exciting new music was played to accompany Irish set dancing. John told me,

> The dance halls in the towns came into existence ... and then all the people from the country was going into the dance halls. In there, they were going. The hall dances would be big *céilí* dances, d'y'see?

The use of the word *céilí* in this context has very little to do with the *céilís* that Glassie describes. These dance halls employed '*céilí* bands' which consisted of a combination of "traditional" instruments such as fiddles, flutes, accordions, concertinas or banjos, and big band instruments such as the double-bass, and drums (Curtis 1994: 14). The piano ubiquitously provided homophonous accompaniment in a strong marching rhythm. Christy Barry remembered a local *céilí* band that had clarinets and a brass section. "It wasn't just fiddles and concertinas", he said, "There was a lot of brass in it ... . Irish music would be dictated by brass."

The way this music was played and performed differed radically from the music played at a *céilí* or a country house dance even though the tunes themselves might have been the same. In these other contexts, musicians would have all played the melodic line simultaneously in unison. This allowed each musician to play on their own or with any combination of other musicians. Also, certain musicians might prefer playing together, but there was no such thing as membership into a group. The tradition of playing different versions of a tune was an aesthetic marker as well. Finally, the order of tunes within a set of tunes might be known beforehand, but quite often not at all. The lead musician might simply call out a new tune or even just a key-signature towards the end of the previous one. *Céilí* band music was different, first because they required membership. One version of a tune was chosen and agreed upon by a bandleader, and tunes would be formalized into arranged sets. Like the big bands of the time, different parts—melodic lines or rhythmic lines—were arranged for the varying instruments (Ó hAllmhuráin 1998: 101–102). *Céilí* bands first became popular in the late 1920s (ibid.), and as the country house dances waned from the mid-thirties onward, the *céilí* bands filled the void. In many ways, the music was very different from that which was played in previous contexts, but to some extent, this was a country house dance formalized and writ large. And popularity bred fame, especially after *Radio Eireann* began broadcasting recordings of *céilí* band music on the air. By the 1940s, classically trained musicians were even auditioning traditional musicians before they were allowed to be broadcast on the air (ibid.: 112–113). Two of the most famous bands of this era—The Kilfenora *Céilí* Band and the Tulla *Céilí* Band—were from County Clare.

Early Collections and Early Sessions

The economic depression in Ireland in the 1950s was severe (Ó Gráda 1997: 25), and it was hard on the *céilí* band scene and traditional music generally. Emigration took its toll on Ireland's stock of musicians. The popularity of rock-and-roll, and the new "sound" coming out of America did not help either as it supplanted Irish music on the airwaves (Curtis 1994: 15). In most of the Republic of Ireland, traditional music became difficult to come by. Most people, faced with yet another cycle of economic hardship, simply wanted to modernize. People began rejecting the symbols of "traditional" Ireland. Live traditional music was now only heard at Christmastime or at weddings. Indeed, one of the only remaining mediums for hearing traditional Irish dance music was in the form of a few radio programs. The radio shows that Ciarán Mac Mathúna and Seamus Ennis broadcast kept a small core audience around the country satisfied (ibid.: 16). The influence of the very earliest of recordings of traditional Irish music cannot be underestimated because the bottleneck effect they had on today's style of playing. Fairbairn has argued that early recordings of Sligo musicians, who tend to use more complex ornamentation, started to influence the performance style of musicians from other counties (1994: 577). Interestingly, these early recordings were of Irish émigrés in New York and were later imported back to Ireland (ibid.).

Traditional music always remained popular around west and north Clare though, as did other "folk traditions" that had long since died out elsewhere such as the Straw Boys ritual at weddings,[10] the Wren Boys (mummers) performances at Christmas, and traditional forms of storytelling (Vaillant 1984: 77). In fact, the west coast of County Clare was considered one of a few places where these traditions still lived on (Curtis 1994: 16). Collectors from the Folklore Commission gathered materials in the area between the 1920s and 1943 (Coady 1996: 8). Local people remember Ciarán Mac Mathúna and Seamus Ennis coming to Doolin to "collect" tunes for their radio programs. Seamus Ennis wrote about his first trip to Doolin in his diary. He stayed out at the tea shop at Doolin Point for two weeks. It was on the day that he left Doolin, September 30, 1945, that Ennis spent most of six hours collecting tunes and talking with a twenty-four year old Packie Russell (Bourke 1986: 55). Packie was one of a number of musicians around the area who played regularly at house dances, Miss Murphy's Tea Shop, and other social outlets. He and his brothers, Micho and Gussie, along with Willibeg Shannon, Steve MacNamara, and also Paddy and John Killhoury formed part of the core of this traditional music scene that was so healthy that it attracted academic "collectors." Without a doubt the fact that collectors were interested in the music encouraged local musicians too.

These were the musicians who would play music occasionally in J. O'Connor's Pub in the 1950s. I asked Gus O'Connor when musicians had started playing tunes in the pub. "Oh, that was always there," he said, "but on a small scale." In her memoirs, the daughter of the local landlord even recalls dancing occurring there before the 1920s (Devas 1968: 27). On special occasions, the locals would have an illicit after-hours "lock-in" and play music and dance. Unlike other musical contexts in which the genders were allowed or even encouraged to mix, women were not normally seen in the pubs in the old days. One older woman in the village told me that "it just wasn't the done thing" for women. As a result, these early sessions took place in the private spaces of the pub—namely, the publicans' kitchen. I asked Seamus MacMahon if it was unusual to have music in the pubs in those days. "It was", he said,

I'll tell you.

I remember now.

They might be playin there of a Sunday night you know, on a special occasion. Maybe it'd be in the Christmastime. Maybe around Easter. Maybe around St. Patrick's Day. And old O'Connor now—Gussie's father—he'd have to be watching in case the Guards'd come. And they'd be playin' down in the kitchen. The Guards were very strict that time with the pub licenses you know ... .

They tried to have long sessions on them nights you know.

I asked if this was happening in pubs in the neighboring towns and villages: Ennistymon, Lahinch, or Liscannor.
He answered,

It is now alright, but earlier on it wasn't happening in Ennistymon. As far as I know it wasn't. Well, I suppose in the sixties it was alright-like but, you know, not before that.[11]

Soon enough, playing music in O'Connor's Pub went from being a special occasion to becoming a regular habit. In this era when traditional music was at best disregarded and at worst disparaged in many parts of Ireland, publicans like Gus and Doll O'Connor who encouraged musicians to play in the pub became some of the only real patrons of the music. This patron-client relationship (an old institutional pattern in Ireland that also included the priests, and prior to Independence, the landlords) was to become appreciably concretized in later years.

The economic depression of the 1950s and early 1960s meant that there was little work to be had in Doolin. Music in the pub helped pass the time. Michael Coady remembers that the three Russell brothers "possessed an enormous body of music" between them, but it was a relatively rare thing for all three of them to play together at the same time "due to personality differences" (1996: 12). Despite this, all three life-long bachelors lived in the same house. As one local put it, "Packie was fond of 'the drop'", and eventually died from drinking related health problems. He was a sharp wit by all accounts and a great musician, and would often spend the afternoons in O'Connor's playing tunes on his concertina. Micho Russell would play the whistle or sing songs during the evening. "Micho was the night man, and Packie was the day man," I was told. Gussie Russell, the third brother, was a brilliant flute and whistle player. I was often told that he might have been the best musician of the three, but that his intense shyness kept him from the limelight throughout the years. Other local musicians would also join in on a regular basis. As recordings of these early sessions were made and broadcast on the radio by Ciarán Mac Mathúna and Seamus Ennis, the word began to spread amongst connoisseurs of traditional Irish music that Doolin was a place to hear a bit of the "pure drop." Others heard as well. Doolin was suddenly "on the map." And then, very quickly and very dramatically, things started to change. Or more accurately, things started to change again. We will see just how they changed in the next chapter.

Conclusions

Dipping back into the remembered history clearly illustrates how political, social, and musical change is nothing new to Doolin, to northwest County Clare, nor indeed to Ireland. The period of social memory that I have delineated as "the old days" was a period in which an older economic structure, a smallholding economy, survived (but was under significant pressure). Likewise, traditional Irish music survived in very small pockets around the country, although largely, interest in this music had dwindled to almost nothing (Curtis 1994: 16).

Local histories and relationships are intimately related to regional, national, and global developments. While we ought not become too enamored with our grand theories of globalization, it is just as intellectually unsophisticated to embed ourselves in the local and forget the extra-local. A truer contextualization ignores neither scale. Life in Doolin in the old days was quite clearly affected by national and international economic shifts, politics, and socio-cultural changes. But the character and actions of local individuals also began to leave their mark in these larger arenas. This will become even more evident in the following chapter.

Notes

1. See Connerton (1989: 2), Glassie (1995[1984]: 59) and Tonkin (1992: 2) for further discussions.
2. Obviously, the War of Independence from Britain and the subsequent "economic war" create a dramatic backdrop to the early twentieth century in Ireland, but it is beyond the scope of this book to delve into those complex topics. Occasional references to pre-war era are made in this chapter, but most of what is discussed follows the war.
3. When local people describe the Burren they like to use a quote often credited to Cromwell: "There aren't trees enough to hang a man, water enough to drown him, nor soil enough to bury him."
4. This excludes those listed as school children, but includes those whose occupation is listed as "farmer's son" or daughter, "farmer's wife", or "farm labourer" ("1901 Census of Clare—Killilagh DED").

5. This was a tea and sweets shop at Doolin pier where musicians would occasionally play. It no longer exists.

6. The exception to this is the refinement of "*céilí* band" music played for radio broadcasts in the 1940s and early 1950s.

7. As the area's Gaelic speakers died, this seems to be a term that was lost to common usage, but the lack of its use today (and its related terms) also indicates the changes that have occurred in musical contexts since the 1930s.

8. I use the term "structure" here in the sense that *céilís* were habitually and regularly attended, not in the sense that the events themselves are formally structured. Having said that, a further qualification is justified: As Glassie describes in great detail (1995[1982]), *céilís* do have their own subtle, informal, rules of behavior.

9. An Anglicized shorthand for the *Gardaí*, the Irish police

10. This is a classic ritual of reversal that involves the groom's male relatives cross-dressing and stealing the bride (Valliant 1984).

11. Note Seamus's chronological qualifications. This is an example of the way in which we "dip" into the pool of remembered history and rearrange it to fit a chronology. First, he talks about the present. Then, he reaches back to The Old Days when "it wasn't happening." Then, he jumps forward to "the 60s" to qualify his statement, and then finishes in the Old Days again.

Chapter 3

The Revival

High Art is very fine but it is not enough in the twentieth century—it was
never enough.
—Ailie Munroe (1984: 33)

Doolin was destined to be the nest for this hatching of new rules to break
the old rules.
—Nicolette Devas (1968: 26)

It was at Gus O'Connor's Pub in Doolin in the 1950s and 1960s that the three
bachelor Russell brothers—Micho, Packie, and Gussie—regularly played music,
told stories and tall tales, and generally passed the time. Other musicians like the
Killhoury brothers and Willibeg Shannon would often join them. For many miles
around, people knew they could hear a little music and enjoy the *craic* and a story
there. Christy Barry was barely a teenager when he first started to play music with the
Russell brothers. He was particularly inspired by Gussie's flute playing. He described
what O'Connor's was like before people began to flock to the area in the late 1960s:

> O'Connor's
> would have sessions,
> would have Packie Russell in there, sittin'.
>
> And you'd have a different kind of group of people going in there.
> A bachelor kind of a group of people.
> who wouldn't be too interested in getting up dancing anyway. They preferred
> to talk, and they preferred to slag and bullshit each other all night long at
> the time, d'y'know?
>
> But they were great company … . It was like long, old stories, and fairy
> stories, and a tune. And Packie Russell was a very wisdom kind of a—and
> a very—a man that wouldn't withdraw. He'd add to the fire, you know.

They'd drive a situation, you know, and make a big deal out of it. And some people'd be confused. Others'd believing it. Others wouldn't know whether it was bullshit, and—. They had their own fun. D'y'know what I mean?

But a lovely social life they had there.

I said,

So it was an entertainment based on talking and storytelling.

He answered,

Yeah.

And they would have set dancing in the kitchen previous years to that. You know, they'd have little bits [of music] for when people'd come around. And a lot of musicians came up from Ennistymon to play there at that time … and they all came up there to play for a few years, for the pints. You know, that was the pay they got.

It was in this setting that the first Revival sessions took off in Doolin amidst these local bachelors who were able to entertain people with sharp-tongued conversations and storytelling, even when there were no tunes to be heard. As O'Connor's Pub in Doolin gained a reputation as the place to go to hear traditional music, regular visitors from across Ireland—and very quickly from across the globe—started to trickle in to hear or learn how to play a few old tunes. Peter Curtin, a publican who runs a family pub called the Roadside Tavern, in the neighboring town of Lisdoonvarna, remembers how this quickly snowballed.

And once it got that momentum going, more musicians wanted to play there because if—they knew if they went to Doolin, there was always a session going on in the pub. They could always join in … virtually all day long, from like 12:00 to closing time, there was always somebody about to either scratch on the fiddle or whatever, d'y'know? It was like that.

Then, popularity breeds popularity. Some people like to go where the action is. You know, if people want to learn music, and they know there's good musicians down there, well then that's the place they'll go to.

So.
And then you get to a certain kind of critical level, and then it kind of keeps itself going there, thereafter, you know?

Very quickly, a small trickle of traditional music "pilgrims" became a flood. The revival, as it has come to be known, landed squarely in Doolin in the late 1960s.

When people discuss the revival, it is, in the first instance, about music, but as Vallely has pointed out it was also "a cocktail of awareness of value, politics, reaction to technology, conservatism, nostalgia, music and commitment. Essentially it involves much more than music, for it can build sub-cultures and new myths" (1999: 318).

The revival of traditional Irish music in Ireland was not an isolated event in other words. Shields and Gershen argued that it was largely the result of four elements: the influence from the folk music revivals that had been gathering steam in the United States and Scotland, the increased recording and broadcasting of traditional Irish music, the beginning of competitive festivals of traditional music after 1951, and the huge impact that the arranged compositions of traditional Irish music by Seán Ó Riada, who founded what was to become the band the Chieftains (Shields and Gershen 2000: 390). Curtis identifies another ingredient that allowed much of this to happen: the underlying current of growing economic prosperity in the 1960s in the Irish economy. A sense of "confidence permeated not only the business sector but also the arts in all forms. For one golden moment, everything was hopeful, everything was possible," he writes (Curtis 1994: 17–18). Locals in Doolin told me that this sense of "possibility and freedom" was an inherent part of the revival. Two other elements brought the revival to places like Doolin. Firstly, the development of modern tourist infrastructures in Ireland increased the ease of travel for people coming from other countries. What's more, an improvement in the Irish economy encouraged masses of Irish emigrants to return home. A bit of extra cash and the continued development of an international tourist infrastructure meant that more people began to move about. A consumerist buzz swept through the nation as shopkeepers and publicans expanded and improved their businesses, and coach tours full of foreign tourists began to roll through Ireland's villages (Ó hAllmhuráin 1998: 127–128). The second element was the countercultural movement that emerged in the 1960s. It was associated originally with rock and roll and the folk revivals which started in England and America, and added an edginess and buoyancy to this heady mix of growing economic prosperity, easier travel, intensified external interest in traditional Irish music, and the internal changes in the music itself through innovative compositions and official competitions.

Peter Curtin described this strange coalescent mix and how it affected northwest Clare:

You had the first inklings of people with money in Ireland—people getting jobs and money, and a bit of inward investment. That was another piece, where people began to come west and enjoy the hospitality along the west coast. The music was there, the music of the—the only music available was traditional music, right? And ah, people in the west coast were into the traditional music … .

And suddenly, there was a kind of focus on Irish music in the broad sense of the word, which helped the popularity of the core of the music itself. And ah, the people could see that there was a genuine relaxation and welcome and a genuine sense of relaxed carefree fun in coming to places like Doolin.

And in particular, O'Connor's Pub—the O'Connor's themselves, Gussie (God Rest Him) and Doll, were really hospitable people. They were very genuine in the way that they behaved towards the people.

And that was largely the ingredients.

Of course, you also had a far more relaxed regime in the country. There was no such thing as drunken driving, breathalyzers, less motorcars than there is now. You know, the safety factor—the caution—wasn't necessarily there. The laws weren't there and things were much more easy. And that was the beginnings of it.

Traditional Irish music gained a wider popularity, and as Peter told me, some traditional musicians brought it to the rest of the world, which propelled the revival to a new global level:

You also, then, had groups going out, like The Furey Brothers in particular, going to Germany. They became very popular. You had agents coming in from Germany to the All-Ireland Fleadh Cheoil in Listowel looking at these groups, taking them back, putting them on the folk-circuit in Germany for example, introducing the European people to Irish traditional music, the younger people in these countries having lost their own ethnic music to a large extent. Looked at the Irish thing. Looked at the mystique of Ireland. Ireland was suddenly made available to European people. They could come to Ireland, particularly university students and people like that, backpacking. Staying in hostels sprung up. Cheap accommodation. You know?

Many disparate things coalesced at once to produce the unprecedented and sudden changes that came to northwest Clare in the late 1960s. The impetus for the revival and the timing of its arrival in Doolin were due to events and shifting patterns that had been occurring internationally and nationally for decades. People had more financial (and therefore physical) mobility as the Irish economy improved. Mass tourism began to spread across the globe to places like Ireland. A new generation in Europe and America was emerging. Some of these young people were searching for new experiences and were drawn to the romance of what might be called "traditionality." Interest in traditional music intensified, both within Ireland and internationally. All of these factors led to more travel to and within Ireland. Very suddenly, places like Doolin became tourist destinations, especially for aficionados of traditional music. These larger societal and economic factors deserve a closer analysis before we return to the music itself.

A Changing Economy

Before the revival, in the era when the Russell brothers entertained locals with a few tunes and good conversation, things were not so good economically. In fact, Doll O'Connor told me that playing music was perceived to be something of a waste of time by many, something that detracted from the endless cycle of farming and fishing and surviving. Musicians, she told me, made sure to carry their instrument cases low at their side when making their way to the pub. That way, the stone walls that line the roads concealed the instruments from the peering eyes of gossiping neighbors. Money was scarce in Ireland and music did not feed families.

After the Second World War, Europe's economic productivity rebounded while Ireland's economy only grew very slowly. In comparison to the expansive growth in Europe, it felt like stagnation. This economic imbalance between Ireland and the rest of Europe led to yet another wave in the pattern of emigration as Irish people moved abroad for better wages (O'Hagan 1995: 34) in England and elsewhere. Largely, wrote one economist, the 1950s were "a miserable decade" (Ó Gráda 1997: 25). Then an important shift occurred. Economic policies in the 1960s, characterized by trade liberalization and increased foreign investment, led to an increase in per capita income that considerably outpaced incomes in Britain even (O'Hagan 1995: 36). Not only did emigration cease, but immigration into Ireland actually began. "For the first time in several hundred years", Curtis wrote, "a generation of young Irish men and women did not have to consider emigration as their only option. A dynamic new energy found release in this seemingly new Ireland, growing in confidence almost daily" (1994: 18).

Trade barriers were actively dismantled throughout the 1960s. Tariffs were cut significantly, a "free trade area" was created between Ireland and Britain, and in 1967, Ireland signed onto the General Agreement on Tariffs and Trade (GATT). This was a clear move towards economic globalization, and the effects are felt today. All of these measures followed the general politico-economic amalgamating trend throughout Europe (O'Hagan 1995: 36–37). Serious discussions about an integrated European entity, discussions that ultimately led to the European Economic Community (now the European Union), and more recently a single currency, began as early as the mid-1950s (Maher 1986: 50). To say nothing of the monetary or political impact that an integrating Europe was to have on Ireland, the shift was psychologically significant. It was the beginning of a new sense of independence, one that was not merely defined in opposition to "Britishness" (Graham 1997: 8). Ireland officially entered the EEC in 1973, and ever since, has increasingly invested itself in a relationship with this emergent European "community" (O'Hagan 1995: 37). Although it would remain a very poor country at the edge of one of the world's most powerful regions for several decades to come, the general commitment in Irish policies to economic globalization would have far reaching impacts.

A shift in attitudes towards tourism had also occurred. *Bord Fáilte* (literally, the "Welcoming Board") was created in 1952 under the auspices of the Tourist Traffic Act in order to "encourage and develop tourist traffic", to "engage in publicity", and to license hotels and other accommodations (Deegan and Dineen 1997: 21).

Things had changed very quickly in the years preceding the act. While discussing the bill to create *Bord Fáilte*, a deputy in the *Dáil* (the Irish parliament) recalled that only a few years previously, tourism was even seen by some politicians as an unwelcome annoyance to Irish society (ibid.). In the 1960s, the tourism industry expanded rapidly throughout Europe, and the Irish government began to give *Bord Fáilte* more funding and discretion as to where monies were spent (ibid.: 36–41). John F. Kennedy even recognized the importance of the tourist industry in Ireland when he visited to country in 1963: "Other nations in the world in whom Ireland has long invested her people and her children are now investing their capital as well as their vacations in Ireland" (Bryant 1979: 1). He was not wrong. Between the mid-1950s and the mid-1970s, the overall number of tourists doubled, and the number of North American tourists tripled (ibid.).

This economic "Golden Age" was to last for almost two decades, well into the late 1970s when Ireland was crippled by rising unemployment and the aftermath of the oil crisis (Ó Gráda 1997: 30). This glimpse of economic prosperity created a buoyant confidence during the revival period. The positive mood was accompanied by other major factors that are important to our history: the revival of folk musics in the English-speaking world, internal changes within Irish music, and an emergent youth counterculture.

The Folk Revival

In 1947 in Scotland, the International Festival of the Arts was founded in Edinburgh, exposing traditional Scottish singers and musicians from the countryside to an urban audience (Skinner Sawyers 2000: 151). Additionally, in the late 1940s, a Scottish Studies program was set up at Edinburgh University, driving a grassroots revival of traditional music (Munroe 1984: 53–54). Like the parallel folk music movement occurring around the same time in the US, the Scottish musical revival had a political edge to it "virtually guaranteed by industrial decline, appalling social conditions, and a powerful socialist movement" (Skinner Sawyers 2000: 152). By the mid-1950s, just a few years after its first introduction to an urban audience, Scottish folk music seemed to have suddenly appeared "with all the force of revelation to audiences of questing intellectuals, industrial workers, students, douce city folk and cosmopolitan culture-seekers", and it "could not be re-submerged" (Munroe 1984: 58). Moreover, it was not limited to Scotland. McCann (1995) documents the emergence of a folk song revival in Belfast at this time as well.

A revival of what simply came to be called "folk music" had emerged in the US decades earlier. Alan Lomax brought his extensive collections of music from the South to Greenwich Village in New York where he enlisted singers like Woodie Guthrie, Huddie "Leadbelly" Ledbetter and others (Cantwell 1996: 4). "Folk music" in the US centered primarily on ballads rather than instrumental dance tunes like in the west of Ireland. Moreover, a clear agenda—pro-union, pro-working class, anti-fascist, and anti-war—began to emerge around the US folk music revival. Pete Seeger, Leadbelly, and Woodie Guthrie (who Munroe has called "America's Robert Burns" [1984: 29–30]) were particularly political. In the 1960s, a new generation of musicians, inspired by these folk-singing forebears, established themselves commercially, and went on to sing the melodies of the counterculture movement. Bob Dylan, Joan Baez, and Peter, Paul, & Mary were perhaps the best known of this circle (Curtis 1994: 18). They created a folk music "boom," which maintained political protest as a central element. The Civil Rights and the Anti-War movements provided enough material to sing about, and a growing youth counterculture provided a growing audience (Eyerman and Jamison 1998: 97, 114; and also see Foss and Larkin 2001). Folk music rivaled rock and roll on the singles charts.

It was during this period that an Irish balladeering group called the Clancy Brothers and Tommy Makem caught the attention of the folk scene in the US. They used harmonies, a guitar, and an American-style five-string banjo for backing accompaniment to adapt Irish ballads. They garnered much commercial success (Skinner Sawyers 2000: 219), appearing on the *Ed Sullivan Show*, and performing at Carnegie Hall in New York and at the Royal Albert Hall in London (Ó hAllmhuráin 1998: 129). They exuded an air of the "ethnic authenticity" and "underclass purity" that appealed to the American folk audiences so much. They wore Aran Island sweaters and sang in a thick Irish accent about oppression and loss. Their international popularity, of course, made them instant celebrities "back home" as well, and prompted other native Irish ballad groups to join the fray. The Dubliners, The Wolfe Tones, and The Fureys quickly surfaced as celebrity balladeering groups. People began to collect in smoky clubs to take turns singing songs from the US, Ireland, England, and Scotland accompanied on acoustic guitars. This was not the instrumental dance music that the Russell brothers played in O'Connor's Pub in Doolin, but given the "folk music" tag that was often pinned on traditional Irish dance music, it was not a stretch for enthusiasts to see the two as related genres. These balladeers, mostly from the bigger cities like Dublin, were keen to hear what they called "the pure drop" and learn to play it, and they quickly went searching for it in places like Doolin.

One of the great ironies about the revivals of folk musics in the twentieth century is that they emerged to a large extent in urban centers and spread outward into the rural countryside, not the other way around. At their lowest ebb in popularity, traditional music(s) tend to survive in rural pockets, places like western County Clare or southern Appalachia. In these places, revival is unnecessary. Christy Barry made this point one day when we talked at his house in Doolin:

> You know, music wasn't that plentiful all over, really. It wasn't. There was counties that never had it, really. It was really Clare and counties like up around Sligo and Galway. Just along the west coast there, up to Donegal, really.

As Livingston has suggested, the specific motivations for involving oneself in a musical revival are infinitely variable (1999: 73). Like Bohlman (1988: 130–135), she suggests that music revivals are even "a particular class of musical phenomenon" (Livingston 1999: 69). Still, there is a common pattern in which people of urban extraction actively seek out the folk music of the rural countryside, learn it, perpetuate it, and create the driving force behind its revival. Urban revivalists desired what they imagined rural people had. The romantic search for the "authentic folk culture" in the rural hinterlands has gone on for centuries, for example giving birth to the discipline of folkloristics in Europe.

In Ireland, the appropriation during the Revival of a mostly rural music by musicians and singers from urban origins began to create a deep rift amongst musicians that eventually led to a politically charged debate over "authenticity." Skinner Sawyers' description of the period is common: "scores of young people throughout the British Isles [were] invading pubs, strumming guitars, wearing fishermen's jerseys, singing watered-down versions of ancient ballads, and, in essence, passing themselves off as the real thing to anyone willing to listen" (2000: 219). Some musicians I talked to in Clare were equally nonplussed. Many others thought that this period was more of an "awakening" though.

Internal Changes in Irish Music

Comhaltas Ceoltóirí Éireann (pronounced roughly *co-altus cyeltory erin* and translating roughly to the "Musicians' Association of Ireland"), or CCE, was formed in 1951 with the goal of supporting and disseminating traditional Irish music, dancing, and language in community settings. It was originally a small organization formed as an offshoot of the Piper's Club, an institution that dates back to 1908 (Henry 1989: 69–70). But CCE grew quickly and became an important element in the traditional Irish music scene, especially in regards to the annual *fleadh cheoil* ("music competition", pronounced *fla cyol*) that it sponsors. Today, CCE is a massive and influential institution with local branches in every county in Ireland (north and south), England, throughout Europe and North America, Australia, New Zealand (Henry 1989: 70–71), and now as far afield as Tokyo, Japan (www.comhaltas-jp.com). Although CCE activities are varied and occur at international, national, and local levels, the All-Ireland *fleadh cheoil* is by far CCE's most publicly celebrated function. "The *fleadh*," as it is more commonly known, is held on the fourth weekend of every August (Henry 1989: 75). There are formally judged competitions in various categories, formalized classes, and an endless series of informal sessions in pubs and on the streets.

Only a decade after its creation, tens of thousands of people were attending the annual *fleadhanna*, and by 1965, CCE was coming into direct conflict with the nascent Revival. In particular, serious tensions arose when a massive crowd descended on the 1965 *fleadh* in Thurles. The town was inadequately prepared. By sheer numbers, the youthful revival crowd appropriated the 1965 *fleadh*, and they clearly brought a different meaning to the music than the founders of CCE. It was no longer a quiet little competition for Irish musicians trying to promote, as one CCE member suggested, the "vision of an Irish idyll" (quoted in Henry 1989: 69). The revival crowd was blamed for all the problems with that years' *fleadh*. The newspapers reported that these "revivalists," described earlier by one journalist as "bearded balladeers" and "guitar-propped jokers" (Paddy Tunny quoted in Curran 1999: 60), were more interested in debauchery and riotous behavior than music. Another journalist depicted the whole row over the 1965 *fleadh* as emblematic of the "internationalization" that threatened Irish society generally (ibid.). Partitions, stereotypes, and battle lines were quickly drawn up. The guitar-clad youths were assumed to be Dubliners: young, depraved, urban invaders corrupting the integrity of the music. The "serious" musicians were perceived to be rural folk: older, wiser traditionalists trying to preserve it from ruination (ibid.). After 1965, many musicians began "saving themselves" for more private sessions after the official *fleadh* weekend concluded. By 1970, the decision had been made to even move the annual competition as far away from Dublin as possible to attempt to limit the magnitude of the crowds. As a result, the town of Listowel in County Kerry, all the way across the island, has become a regular host (ibid.: 61–62). But by then, "the spirit of the age" as one Doolin musician described it to me, had taken over the younger generation. The ballad boom and a full-blown revival of traditional Irish music had blended and gained a singular momentum.

The episode at Thurles, and the consequent tensions between "revivalists" and "traditionalists," reveal a change in musical meaning. As Bohlman has pointed out, the emergence of new ideologies about folk musics are in fact a central feature of revivals (1988: 134–135). Not only was there a new kind of division between the knowledgeable "keepers of the tradition" and these teeming masses, but also what was deemed to be "authentic" Irish music was being contested by a new generation (ibid.: 62). An official, institutionalized definition of what the music was "about" was running headlong into a grassroots revival that had as much to do with lifestyle as it did with the structures of a particular musical form.

CCE is a bureaucratic institution, an organization, and while Irish music had been institutionalized before in various other ways, no musical organization had been so broad or influential in its coverage. In many ways it helped promote Irish music to a wider audience and even saved it from possible extinction (Ó hAllmhuráin 1998: 123; Curtis 1994: 17; Henry 1989: 69). In that sense, CCE played an important role in laying the foundation for the revival that it eventually came to resent. Institutions are by nature authoritative, and as one recent journalist wrote of CCE, they "jealously guard" their "territory from threats internal and external. Border disputes have been frequent and sometimes bitter" (McNally 2003: 12). According to Bohlman, two central responses in folk musics to culture change are institutionalization and what he calls "classicisation", a move towards the standards of western classical music (1988: 134). Clearly, CCE and the competitions are representative of this shift.

Two other points can be made here. First, the conflict between the "traditionalists" and the "revivalists" is a good example of how social structures buckle and collapse in periods of rapid change in cultural meanings. New generations may altogether reject what Bourdieu has called the previous generations' "structuring structures" and dispositions, or as is at least partially the case here, they may fundamentally alter their meaning in the zealous attempt to (re)locate and adopt older traditions. Second, due to strongly held conviction that traditional Irish music is a public resource, owned collectively in a kind of "commons," institutionalizing it in any form causes conflict. To this day, opinions about CCE and the competitions can sometimes be bitter. Some musicians I know regularly attend *fleadhanna* and look forward to the exciting atmosphere that surrounds them, but many musicians are also equally dismissive. The latter feel strongly that the very act of competing and judging fosters a misguided elitism in the music and erodes its original evocation of a sense of community. One man even suggested to me that "the better musicians" avoid competitions altogether today because "there are always too many musicians just showing off". Another person, not a player herself but and avid connoisseur, told me that she was concerned about what the act of competing was doing to the music:

> Competitions never made music better. Competitions are still destroying music as far as I'm concerned. You can't play Irish music in a competition. Sitting down to play a tune for two or three people listening to you, sitting down to judge you, couldn't make it better.
>
> No.
>
> It doesn't make it better. It takes the energy out of the music because people are too nervous and too careful and too everything.

On the other hand, the younger musicians in the 1960s and 1970s, whether they attended the *fleadhanna* or not, were exposed to this higher standard of musical ability, and were poised to take the quality of the music to new heights. Christy Barry suggested that, through various means, these musicians were pushing things beyond what the older generation had taught them:

> I think the younger musicians of the time were great. The younger lads took it further. They peaked. What the other guys were trying to do, they made it happen kind of, d'y'know? They developed the music into what it should be, really. They were a little bit more educated … . They mixed more, and they learned more from each other than the older crowd did. The old crowd would be set in their ways in their areas and they'd have their own little things going … . They wouldn't have tape recorders or anything up 'til then, really anyway, would they? D'y'know? They wouldn't have anything to learn tunes off of. They wouldn't have a great variety of music, the old people. They might have a couple of tunes, d'y'know, and that was it.
>
> But the younger lads started to do more research and fuckin' bring out more stuff. And old stuff that was in books and stuff like that, d'y'know, and really get into it. And they'd come and put a little enthusiasm in the music. A bit of life and energy.

Christy adds to what Peter Curtin described earlier in that various extra-musical social factors coalesced during the Revival.

In a sense, the establishment of the *fleadhanna*, and CCE's failed attempt to initially keep vast audiences away from them, actually helped reinforce what was to become one of the basic behaviors of the revivalists: traveling far and wide for a bit of music and a bit of *craic*. The increasing mobility of musicians added an important element of excitement to the Revival. Again, Christy Barry described how exhilarating it was to hear, for the first time, music from other parts of the country:

> And you were traveling a bit more to meet other people, other musicians. You were havin' the get-togethers not just in the house. You were having the get-togethers publicly, [with musicians] from other counties and places we hadn't heard music comin from, that nobody had ever been-like before that. Like Donegal and places. And we were getting their influence a little bit. And we were starting to hear where they were at.

> And 'twas all great music. D'y'know? 'Twas all fuckin' great stuff. Their tradition was different from ours, but you could—you could shake hands on it. You knew what they were about and they knew what *we* were about. And we were both doing the same job-like.

> D'y'know?

Eventually, the distinct regional styles within traditional Irish music began to fade somewhat (Ó hAllmhuráin 1998: 124). Partly, this resulted from these interregional influences. It was also due to the increasing number of recordings of traditional Irish music after the early 1970s. But during the early years of the Revival, it was an exciting time of interregional musical communication, education, and experimentation.

Another big change occurred within the music starting with the innovations of the composer Seán Ó Riada. He was born in Cork and raised in Limerick, where he learned traditional Irish music on the fiddle. He got his first formal music degree from the University College Cork, later studied music in Italy and France, and eventually returned to Ireland where he worked for the Abbey Theatre and finally for his alma mater in Cork. During his lifetime, he composed liturgical works, pieces of classical music, and film scores. Ó Riada became something of a musical celebrity in Ireland, and in 1960, he formed a group called *Ceóltirí Chualann*, made up of Dublin-based traditional musicians (Ó hAllmhuráin 1998: 125). This group, or "folk orchestra" as some have called it (Skinner Sawyers 2000: 251), performed Ó Riada's ensemble-style compositions of traditional Irish tunes. They exposed traditional music to a "'brave new world', away from the country house session and into the 'high art' concert halls of the nation" (Ó hAllmhuráin 1998: 126). His compositions took traditional Irish dance tunes and interspersed them with polyphonic harmonies, solos, and improvisations (ibid.). For all of the changes in context and performative style that Irish music had undergone in the years since the "old days," this departure was perhaps the most radical because it changed the very structure of the music. The group changed their name to The Chieftains following Ó Riada's death in 1971 (Cowdery 1990: 24). When they were first formed, it was clear from the start that this was an entirely new kind of Irish music, a new way of playing the old tunes.

Through *Ceóltirí Chualann*, Ó Riada was able to bring traditional Irish music to a larger audience, but he also earned the respect of many traditional musicians by recovering and re-popularizing lost tunes. Of course, he did not earn everyone's respect, and in particular his vocal disdain of the *céilí* bands ruffled a few feathers (Ó hAllmhuráin 1998: 126–127). He was only forty when he died, but he had introduced a fundamentally new idea into Irish music: that one could experiment with its form, its melodies, and its arrangement.

So, outside Doolin and northwest Clare, shifts were taking place in the national economy, more and more tourists were coming to Ireland, revivals of folk music were emerging elsewhere in the English-speaking world, and changes within traditional Irish music were occurring. This complicated milieu of social and economic change was the subtext to life everywhere in Ireland, but in the day-to-day existence of the people of northwest Clare, these changes had not yet "arrived." When they did, in the form of massive crowds of revivalists, it was by all accounts sudden and intense.

The Revival Arrives

When revivalists "discovered" Doolin in the late 1960s they brought the Revival with them. Again, it was by its very nature something from the outside, because the music never needed reviving in northwest Clare. Playing music was simply something people did as part of their social world. As Michael Coady wrote, "Backpackers from all over the world were amazed and delighted to find such a thing: a place where 'real' folk musicians played music which was a living communal reality and not something dead for generations and self-consciously resurrected by scholarly types who met in folk clubs at weekends" (1996: 15). As Doolin's reputation spread throughout Ireland and abroad, it became a kind of pilgrimage site for traditional musicians, novice musicians wanting to learn tunes, connoisseurs of the music, and hippies looking for the "good life." In turn, Doolin's popularity attracted more of the same. A feedback cycle was created in a very short amount of time, solidifying Doolin's reputation as the "traditional music capital of Ireland." It was a relatively sudden change and a monumental one. The crowds swelled and music became ubiquitous. Sessions and audiences overfilled Doolin's three pubs. It was an unannounced, unplanned, unending festival. "Anyone could turn up," wrote Coady, "players famous or unknown from all over Ireland, musicians of all kinds from America, Britain, or continental Europe, painters and poets, journalists and photographers, drop-outs and millionaires, academics or judges or politicians" (1996: 15). Christy Barry told me what it was like during the revival in Doolin:

> Well, you'd have the odd fellow come with his—his accordion, a big hippy-like guy coming with long beard and his knaversack and he'd be after hitching, maybe, from Galway or hitching from Sligo or wherever. Or Dublin or wherever.

And he'd stay. He'd bring a tent with him and he'd stay. He'd stay. And there were plenty of places for camping at that time. You didn't have to pay for it even.

D'y'know?

You could find anyone's field, they'd just tell you, "Fire Away!", d'y'know? We had very little showers, but rivers that they washed in.

All those people came in and they played everyday then. They came in and played and it was beautiful-like … .

We'd lead off the session everyday. And every time you'd look around, there'd be a new bunch of musicians there after arriving, and they'd be there a week or something. The sessions would be so good at some times that it would be unbelievable. There'd be no hang-ups, or no—.

And if we wanted to learn tunes, we learned tunes off each other. If some guy had a nice, new tune, we'd listen to it. And we'd ask him if we could learn it. And maybe in the course of a week, we'd pick it up. We would get something from him, and he'd learn one from us, and we wouldn't see him again for a couple of months again, or maybe five months, six months, and he'd show again. But there was always a constant flow. And they were all—.

They'd be great names now in music-like … .

There's not one star that you can buy their record that has not played in Doolin.

This passage illustrates a number of interrelated things that need to be addressed in more detail. First, there was a lack of infrastructure in Doolin to accommodate this new class of tourist, or even an easy means by which to travel to the village. Second, a radically new (and radical) type of tourist arrived in Doolin: the hippy. Third, this all created a buzz of excitement, and Doolin became one of the most important geographic locales for the manifestation of the Revival.[1] Fourth, what was happening musically in the pub sessions in places like Doolin spread outward, was reproduced elsewhere, and helped change the very nature of the music itself.

Hitch-hiking was a common means of getting to Doolin in those days, and for many, the only means. The journey to Doolin was itself an adventure. Once they finally arrived, there were few places to stay. Locals with their own houses sometimes let these new visitors camp out for awhile. One local man described his own participation:

All of 'em used to come stay with me that time when they came here. They stayed with me. That was the first hotel they came to! (laughs)

Well, they'd camp out back if there wasn't room in the house. Or, they'd put their caravan around the back into the field in the back, and they'd wash in the house, and they could eat and cook and put stuff in the 'fridge. We looked after 'em all, everyone one of 'em: Americans, Australians, Canadians, French, Germans, the whole lot.

Tents in cow pastures became a common sight. Locals were very accommodating, and they were well aware of the business opportunities that had, quite literally, arrived at their doorsteps. Very quickly, tourist accommodations were being built or created out of old buildings.

Doolin was difficult to find in the early days and lacked the amenities of typical holiday destinations. On the other hand, tourists did not travel there by chance. A tourist to Doolin in the late 1960s or early 1970s would have heard enough about the place to know that they needed to be self-sufficient. These were people who were very serious about hearing or playing some traditional Irish music, and were determined enough to find their way there and then deal with the lack of amenities once they'd arrived. Many although by no means all of these new tourists were labeled "hippies," caught up in the larger, international countercultural movement and the other folk revivals that were occurring elsewhere. Christy Barry told me that he proudly identified with this movement:

My generation really broke up the melting, and they went fuckin' crazy .... They totally went against Church and everything. Free love. The whole fuckin' lot started big-time-like. And that was the late 60's and early 70's stuff. D'y'know? I think it was the nature of people at the time around the world.

I asked him why he thought the music was so good during the Revival. He answered rather dramatically, not by describing a change in the music but a change in society: "I think people were starting to come out of slavery," he said. He described how his generation was beginning to become aware of the cultural, political, and especially the religious hegemony that previously had such a strong hold over Ireland. He put it another way: "The music came out of the times," not the other way around. From a Marxist perspective, this might be considered an "awakening" of sorts that led to the poor to wrest themselves from the psychological control of Church and State. Again, it also provides a critique of the Bourdieu's "structuring structures" because the change was too radical to allow much of the old structures to remain. Perhaps more explanatory than either of these perspectives though is the notion of "cosmopolitanism," the state of being in which one rejects, or at least does not rely solely upon, received structures like traditions, history, cultural values, or other "identity markers." The revival was a period when traditions, histories, and societal structures were very nearly rejected altogether. Some remained, like traditional Irish music, but even the music was undergoing radical transformations.

Despite the stereotype that a suffocating cultural conservatism was uniform in the west of Ireland (cf. Messenger 1969), Bohemianism and "alternative" lifestyles were actually nothing new to Doolin. The son of the local landlord, Francis Macnamara, who had a house in Doolin, used to invite his artist and painter friends there (including Augustus John and Dylan Thomas) in the early years of the twentieth century (Curtis 1994: 151). Their behavior included heavy drinking, dancing, and storytelling with the locals at O'Connor's Pub, and nude bathing down at the shore (Devas 1968: 27–30). As a result, the influx of "hippies" and other bohemian types at the end of the 1960s and 1970s, a new variant on an old idea, was not as shocking as it might have been in other places in Ireland.

As more and more people, musicians and otherwise, poured into northwest Clare during the summers, there were sessions of Irish music being played in the pubs daily, and this too was a change. Musicians, Irish music connoisseurs, and those searching for what they perceived to be a kind of "cultural authenticity" were arriving from all over Ireland and all over the world to listen to sessions, play in them, trade tunes, and soak up the exciting atmosphere. As Koning wrote about east Clare a little over a decade later, "The abundance of informal sessions in East Clare … is a result of the interference of visiting musicians with local culture rather than a feature of the culture itself" (1980: 421). Koning's use of the word "interference" here polemically overstates his case, but otherwise, he is correct. Before the Revival in Doolin, entertainment in the pubs consisted largely of a bit of conversation peppered with a few tunes from one of the Russell Brothers and others, and on some occasions, musicians might accompany a night of set dancing. After the Revival arrived though, sessions started as early as mid-morning and went on all day as visiting musicians came and went. The sessions might swell to include dozens of aspiring players, and this went on until the pub closed. It was, as people often described it, "one constant session." Christy said,

> We'd play eight hours a day at that time. That wouldn't be a 'night session' like now. That'd be all day … . Seven days a week, d'y'know? You wouldn't know if it was Monday or Friday sometimes.

After the pub closed, there might even be a party to go to at someone's house, or at a visitor's campsite.

Sessions started to be played anywhere where musicians could find a small corner to huddle into. Music became big business for the publicans during this period too. Gus O'Connor remembered when, in the 1970s, Guinness Corporation told him that his pub sold more Guinness than any pub in County Clare except "Dirty Nellies" at Bunratty Castle near Shannon International Airport. Advertisement was unnecessary. Word of mouth carried the names of these pubs worldwide. As Gus O'Connor told me,

The people who came there advertised it … . I think we must have had someone from nearly every country in the world at some stage. And they wrote about in their different newspapers in their own country … . Of course, the Russell brothers were the main attraction.

Even before the Revival hit Doolin, the Russell brothers were attracting people to O'Connor's Pub. Collectors of traditional music were coming to record tunes from them. Ciarán Mac Mathúna, according to Gus O'Connor, was the first to come to broadcast a recording from O'Connor's on RTÉ, the national radio station. But other radio and television crews from all over the British Isles quickly followed suit.

Through broadcast recordings, word of mouth, and journalism, the Russell Brothers, especially Micho, became celebrities.[2] People often said to me that the Russell brothers are responsible for the thriving economy in Doolin today. Whether or not this is a bit of hyperbole is debatable, but regardless, the Russells remain the centerpiece in the discourse about Doolin's music scene. Micho Russell attracted particular attention. People told me that his personality was somehow suited to performing. He was gentle and had a deep love for traditional music, song, and storytelling. His seemingly simple (although truly complex) whistle-playing earned him the title of All-Ireland Champion at the *fleadh* in 1978, and as his fame increased, he was asked to go on tour. During his lifetime, which was tragically cut short in 1994, Micho traveled throughout the United States and Europe many times, always to return home to sit around the fire at O'Connor's Pub. He is often called "The Ambassador of Traditional Irish Music" as a result (Winters 1997[1986]: 1). Illustrative of Micho's renown, a postcard from continental Europe was sent to him with the woefully inadequate mailing address "Micho — Ireland" but it actually got to him (Winters 1990: 17). The other two brothers, Gussie and Packie, preferred to stay home and let the world come to them. Michael Coady remembers watching his friend Packie sitting at the pub "through this non-stop feast, playing or listening, meeting and drinking and talking with thousands of people from the four corners of the world" (1996: 15).

In only a few short years, an amazing change had occurred. The music had somehow been "revived." This tradition of Irish dance music, commonly belittled in many circles only a few decades before, was now popular throughout the world, and Doolin was at the centre of the excitement.

Turning the Tune

Places like Doolin acted as crucibles during the revival, but what occurred there could not be contained. The music spun out of northwest Clare, carried off by the constant ebb and flow of people. And the Revival, having been partly motivated by other folk music revivals elsewhere, now began to graft elements together from other musical traditions. A new sound emerged which was widely popularized in 1972 when a new group called *Planxty* released a self-titled album amalgamating traditional dance tunes and the kind of ballad singing that had been occurring in the United States, Scotland, and Dublin. This mixture of styles was instantly popular, even though it was not altogether novel. Seán Ó Riada had formed the precursor to *The Chieftains* well over a decade previously, and Johnny Moynihan, Andy Irvine, and Joe Dolan had formed a band called *Sweeney's Men* in 1966 which also began to combine elements from the Ballad Boom with traditional instrumental dance music (Rice 1995: 1). The difference was in the timing and the presentation. *Planxty's* youthful and energetic sound appealed to the new countercultural audience. They grew their hair long and had hippy moustaches and beards: they looked like rock stars. They were members of that very generation, and they were "radicals." Their charisma as a group and their musical virtuosity made them instant stars throughout the British Isles and Europe. Other groups soon followed suit. *De Danann* and *The Bothy Band* in particular became influential. These groups brought the appropriation of traditional music by the younger generation full circle, an appropriation that arguably began at the *fleadh* in Thurles in 1965. *Planxty* and *The Bothy Band* were named repeatedly by musicians I know as the inspirational reason they first started to play traditional Irish music. A local musician named Micheál told me how this new, energetic, youthful brand of music, both in these early revival records and the lively Doolin scene, inspired him to pick up a guitar for the first time:

> Doolin was certainly, kind of, my instruction, where I fell in love with it … .

> I suppose you're well aware of the 60's Revival with *Planxty* and *The Bothy Band*, and it brought a whole new energy on the music. I suppose the music here was coming more from that vein than it was from the *céilí* band era or—ah, people playing the older style. And I suppose it just appealed to me more … .

> I suppose it had a lot more energy in it.

> There was more "music" in it, played more for the music rather than for the dancing. A lot of the older music would have been "pumped out."

> Yeah, some of the older musicians—or, my perception of it—the tuning wouldn't have been as fine. It's just a rougher sound all around, where [later] people played somehow more dynamic music,

> which is, yeah, more appealing.

The revival began to separate the dancing from the music. Music became an art-form in its own right. Coady described how, as more and more people arrived to hear the music, "[d]ancing became impossible in a jam-packed pub, though there was never any lack of music—often two or three sessions going simultaneously in different corners" (1996: 15). A concentration on the music allowed for a refinement of its tuning and timing. With the entire focus on the music, things like the "rougher sound" and the poorer tuning became less acceptable. Some still lament this change as the "end" of traditional Irish music. Others, like Micheál, celebrate it. For him, the revival was when traditional Irish music first became exciting and its heyday began. I would suggest that the difference in opinion is partly explained by a generation gap, and the emergence of new aesthetic sensibilities and meanings attributed to the music.

Even as folk music was increasingly marginalized by rock-and-roll elsewhere in the 1970s, the emerging new, traditional Irish "supergroups" began to record albums and top the charts in Ireland. They inspired musicians like Micheál to pick up instruments, and they helped maintain the revival itself and even drove it further. They were treated like pop stars in many ways, and adopted all of the trappings of pop music. The pop sensibility became embedded in traditional music to some extent. These "bands" went into the studio to record new albums, they were interviewed by music magazines, albums were listed on record charts, and they toured. The following excerpt from a book on the history of Irish music reads like something out of *Rolling Stone* magazine:

> By 1976, other dramatic changes had come about. Planxty had decided to call it a day; Dolores Keane had departed from De Danann, to be replaced by Andy Irvine. And so the wheel continued to turn. Christy Moore, Paul Brady and Mick Hanly pursued solo careers. Prior to going solo Paul Brady joined Andy Irvine for the recording of their much celebrated album for the Mulligan label (Curtis 1994: 29).

Some groups took this move towards a pop music ideology even more literally and attempted to fuse traditional music with rock and roll. *Moving Hearts*—an offshoot of *Planxty*—is an early example (Ó hAllmhuráin 1998: 138). They opened the doors to a kind of Celtic/pop fusion in later years.

According to Bohlman, diversification is another central feature of folk revivals (1988: 133), and this kind of musical experimentation is a classic example. The revival brought other diversifying changes as well. The bouzouki, an instrument from Greek traditional music, was introduced by Johnny Moynihan and Andy Irvine of *Planxty*. The acoustic guitar came in to the sessions straight out of the Ballad Boom. Today guitars are almost always used as purely "backing" instrument, whereby chords are strummed to create a homophonous foundation for a tune's melody. The guitar is still a highly contested introduction into traditional music (cf. Commins 2004a). However, its introduction during the Revival helped merge the Ballad Boom with the session context, and songs accompanied by the guitar became a way to break up the sets of instrumental music. In that sense, its influence on the way sessions are performed today has been significant. Other new instruments that were introduced during the Revival and which are now commonly used are the mandolin and mandola. The "low whistle" is also a relatively new invention, popular with flute and whistle players for "slow airs." Even the didgeridoo and the djembe, originally from Australia and Africa respectively, are not uncommon. Moreover, once the music was introduced to studio technology, nearly anything became possible. For example, modern recording effects like "reverb" are commonly used. Every type of instrumentation has been used in recordings from electric guitars and basses to synthesizers and trap-sets. As can be expected, this is an offensive erosion of tradition for some while others perceive it as a terribly exciting and innovative expansion of the music.

It is difficult to know when to mark an end to the Revival. Clearly, a different era has emerged. The music has been revived, but as we will see in the following chapters, the meaning of the music and the social relationships surrounding it changed yet again. During the Revival period, Doolin became a site of creativity, one that had gained credibility (Connell and Gibson 2003: 43–44). To some extent during the period since the revival, the credibility of the "Doolin scene" has been questioned. Doolin is now world-famous and is very much a commercial success-story, but as a result, in traditional Irish music circles, in neighboring towns and villages, and in tourist guidebooks, it is not uncommon to hear negative assessments about its music scene.

In local narratives, some people mark the end of the Revival sometime between 1978 and 1983, when a series of massive music festivals were held in a farmer's field in between Lisdoonvarna and Doolin. The "Lisdoonvarna Festivals" became the annual Irish version of Woodstock. They started out as traditional Irish music festivals, a popular venue for the new revival bands to play. They were a huge success, and as time went on, more rock groups were signed on. By the end, Van Morrison, Rory Gallagher, Emmy Lou Harris, and Jackson Browne had all played there. Unfortunately, in 1983, two things happened that compelled the organizers to end the annual festival. Biker gangs descended on northwest Clare and reportedly caused chaos, which the authorities could do nothing about because the roads were too choked with parked cars to get through. Also, despite local warnings, people went swimming off the coast at Doolin in a particularly dangerous spot, and nine young men drowned. These events effectively finished the festival. Those who suggest that this marked the end of the Revival also tend to argue that the Lisdoonvarna Festivals had more or less over-commercialized and over-regulated the revival scene. For them, the festivals were an attempt to create an institution out of the spontaneity of the revival. These individuals argue that a more general kind of commercialized capitalist mentality crept into northwest Clare and undermined the "unguarded hospitality" that visitors once received. Other Doolin residents are quick to disagree though, and there is no consensus. For some, the festival period was when the Revival found its stride. Some locals mark the end of the Revival with Micho Russell's tragic death in 1994. Packie had died years earlier. More recently, Gussie Russell, John Killhourey (the last of the Killhourey brothers), and Gus O'Connor also passed away. For some, the loss of this older generation has also meant the loss of the spirit of that earlier age. Peter Curtin, ever the pragmatist, put it to me this way:

> I mean, life has changed a good bit since. Life is more commercialized in some ways. The musicians as such have regular jobs that you have to pay attention to nine-to-five, and—you know—the spontaneous session doesn't happen quite like it used to.

But that's life. Life changes—you know?

In the chapters that follow we will see exactly how life has changed.

Conclusions

When we speak of the revival of the music in this context, we are not really speaking about revitalizing anything in northwest Clare itself. The music survived there. A term like "Revival," although commonly used, implies that something from the past is resurrected and expressed in the present (Jabbour 1993: xii), but it is perhaps too strong in this instance. What happened in Doolin, from the local perspective, was much more fluid. This desire to locate and revive came from the flood of musicians, Irish music connoisseurs, and interested tourists that came to northwest Clare during this period, but the music had existed continuously there. For locals, it was not in the past but the ever-present. What the revival did for locals was to change the way the music is performed and perceived. It also ushered in important new economic opportunities.

The revival that began to descend upon northwest Clare in the late 1960s was of a different nature to its counterparts elsewhere. There was no local organizing body that made an attempt to stir up interest. This was no academic endeavor, or one with an overt political message. It was in that sense, organic, and undoubtedly that was part of the attraction for many people. It felt "authentic." Others have suggested that far from being isolated events, twentieth century urban folk revivals are descended from a 200 year history of romanticism of the rural musics in the West (Allen 1981: 71), which are part and parcel of the increased disillusionment of urban-modern-commercial hegemony, a search for the rural idyll and its supposedly organic, community-based "authenticity" (Allen 1981: 78, Blaustein 1993: 272). For some, this idyllic romance may have links to an ethnic identification with the particular music being revived. People who identify themselves as Irish-Americans for example may feel a strong link to the "Irish" portion of a self-constructed hyphenated-identity. The music might be one of many markers of that identification. For others, with no ancestral attachment to Ireland, this music and the globalized traditional Irish music "public" that was to some extent solidified and certainly widened during the revival, might have replaced a lost sense of "communal relationships grounded in kinship and territoriality" (Blaustein 1993: 271). In other words, an association with a chosen folk music, even if it is "someone else's" music, can bring one into the fold of a new kind of community of like-minded individuals.

Romanticism continues today, and the tourism industry capitalizes on it. Indeed, the marketing of a romanticized version of Irish music is "inseparably linked to the marketing of Irishness" by the tourist industry (Foster 2008: 155). As we will see in the following chapters, things have become regular and regulating to some extent, and this includes musical performances. Things have also become extremely profitable. In what follows, we will begin to explore this modern stage of development and its many consequences. Part Two of the book takes a closer look at the tourists who visit Doolin (Chapter 4), and also at the people who have stayed and their relationships with locals (Chapter 5). In Part Three of the book, we return to some of the deeper implications that all of these factors have had on Doolin and the modern performance of traditional music.

Notes

1. Doolin was not alone as a site for the Revival. Places primarily along the west coast like Dingle in County Kerry, Galway City, and Sligo were "hot-spots" for revival sessions as well.

2. Innumerable books and articles have been written about the Russell Brothers. I would not do justice to them by telling their story. Michael Coady (*The Well of Spring Water*, 1996) and Dennis Winters (*The Piper's Chair*, 1986; *Doolin's Micho Russell*, 1990) were their close friends, and I would refer the reader especially to their tributes.

PART II

Moving Through and Moving In

Chapter 4

The Celtic Tiger

> When I was a kid, just down the other side of that bridge, my grandfather
> (God Rest Him) had built a little piggery to rear a few little pigs ... and like,
> forty years later, I end up with a little office down there with about eight
> computers in it and about ten printers and a huge server inside the same
> space, d'y'know? So, you've gone from pigs to computers in forty years!
>
> —Peter Curtin

If globalization simply means having deeply interactive relationships with other nations and peoples, then local places in Ireland like Doolin have been fully globalized at least since the Famine. This is an obvious point when one stops to consider, for example, the sad, rich, local history of "American Wakes," and the resultant relationship between this small village and its Diaspora population that has been migrating to England, Australia, America, and elsewhere for well over 150 years. What's more, "Irish culture" cannot be considered conterminous with the isle of Ireland. It is one example of how earlier perspectives, relying first and foremost on the concept of the nation, are too simplistically bounded. "Much of social science," writes Sassen, "has operated with the assumption of the nation-state as a container, representing a unified spatiotemporality. Much of history, however, has failed to confirm this assumption" (2001: 260). All of this is sometimes veiled by the fact that globalizing processes have quickened since the 1990s. In "the old days," economic and social connections were mostly a unidirectional exchange of people emigrating and then sending money back home. During the Revival, the pattern changed as musical pilgrims began to travel to Doolin. During the more recent Celtic Tiger period—the subject of this chapter—mass tourism streamlined the ability to travel within Ireland to places like Doolin. The trickle of money that flowed in from the Diaspora in the old days became a flood, pushed along by a tidal wave of visiting tourists. Obviously, this has had enormous economic impacts, but it has also had important social impacts. One important result explored at the end of this chapter is that the categorical spaces between "insiders" and "outsiders" have become highly nuanced.

In Part II, we look at the complex movement of people into and through Doolin. Chapter 4 focuses on the impacts of tourism. In Chapter 5, I take a closer look at the impacts of incomers who have made Doolin their home, some of whom started out as tourists. In this way, these two chapters begin with a discussion of those people who spend the least amount of time in Doolin, such as mass tourists, and then move slowly across a spectrum towards those who live there permanently. Understanding the different temporal relationships to the locale becomes key when we return to an analysis of the music in Part Three of the book.

Tourists are often mischaracterized as monolithic and uniform when in fact the term condenses an incredible diversity. Any valuable discussion of tourism must recognize that a "tourist population" is made up of individuals from a wide variety of backgrounds with a wide variety of motivations. One way of characterizing that diversity is in terms of intensity. Some tourists come for an afternoon. Others stay longer, or return year after year and form long-lasting relationships with locals and other tourists. Some get seasonal jobs. As Chapter 5 highlights, others even decide to stay permanently. Some marry locals and enter into new social categories. So, in Doolin at least, the "tourist" lies at one extreme on a broad spectrum of categorizations that are by no means distinct.

Celtic Tourism

I borrow the title for this chapter, "the Celtic Tiger",[1] from a common description of the recent and explosive economic expansion in Ireland, but ultimately I am concerned with the social impacts this new economy has had. I will not spend time here analyzing in detail the radical seachange that the Irish economy managed in the 1990s and into the 2000s (or its apparent collapse more recently). Others have done an excellent job documenting the underlying reasons for it (Allen 2000, Deegan and Dineen 2000, Gottheil 2003, O'Grada 1997, O'Toole 2002). To say that Ireland prospered in the early 1990s is to understate the drama of this period. However, some pundits worry that it has been more of a flash in the pan than a permanent shift (Woods 2002, Crawford 2003, Keenan 2003) or point out that along with new wealth came rapidly rising prices (King 2002). Importantly, still others have pointed out that the new wealth has not been distributed equally (Mac Laughlin 1997, Siggins 2003, Wilson and Donnan 2006: 69–90).

The economic "reading" of the Celtic Tiger by these and other analysts and commentators is—to put it mildly-a mixed bag. So is the assessment of the social changes that have accompanied it. All of these issues are popular topics for conversation in Doolin and elsewhere in Ireland. There are many theories about government corruption and the increasing power of the new Celtic-Tiger-upper-class. Still, despite this widespread skepticism, a "quality of life" survey suggests that the Irish are happier than ever before (as reported in Crawford 2003: 3).

Again, I will leave the detailed economic analyses of the impressively expansive Irish tourism industry to others, but a few brief words might be worth mentioning here. The phenomenal growth in the tourism sector began to take off in the mid-1980s, well before the arrival of the Celtic Tiger, which no doubt helped prime and then later fuel the engine. For example, thirty-five per cent of jobs created between 1987 and 1994 were tourist-related (Deegan and Dineen 1997: 78). According to one report, between 1985 and 2000, annual visitor numbers rose from under two million to more than six million (Tansey et al. 2002). Tourism averaged an incredible twelve per cent annual growth rate from the early 1990s to 2000 (Deegan and Dineen 2000: 163). Not only did more and more tourists come to Ireland during the 1990s, but each year visitors spent increasingly large amounts of money (ibid.). As a corollary, tourism provided even more employment opportunities. By 2001, approximately 137,000 people were officially employed in the tourist industry in Ireland, making it the sixth largest employer in the nation, even ahead of farming (ibid.).

Locally, before the Celtic Tiger era, a few key developments solidified Doolin's nascent tourism "industry".[2] Josephine Moloney, who married a local and settled in Doolin, met numerous times with officials from *Bord Fáilte* (the national tourist body) in the early 1980s and persuaded them to include Doolin on the organization's holiday maps. It was in 1982 that Doolin was included for the first time on the Ordnance Survey maps as well (Danaher 2002: 22). In this very literal way, Doolin was "put on the map." This is a dramatic example of how the local actions of individual agents can influence the "structure" at key points in the historical development of a place. Two years later, Josephine and another woman, Helen Browne, formed the Doolin Development Company, which aimed to promote Doolin tourism interests (ibid.). Significantly, this organization, which was later renamed the Doolin Tourism Co-operative, is by far the most influential and far-reaching local committee in Doolin today, a village that is run on less than a dozen small voluntary committees, not by a formal political structure like a village council or by any formally recognized leadership roles.

Until the owners of the Doolin Hostel in Fisherstreet convinced *Bus Eireann*, the national bus service, to make Doolin a serviced destination in 1987 (ibid.), one of the local hostel owners personally drove people to Doolin from Lisdoonvarna. By 1990 though, Doolin was included on the timetables of the national "Expressway Network" as its own destination. When I lived there in 2002–2003, there were three daily services year-round and an additional four services to handle the increased tourist traffic in the summertime. Like most things in Doolin, the bus service reflects the seasonality of tourism in the area.

Economic figures that deal specifically with Doolin or Killilagh parish are nearly non-existent. When I first began fieldwork, I innocently envisioned doing a house-to-house survey, but quickly realized that discussing money is "just not the done thing." Even close neighbors typically only know the basic facts about each other's business dealings. Prying can end long-standing friendships and create family feuds. So, it was a stroke of luck that Tim's brother Mattie had personally taken a census of the main part of Killilagh Parish in 1991 (in order to prove that the village had a high enough population to host its own school football team). He updated his figures to include all of the new development and changes in the local population of the area for a local development plan submitted to the Clare County Council in June of 2003. The following material is largely derived from his data, and while there are no specific economic numbers, it does give an idea of how things changed locally during this period.

According to Mattie's figures, the development of local tourism interests grew rapidly in the 1990s, seeming to outpace national trends. In 1988, one bed & breakfast proprietor told me, there were only five small B&Bs in Doolin, two in Fisherstreet, and three in the Roadford part of the village. In 2003, there were around fifty, and today, they typically have at least four or five rooms each. Since 1991, an estimated ninety-three new buildings were constructed in the immediate area in and around Doolin, and almost half of those were devoted, at least in part, to commercial activities. In 2003, four hostels catered to tourists in Doolin too, as well as two campgrounds. Additionally, some of the B&Bs and hostels rented out a space in their back fields for overflow campers in the summer. Significantly, at the same time, the permanent population of the area remained relatively stable, growing from roughly 510 to around 570 permanent residents.

Much more accommodation has been built since 2003, including two new hotels and several dozen "holiday homes." Due to the expiration of a nationwide tourism investment initiative, the new Irish bourgeoisie flooded the County Clare development office with plans to develop literally hundreds of holiday homes in Doolin alone. Most of these were successfully thwarted by fierce local opposition (which even included some local businessmen who stood to reap huge financial rewards from the developments). Still, the approval of even a smaller fraction of planning permits to build summer holiday homes hails a significant change for Doolin. First, what was once a local, grassroots, family-owned and operated tourism industry is now being appropriated by corporate developers. Second, the sheer number of non-B&B tourist accommodations like holiday homes and hotels, in which no one lives permanently, threatens to turn Doolin into an overdeveloped ghost-town during the "off season."

To say the least, a tourist-oriented business infrastructure was built up rather rapidly during the last twenty years, and extant buildings were restored and rebuilt for tourism purposes as well. For example, every building along the main road in the Fisherstreet section of Doolin now houses one type business or another: B&Bs, craft and music shops, a grocer's, a coffee shop, a sweater shop, and a bookstore. This fact is in stark opposition to the simplified rhetoric of tourist guidebooks. The 2003 edition of *Frommer's: Ireland* for example describes Fisherstreet as "a row of thatched fisherman's cottages" (Kelleher 2003: 381). But one quick glance along Fisherstreet would disconfirm this claim immediately. The village's pubs expanded over the years as well to accommodate the increasingly large crowds.

Unequivocally, tourism changed the built environment and the landscape. One friend who built a bed and breakfast on the Roadford side of the village back in the 1980s often comments on how when the house was first built, she could see nothing but green fields from her front door all the way down to the sea. Today, her view is increasingly obstructed by the dozens and dozens of buildings dappled across the valley. Like the pubs, the B&B's also regularly expand to accommodate more guests.

Figure 4.1 Expanding Doolin's Carrying Capacity

It is difficult to accurately calculate the exact "carrying-capacity" of tourists in Doolin since the campgrounds (and overflow camping) can take in large and indefinite numbers of campers, but excluding the campgrounds, Doolin had an estimated 770 tourist-beds in 2003 (up from roughly 375 beds in 1991).[3] This is well over the permanent resident population of around 570 villagers, and if one were to venture a guess at how many people could stay each night in Doolin's campgrounds and "back fields," the figures at the height of the tourist season in the summer could easily double or triple that of the local population. In other words, during the busiest time of the year, generally June through August, when it is difficult to find a place to sleep in or around Doolin, up to two out of every three people staying in Doolin are visitors. That does not include those tourists who take daytrips to Doolin from other neighboring towns and villages, who pass through for an afternoon on their way to somewhere else, domestic tourists from neighboring towns and villages, and tourists who stop through for an hour or two as part of a packaged coach tour. Since most locals work long hours during the summer months, one might only see the occasional permanent resident amidst the heaving crowds. The seasonality of this picture is stark. The tables are turned and tourists are rare in the "low season." In the depths of the winter of 2002–2003, only four B&Bs were open for business, and even these were rarely full. Due to the poor Irish winter weather, camping is not an option. And the two hostels that stayed open only took in very small numbers.

Other tourist-oriented businesses grew up around the burgeoning mass tourist industry in the 1990s as well. Numerous gift shops opened. Two traditional music shops now run successful businesses in the Fisherstreet end of Doolin selling CDs, tapes, books and traditional instruments. A number of restaurants, serving international and local cuisines, have opened in and around the village. Like the accommodations, most shops and restaurants close sometime in October or November and do not reopen until March or April. Likewise, even the most visited pubs in northwest Clare close off whole rooms for the winter. O'Connor's Pub for example reduces its carrying capacity by about two-thirds in the wintertime by closing off the more recent additions. In a very real sense, the constriction of the village's interior spaces in the wintertime creates a closer, more intimate physical context for social interactions, one that is confined to the older spaces. As a result, temporality in Doolin is odd in that seasonal shifts feel like shifts in whole decades. As we shall see later, this has a very real psychological effect on social interactions and musical performances.

As businesses developed in Doolin itself, it was natural that regional relationships with other tourist-interests developed as well. O'Connor's Pub, and later McGann's Pub and McDermott's Pub, began to cater to packaged coach tours, building up relationships with companies that needed somewhere to stop for meals.[4] When O'Connor's was sold to its present owner, those relationships were built up further, and today at the height of the tourist season it is not unusual for even six or seven coaches carrying up to fifty people each to stop at the pub to feed their customers during the daytime. Some coach tour companies originate as far away as Dublin, but most have a more regional base like Galway or Ennis. The business that they provide is highly profitable. A typical tour group will be offloaded in Doolin for an hour or more, eat lunch at the pub, do some shopping at the gift shops, and then move on. Coach drivers are asked to call in the morning to let the pub staff know how many tourists they are carrying that day, and over time, these daily encounters between the coach drivers, tour-guides, publicans, and the pub staff develop into personal relationships.

Regional relationships between B&Bs were cultivated over the years, too. An informal but vital system of recommendations has been created between B&B proprietors in other parts of Ireland. One B&B proprietor explained how this worked:

> That usually starts when I have someone come in and says, "I just stayed in Clifden and this is a really nice place". And "here's some cards". And then you start—and then you start talking to them over the phone. And most of these places that I recommend, I haven't met the people. I've only spoken to them on the phone … . And it's good to only have one [business relationship] in a place. In a place that's really busy like Clifden or Dingle, you might have two. But you stay really faithful to those two. They'll recommend you, too. But if they find out that you're recommending four or five, it just doesn't work. You have to stick to one or two.

Relationships are built up between tourist "hot-spots" and recommendations are given out to new tourists to visit those destinations, building their word-of-mouth reputation. This further cements certain locales as tourist destinations and reinscribes the tourist pathways between them.

Mass Tourists

The build up of the tourist infrastructure—and by that I mean the ease of access to Doolin, the build-up of accommodation, and the availability for consumption of food in restaurants and souvenirs in shops—has led to a situation whereby Doolin now caters more to "mass tourists" (i.e., a general tourist market with diverse motivations) rather than the specialized "music tourists" (i.e., those who came primarily to listen to or to play music) that characterized the revival period. It is difficult to say, and maybe pointless to dwell on, whether or not mass tourism came first or whether the build up of the tourist infrastructure led to mass tourism in Doolin. The change was not immediate, and most likely there was a mutually expanding relationship between the two.

The phrase "mass tourist" is common but misleading. As stated earlier, tourist populations are inherently complex in make-up and motivation. Moreover, the "tourist-site" is not fixed. Tourists rarely stay in one place for long, and therefore, the "site" of tourism is a mobile one.[5] Tourists pass through physical spaces like Doolin, and each group may travel a different route. Seen "from below," from the perspective of a physical site fixed in space like Doolin, the tourist population is constantly shifting as the crowds continuously reconstitute themselves. Americans may dominate the crowd one week. The next, continental Europeans may be common. Sometimes these patterns are predictable. Other times, they seem random.

Authoritative answers to even simple questions like, "Who are these tourists?" are therefore difficult to answer. However, despite the fluid and dynamic nature of this population, certain patterns can be discerned from a mixture of qualitative and quantitative data. In a survey of tourists that I conducted in conjunction with the Doolin Tourism Co-operative over a two-month period during the summer of 2003, we gathered basic data about Doolin's tourist population: what country they originated from, why they chose Ireland as a destination, what things they wanted to experience in Ireland, what attracted them to Doolin, how they traveled, and what type of accommodation they stayed in, amongst other things. Much of the qualitative information in this section is supported from that dataset. For example, quantitative data gathered from tourists in Doolin strongly supports anecdotal evidence about common tourist routes in the west of Ireland. Predominantly, tourists who come to Doolin travel along the coastal counties in the west. Doolin becomes one stop on this coastal journey.

One way social scientists have looked for patterns in the seeming chaos of tourist crowds is to create taxonomies of "tourist types." Indeed, this has become something of a cottage industry. Disagreements have arisen in the literature primarily over which metaphors to use to describe tourist behavior (the gaze, staging, etc.) (Chaney 2002), how to create these taxonomies (e.g. modes of travel vs. motivations for travel), and whose taxonomy is more "correct." In my experience, only very rarely did tourists I spoke to in Doolin have one motivation for being there. Labels like "cultural tourists," "heritage tourists," "eco-tourists," etc., common in the tourism literature, are adjectival rather than categorical. Creating taxonomies based on tourist motivations for travel is another common way to see order in the complexity; however, once again I would argue that we ought to base our models on what the ethnographic data tells us rather than the reverse.

When I asked permanent residents in Doolin how they would describe various types of tourists, the *emic* response consistently began with nationality. In this regard, Doolin's tourists reflect the make-up of tourists for the region generally in that the majority are overwhelmingly North American. According to a 2003 report, 44 per cent of tourists landing in Shannon Airport were North Americans ("National Tourism Policy Review" 2003: 3), coinciding with the 48 per cent of North American visitors to Doolin that same year. Doolin's other tourists come mostly from other European nations, but long-haul tourists from every continent (especially Australia) come as well. Beyond this, descriptive qualifications are normally used in conversation. In other contexts, someone might talk about tourists by their mode of travel such as "backpackers" or "coach tourists," or by other means such as "pensioners" or "hippies."

Tourists who I talked to and surveyed had mixed and very general motivations for traveling to Doolin. A typical example is a middle-aged Swedish tourist who said she came "mainly [for] the trad music and beautiful scenery, and also it's convenient for going to Galway and Limerick." A young New Zealander said that she came on the recommendation of a friend "to see the Cliffs of Moher and Doolin and the Burren." Others had little choice in the matter as is revealed by a young New Yorker on a coach tour who simply wrote, "It was one of the places on the tour." In my year in the village, I often heard tourists say that they had no idea why they were there. They were simply "told" to go. This extremely generalized (or sometimes even confused) basis for visiting a destination is a common characteristic of mass tourism. It is a far cry from the intentional, pilgrimage-like inconvenience of the tourism that characterized the revival period.

According to the survey, Irish music is the second most important draw to Doolin after the landscape. This is not surprising. Quinn notes that even as far back as 1993, 69 per cent of visitors surveyed by *Bord Failte* indicated that "traditional Irish folk music was either 'a very important' or a 'fairly important' factor in considering Ireland as a holiday destination" (1996: 386). The appeal of the region's landscape cannot be underestimated though. Five out of seven of the top attractions, according to the survey, were natural environments like the Cliffs of Moher. This increasing interest in the landscape also marks a difference from the revival period as well. Recently, one local family has even opened up a new "landscape" for tourists to explore: a cave system called *Poll an Eidhneáin* in the eastern part of the parish that leads to what is stated to be one of the world's largest free hanging stalactites.[6]

Tourists often speak very laudably about Doolin. This American's comments are representative:

> I have to say that Doolin was exactly what I expected, which surprised me. It really was tiny. It really did have only three pubs. The music really was extraordinary.

Figure 4.2 Tourists Consuming the Landscape and Crossing Borders at the Cliffs of Moher

Others, like this German tourist did not seem to know what to expect, resulting in mixed reactions:

> I was a little disappointed in it at first … . But Doolin developed some charm after a while mainly through the nice experience in the pub … . I didn't expect music for I didn't know before that it is famous for it. I came for the Cliffs, but was very pleased when the music session started. Then I found it quite traditional.

Others were not without a critical voice. In particular, the survey supports what many tourists told me in conversations in the pubs. They were concerned that Doolin was becoming too touristed and too developed. One representative example comes from an American tourist who wrote:

> I live in a tourist town … in northern California, 900 population, but on a Saturday in the summer, 3000 … . In 1988, [it] was a wonderful town. With tourism came development and now [it's] not so nice. Don't let Doolin become Disneyland … . Don't become California with lots of houses. Also no tacky leprechaun tourist shops. Keep it real. Keep it local.

One tourist put it more succinctly: "More Irish, less tourists." The underlying implication to this kind of comment is that a sense of "authenticity," a sense that one is keeping the community "local" and "real," is derived from the production of the lifeworld for oneself and not for others' consumption or for profit. The tourist-oriented built environment and the increasingly tourist-oriented production of the music are sometimes perceived to be "inauthentic" because they are being produced for others and for profit. Of course, the age-old irony that tourists are often the most vocal critics of tourism is not lost here.

Coach Tours

The data gathered from the survey has a significant bias towards those tourists who stayed overnight in the village. This is because the surveys were distributed to B&Bs, hostels, and campsites where customers filled them out. A smaller proportion were filled out at the area's restaurants and pubs. In other words, the coach tourists who pass through the village for extremely short periods (an hour or two) are barely represented. On the other hand, I had extensive, daily experience with coach tours as a member of staff at O'Connor's Pub. Since this kind of tourist makes a significant contribution to the local economy, and since they have significant impact on the daily life of the village, they are worth looking at in some detail here.

The coach tour business is technically year-round in the sense that packaged tours come through Doolin even in the winter. But it is a seasonal business for all intents and purposes. During the winter of 2002–2003, it was common for only one small coach per day with 15 tourists or so to stop into O'Connor's Pub for lunch.

In proportion to the amount of money coach tourists leave in Doolin, their time there is very short, their impact is minimal, and for some publicans and shopkeepers, they are a consistent source of income. Ironically, other tourists commonly belittle those who take coach tours as the very representation of the factors that supposedly "ruin" places like Doolin, but the truth is that coach tourists spend huge amounts of money in proportion to the relatively small "footprint" that they leave. By contrast, the tourists that locals find exasperating are the ones, like backpackers, who spend as little money as possible but are also inclined to "explore" (from the tourists' perspective) or "invade" (from the locals' perspective) the more private areas of the village. Tim told me that he has had tourists walk right into his cottage for example. Other tourists may have a negative opinion about those who take coach tours, but it is rarely the coach tourist who is accused of this type of invasion of privacy. By their very nature coach tours are more disciplined and directed experiences, which may be a factor in individual tourists' interactions with the locale.

When a tour group comes into the pub for lunch, the driver (and in some cases, a separate tour-guide) will rhetorically "direct" the tourists' luncheon "performance" by handing out menus, telling them where they can or cannot sit, informing them of the daily specials, and telling them to order their food at the bar. I recorded the following monologue from a coach tour guide as a bus pulled into the village one spring afternoon. The instructions are extremely specific and highlight the fact that a clearly defined symbiotic business relationship between this coach tour company and O'Connor's Pub.

When we get to Doolin, [We'll] bring you in and give you the menus.

And the first thing you do is pick a table.

And the number's on the table.

So when you go up to place your order, the first thing the barman will say to you is, "The number of the table where you're sitting?" So make sure to have that in your head.

As I say, [we'll] give you the menus.

Now, the fish-and-chips here is fantastic. The fish is fresh from the Atlantic Ocean every day, so it's quite good. Fish-and-chips—the best in the country. The Seafood Chowder is fantastic. Of course, the Beef Stew in Guinness is good too, and our traditional meal, which is Bacon & Cabbage.

But anything you order here is really good. You can tell me when you come out if you enjoyed it. And anytime I ask them when they come out, they really enjoy their food in Gussie O'Connor's.

You never hear a complaint.

As the bus makes its way down to the village, the tour guide also provides a narrative framework to contextualize the experience, talking about the Russell Brothers and traditional Irish music. After unloading the tourists, the driver sits down to a complementary meal and a chat with the bar staff. In the meantime, the influx of customers causes an explosion of activity in the kitchen and on "the floor" for the staff. If the drivers and tour guides have a long-standing relationship with the pub, they always sit at the bar. The topics for discussion between the drivers and the staff are often the weather, driving conditions, the nature and make-up of the day's tour group (e.g., "A lot of Germans today"), gossip from Doolin, and general news headlines. As casual as they sound, these chats can be very important because the health of the coach tour business can be an anecdotal barometer of the regional tourism industry. If drivers originating in major tourist hubs such as Galway or Dublin complain of dwindling tourist numbers, it can indicate low tourist numbers for Doolin in the short-term future.

Meanwhile, as the driver has a meal and a chat, the tourists are left to their own devices. Generally, they are hungry and order food and a drink. But they are normally given at least an hour to spend in Doolin, so depending on the instructions of their guides and partially upon the weather, they often finish their meal and then take a quick walk around Fisherstreet to snap a few pictures or stop into one of the shops. At O'Connor's Pub, the interior and exterior of the building itself becomes the subject of many photographs. Tourists like to document where they ate as a mnemonic device for the telling of subsequent "tourist tales." The tour guides' narrative framing of

Doolin's place in the history of traditional Irish music give the pub and the village a point of reference, and a reason to photograph it.

Edensor might describe this as an "enclavic tourist space" in the sense that there is a "continual maintenance of a clear boundary which demarcates which activities may occur" (2000: 328). The space is:

> organized to provide a self-contained environment where tourists are encouraged to spend as much money as possible. Thus their activities and movements are arranged to facilitate maximum expenditure by circulating them between enclavic attractions and by setting up institutional arrangements where services dovetail with each other (ibid.: 329).

Coach tourists are led directly into the pub for their lunch, and their time limitations only allow them to wander so far. In this way, they are confined to the semi-enclavic space of Fisherstreet where they are encouraged to spend money in the pub and shops. I want to be careful not to overemphasize the limitations of the coach tour experience though because as Oliver (2001) has shown, coach tourists do not travel through places in a impermeable "social bubble" (ibid.: 237). In fact, the coach tour experience in Doolin only partially matches Edensor's definition, because pure "tourist enclaves" have heavily policed boundaries that prevent unwanted interaction between locals and tourists. That is not the case in Doolin. Permanent residents are often found in the pub or along the street (and sometimes become photographable subjects themselves) when coach tours arrive. In fact, "people watching" in the pub is a constant form of entertainment for Doolin bachelors. While the coach tourists often perform what Edensor calls a "disciplined ritual" (ibid.: 334), for the most part keeping to themselves and "gazing" at their surroundings through the camera lens, opportunities for more "improvised performances" (ibid.: 335), albeit short ones, are available to the more outgoing tourists who wish to interact with locals.

Figure 4.3 Consuming the Locals

"Travelers," Working Tourists, and Visitors

It was with some surprise that the first people my wife and I met on the day that we arrived in Doolin to begin fieldwork were not Irish at all. We drove into the village in late June of 2002 and found our way to the little house in which we had made arrangements months earlier to rent a room. When we knocked on the door, we met our five new housemates who, as it happens, were a New York chef, an Australian backpacker, a Swedish musician, two Czech women, and a Congolese-Frenchman. Only one of them intended to stay in the village long term. For the most part, they were on extended tours funded by whatever service industry jobs they could pick up along the way. Admittedly, this came as quite a shock. We were wholly unprepared for this introduction to social life in a small village in western Ireland. After they showed us to our room, we all watched a World Cup match on the small television in the kitchen and shared cigarettes. We made small talk and I wondered nervously if we had made a poor choice of field sites. However, far from being unusual, working tourists from far-flung places are now common in many Irish tourist destinations. An *Irish Independent* reporter wrote that "Irish hospitality is now being doled out in bars, hotels, and B&Bs by non-nationals" all across Ireland (Collins 2002: 4). The reporter quoted a politician who worried that it "could seriously damage [Ireland's] image with tourists" (ibid.). Be that as it may, employing international workers in the service industry is a fast-growing national trend. In retrospect I suppose I was surprised in part because, as Nelson Graburn once wrote, "our conception of tourism is that it is not work" (1989: 22). But once again, the term "tourist" disguises much deeper complexities. Some people do not simply pass through a place as most tourists do. Some stay. They sit between categories and are not easy to pinpoint or label.

For the most part, these tourists come to Doolin for the summertime when there is more than enough available work. This pattern of behavior is nothing new. Young Australians and New Zealanders for example are well known for traveling for long periods through Europe, and often supplement their funds by working for relatively short periods in the service industry. "Working tourists"[7] from continental Europe have also significantly increased in recent years since Eastern European countries like Poland have been included in the European Union. In Doolin, working tourists most often take on unskilled or semi-skilled service jobs in the pubs, restaurants, B&Bs, hostels, and shops. Usually, these are temporary low-paying jobs, taken on for a few months during the summer.

The reasons for combining work and travel vary. For some, the attraction can be solely monetary. Some working tourists arrive annually in the spring and work through the summer to save as much money as possible, for example to fund university tuition. Others make an annual circuit around European tourist destinations as the seasons change. More often though, I found that working tourists are more motivated by the travel experience itself rather than gaining work experience or building long-term savings. Some also conceptualize employment as a powerful means to experience a place, immediately embedding them in intense, interpersonal relationships. Others want to improve their English language skills. In other words, work experiences and travel experiences are not separate activities for them. Even though they are employed locally and live in the village temporarily, most permanent Doolin residents still categorize these individuals as "tourists." Working tourists on the other hand often preferred to describe themselves as "travelers," creating a contrast with "mere tourists."[8] This is a common label in other tourist destinations as well (Riley 1988, Tucker 1997).

In many ways, an Australian woman named Sara who I got to know well is fairly typical. She explained that since she had a relatively indefinite period of time in which to explore Ireland, she felt free to stay in one place longer if she liked it. Before even leaving for Ireland she intended to get work to cover any living and traveling expenses. She felt that it was important to stay longer in certain places to, in her words, "get to know the Irish better." The relationships she could develop would then give her a more personal access to "real life in Ireland," not the relatively "superficial" experience afforded to tourists. She felt that her more outgoing, adventurous personality had led her to travel in this manner. For Sara, these factors distinguished her from "mass tourists" who were on a tight itinerary due to a shorter holiday and an imminent departure date.

In Doolin, seasonality dictates everything. During the winter of 2002–2003, only a few working tourists were able to keep their jobs since employers naturally give preference to permanent residents when there is less work to go around. Many working tourists do not intend to stay on for the winter even if they could, and many of them have obligations at the end of the summer anyway: university programs or permanent jobs back home. When the tourist season begins to quiet down in the autumn, "leaving parties" for working tourists become common as they begin to return home.

Another important classificatory term in Doolin, "visitors," also falls in the gray areas between a standard understanding of tourists and other categories. The term is commonly used to describe those tourists who come to the village on a semi-regular basis for their holidays. Some of these people might have in fact lived in the area for a longer time-period in the past and now return to visit their friends. Other people who are labeled in this way are simply tourists who have holidayed in Doolin for so long that they have become known consociates. They have personally come to know the community to a level that is far deeper than the standard first-time or "one-off" tourist, and certain members of the community have come to know them as well. "Tourist" becomes an inappropriate label for them as it would deny this deeper relationship.

In the 2003 survey, only just over 2 per cent of tourists had visited more than three times, so those who might be labeled "visitors" comprise only a small fraction of the tourist population. However, the qualitative distinction in their relationship with the locale and with locals is vastly different from one-off tourists or even those who have come back once or twice. For example, an American visitor wrote me and explained his relationship with Doolin:

> My feelings about Doolin are very complex. I made … three trips in the last year and a half. It is far too crowded there during the summer months. Unfortunately, it has become a "trendy" place to go and so it is fast losing the original charm that made it so special. Many of the tourists who go there to see and experience a session don't really have any understanding or

appreciation of traditional Irish music. It's just the thing to do. Doolin can't handle the increase in growth … . I'm also disappointed to see all of the new construction and holiday homes … . I know that the residents of Doolin are appalled by this growth as well. I'm worried about Doolin's future and I don't want to see it become a tourist trap.

Such visitors often develop less romantic, more concerned opinions that are created by getting to know locals and the local discourse about the place. These assessments are also created by their own longitudinal experiences. Unlike most tourists who do not come back, visitors like this American are able to see Doolin change over time. What is more, that change is seen not in increments but more dramatically in annual or semi-annual snapshots. "Last year," they might say, "that was a green field. This year, there is another B&B there." Certainly, this American visitor is correct to note that the rapid rate of development in Doolin concerns many locals (and tourists too), but it is also interesting to note the romance of first impressions tends to become the gold standard by which later impressions are judged. As we will see later, this is sometimes true for blow-ins as well.

Conclusions

Although it is my contention that Ireland has to a certain extent, always been globalized, the Celtic Tiger accelerated this process dramatically. Economic prosperity brought wealth to Ireland, but it has also had complicating consequences. Perhaps most significantly, the chasm between the rich and poor has widened extensively. A more general shift in identification seems to have occurred as well, one that is confident about its "Irishness" but at the same time yearns for all things perceived to be modern, European, and global. These shifts are contradictory, ironic, and fraught with tension.

Due to the historical circumstances of the revival of traditional musics globally and the increasing popularity of Irish music in particular, Doolin has become a premiere destination for tourists in recent decades. The revivalist crowds of the late 1960s and 1970s evolved into a flood of mass tourists later on. Capitalizing on this, the permanent residents of Doolin built up the tourist infrastructure that allowed for the growth of mass tourism. A feedback cycle was created, fed in large part by the burgeoning Celtic Tiger economy.

Globalization—and more specifically, the globalization caused by tourism—is too often discussed in terms of the actions of faceless corporations, government policies, or at best global cultural "flows," but real people with real biographies embody it. It is important that we move beyond a basic analysis whenever possible. The diverse identities of tourist populations must be recognized. As Gussie O'Connor said to me once, "I think we must have had someone from every country in the world in the pub at some point." Tim once said to me, too, "We don't have to go see the world, because the world comes to Doolin."

Viewed from a single place like Doolin, it is understandable how one might become obsessed with the "tourist destination" itself. One begins to see crowds rather than people. One begins to focus on the "mass" rather than on the "tourists." However, tourism creates ever-changing connections between diverse individuals and diverse places. Individuals and groups from all over the world travel to the same area but along different routes, and the totality of movement begins to evoke metaphors of webs, warps-and-wefts, corridors, highways and byways rather than simplistic dichotomies between destinations and homelands. What is more, the make-up of this totality changes day-to-day, week-to-week, and season-to-season.

There is also a great deal of epistemological and experiential diversity within the tourist population that comes to Doolin. Not all tourists have the same relationship to a destination. Most are "one-off" tourists who will not return. Some carry with them a narrative about the place derived from tourist guidebooks. Others bring the narratives that friends and family brought back with them from past trips. Still others may have visited Doolin before and expect to return. Some have made friends or have even been employed there. These different understandings of what a place is "about" cannot be overlooked.

The local discourse and perception of tourists is important as well because it forms another layer in this interaction. In this chapter, I highlighted the local categorizations of tourists rather than attempt to frame them in terms of the taxonomies in the social science literature. Surely tourists are discussed, labeled, and categorized differently in other places. This suggests to me that instead of attempting to refine taxonomies of tourist types or worse, create new ones, we ought to return to a careful reading of our own ethnographic data.

Through the medium of travel guides, tourist advertisements and the like, tourism has even consolidated an understanding of the "place" of Doolin and what it is "about." These processes do not simply happen on their own though. People make them happen. Doolin's publicans and musicians made their mark on the global Irish music scene by being welcoming hosts to a Revival. The economic buoyancy of the 1960s, the counter-cultural casting off of earlier hegemonies and the resurgent interest in traditional Irish music helped amplify their quiet agency to the world. Later, through the action of other individuals, Doolin became an institution on the Irish tourist trail, and to some extent, it was individual agency that even concretized the very notion of Doolin as a place.

In the next chapter, I continue this exploration of the people who come to Doolin, but focus on those who stayed.

Notes

1. The name is derived from the burgeoning "Asian Tiger" economies of Thailand, South Korea, Malaysia, and Singapore.
2. In 2003, the tourism interests in Doolin could not be described as an "industry" as such since there was a non-centralized, laissez-faire approach to infrastructural development and tourism marketing. But this has begun to change recently.
3. Again, the addition of two hotels and dozens of holiday homes since 2003 has added significantly to these numbers.

4. In the old days, food was never served in the pubs. I was told that it used be embarrassing for locals to be seen eating food in a pub because it implied that one's domestic life was either inadequate or "on the rocks". So, serving food in general was another expansion of the tourist trade.

5. cf. Oliver 2001 for an interesting study on the roving "tourist-site" of a coach tour through Ireland.

6. In fact, Killilagh parish is undercut by a warren of cave systems, and spelunking is one of the area's more specialized forms of tourism, a form of tourism that Coleman and Kohn might call "disciplined leisure" (2007).

7. It has been noted that this kind of tourism has not been adequately studied (Uriely 2001: 1). Uriely cumbersomely labels them "non-institutionalised working tourists" (2001: 1) who "tend to engage in unskilled and manual labour during their excursion ... primarily as means to travel" (ibid.). Terms like "wanderer" (Vogt 1976), "tramp" (Adler 1985) or "backpacker" (Loker-Murphy and Pearce 1995) have also been used, but these describe more of a mode of travel rather than anything to do with the tourists' behavior in relation to leisure or work. For that reason, I suggest that "working-tourist" is much more accurately descriptive.

8. The term "travelers" in Ireland generally describes Irish Gypsies. The term's use here is not derived from this Irish nomenclature but a tourist one, and should not be confused.

Chapter 5

Locals and Blow-ins

> Insiders and outsiders have had different meanings at different times, and
> the conflicts and resulting compromises have provided a sense of history
> which allows each group to define, develop, adapt, and sustain their sense
> of belonging to a community ... .
>
> — Jacqueline Waldren (2006[1996]: 244)

As the previous chapter showed, the line between who is a tourist and who lives in a place is not clear. Upon close examination, some people cannot properly be called either "tourists" or "locals." This chapter continues the exploration of these areas of gray between social categories, extending the discussion to permanent residents. In Part Three of the book, it will become apparent how changes in the local social structure are intimately tied to changes in the performances of traditional music. In Doolin, as elsewhere in Ireland, large areas of gray exist between non-residents and locals in what Peace has called the "social architecture" (2001) of local places. This area of gray is occupied by a category of people known throughout Ireland as "blow-ins."

In Doolin, blow-ins are classified as people who were born elsewhere but now live permanently in the village. They cannot become "local" in their lifetime, but their children are sometimes considered locals. In other places in Ireland, the boundaries and usage of these categories vary slightly. Therefore, to a certain extent, the terms are polysemous and negotiable. This chapter is not only about the different ways in which these identifications are defined in Doolin, but how people maneuver within them, and the limitation of those maneuvers. Indeed, in no way do I wish to suggest a reification of the categories discussed here. In Doolin, while there are relatively clear boundaries between the categories, these boundaries do move. Further identifiers, such as being an Irish blow-in or being the child of one local and one blow-in, create a shifting negotiation and usage of these terms in different contexts and among different groups of permanent residents. Likewise, I agree with Gefou-Madianou that internal diversity within groups creates a kind of "cultural polyphony" (1999). What I observed in Doolin is also in line with Kohn (2002a) and Strathern (1981: 7) who have argued that successful entrance into a community, regardless of one's status, depends more on daily praxis than on categorical roles. In other words, as Waldren suggests (2006[1996]: 244), the basic distinction between "insiders" and "outsiders" is only the starting point for exploring finer differences.

The distinction between locals and blow-ins is given special attention in this book for the simple reason that it is the most salient and important distinction between permanent residents. Blow-ins have become prominent and influential in the social, political, and economic life of the village. Furthermore, the focused analysis on the relations between these two groups feeds into the rest of the book because in Doolin it is the blow-ins who have all but completely appropriated the traditional Irish music scene.

The complex changes incomers have had in European contexts on local social structures has received some ethnographic attention in the British Isles, particularly in England, Scotland, Wales, and the Isle of Man (Frankenberg 1957; Ennew 1980; Strathern 1981; Phillips 1986; Nadel-Klein 1991; Ahmed and Mynors 1994; Kohn 1997; Dawson 2002; Lewis 2002; Kohn 2002a, 2002b; Rapport 2002), and elsewhere in Europe (cf. Waldren's work in Spain 1996, 1997) but rarely has it been mentioned in the context of the Republic of Ireland. At first blush, the lack of analysis of incomers in Ireland might not seem unreasonable given Ireland's extensive and intensive history of emigration rather than immigration. However, largely due to the new Celtic Tiger economy this trend has reversed, and quite dramatically. Ireland is no longer on the "decline" as Hugh Brody put it over thirty years ago (1973) (if indeed it ever really was "declining"). In fact, the Republic of Ireland now attracts workers and refugees instead of sending them abroad. The issue of immigration receives a great deal of attention in popular culture and the news media in Ireland. What is more, the colloquial term for incomers in Ireland, "blow-ins," is very commonly used and indeed has some antiquity, most likely reaching back to the Gaelic term *séid isteachs*.[1] Recently, the return of so many Irish emigrants-turned-immigrants who once followed the lure of prosperity elsewhere but are now following the money back to Ireland, has led to yet another variation on this term: the "blow-back." So, the continued lack of analysis of blow-ins is even more glaring given their increasing numbers, the salience of the topic in Ireland, and the influence they have had in the development of heavily touristed communities like Doolin.

The notable exceptions to this are Peace (2001) and Casey (2003), who do discuss blow-ins, and Shandy and Power (2007) and Lele (2008) on the more general topic of immigration. For Peace, they are clearly a secondary distinction in his analysis of social structure. It may simply be because blow-ins do not make a major presence in the village he calls Inveresk. This would not be surprising. Certainly, some communities have very few blow-ins while others, like Doolin, are made up of a significant number. (In Doolin approximately one fifth of the total population of permanent residents are blow-ins). In the follow-up volume on *Irish Tourism* (2003) edited by Cronin and O'Connor, Casey briefly addresses the issue of incomers as well, and indeed, in the context of another County Clare village. She reports that blow-ins are described there as situated somewhere in between returning visitors and tourists on a kind of classificatory spectrum (2003: 50). Casey also describes "outsiders" or "newcomers" as a "new type of 'local'" (2003: 50). This is in stark contrast to the assessments of the permanent residents in Doolin (including incomers and locals there), where I was told that blow-ins could never become locals. The differences in definitions and treatment of incomers described by Peace, Casey, and myself highlight the polysemy of the term "blow-in," the meaning of which may change slightly depending on the way in which different communities have negotiated the relationship between different categories of people.

Locals

After a long hike across the parish one rainy day with Tim and his dog Oscar, we were sitting in his cottage with glasses of whisky. The cold autumn air crept in through the stone walls and from under the doorjamb. We had been talking about his family for a while and the fishing techniques they used in the "old days." I asked him how long his family has lived in Doolin.

> We're supposed to have been here for the last five hundred years and a bit over it. So, yes, in that way, I suppose, I am a local at this stage, but there's still some people who—their families have been here a lot longer than that.

I laughed at his characterization of himself as only tenuously "local," confident that he must be joking. Instead, he ignored my laughter and continued in all seriousness, "And ah, they would consider themselves the real locals. Which they are."

I sat up straighter in my chair. Completely amazed, I asked, "So — so they would actually say that 500 years is not enough to be a local?"

"Well, you'd be just about," he responded, changing his mind slightly, qualifying his statement. "Yeah, you would be considered a local at this stage." He paused then to choose his words. "But like, a true local is where you come from the ground itself-like, the ground itself. You're a part of the root. Put it that way."

Tim explained that the "true local" is from the ground, shaped and fed by it, but they also change and shape the ground, "build part if it" themselves. The ground and the local become physically connected, and made of the same stuff. It reminds me of something an Irish journalist once wrote: "When you look at beautiful scenery in other countries, you appreciate it in the way that you would a painting or a postcard, whereas in Ireland, you appreciate it as something that is actually *in* you" (Molony 2003: 16).

Putting the notion of localness in these naturalistic terms is intentional, and only secondarily metaphoric. Interestingly, the word "ground" is used to refer to the specific locale of Doolin, the place itself, not generally as in "the earth" or "the dirt." People call their plots of land their "ground." Fishermen call their specific fishing-grounds their "ground." There is a belonging and an ownership all at once. The Doolin ground is bordered along the church parish lines. Someone said to me once, "You get people living in Ennistymon or whatever below in the pub and 'Oh, they're locals'. They are not locals! How can you be local when you're from another parish?" For some, the boundaries are even more constrained. "If you got someone who, say, lived anymore than four miles from here," Tim told me, "three miles from here, two miles even, they wouldn't be considered locals at all-at all," he said. People from neighboring towns and villages are not locals. They have their own ground. Even people in the countryside between towns might only be considered local to that ground.

Not everyone is purely local though. A "half-local" is someone who is descended from one local parent and one non-local parent. However, even if someone were to make this distinction, in practice that person would be treated as a full-on local in every respect if they had been raised in the parish. Another informant explained that only the children of half-locals would be considered full locals. So by this reckoning, it takes at least three generations to become local. This mirrors the definition presented in a report for the European Cultural Foundation which states that "[t]here is a time-honored custom in many Irish communities of describing anyone whose family has not belonged to the locality for at least three generations as 'outsiders' or 'blow-ins'. This is not confined to rural areas but flourishes in tightly-knit groups throughout the country" (Burke, no date).

In the local discourse, this is all tied into kinship of course. When permanent residents of Doolin are speaking to each other, one's localness might be debated and defined in fairly specific terms. It is not unusual for the exact parameters of the parish lines and the location of a person's natal house to be brought into the conversation as evidence for or against a person's local status. Their ancestral pedigree might be recalled, and their relations in other districts might qualify their standing. Significantly, these conversations will not generally occur when the person being discussed is present. Indicative of its value, to question someone's clout as a local by even discussing it can cause offense. Not surprisingly, the importance of kinship as an indicator of belonging to a locale has been illustrated in other contexts in the British Isles as well. In an English village in north Yorkshire, Phillips noted that "[k]inship is one of the central markers of difference" between insiders and outsiders (1986: 143). Doolin, like many small communities, is a place where people claim that "everyone is related to everyone else" in one way or another. Of course this is not true in an absolute sense, but the "rhetoric of interrelatedness" reveals the centrality of kinship as a marker of belonging.

For many younger people especially, the term "local" is a more expansive category that might include everyone from northwest County Clare. It is conceivable that delineating clear boundaries becomes more important as younger villagers enter more seriously into local economic and political affairs. However, it is not unreasonable to argue that the symbolic capital of localness is simply decreasing among the younger generations who have grown up in a more globalized Ireland flush with cash. Moreover, exceptionally fastidious determinations of people's status like calling someone a "half-local" are only rarely heard amongst younger residents. This generational difference in reckoning who is or is not a local was highlighted sardonically by a young man in the village:

Say "subject A" moved here twenty years ago, brought up a family ... .
All their kids are born here. They'd probably be considered blow-ins—the

kids—by the older locals. The kids their own age don't care. They're locals as far as they're concerned. But … more elderly people, the older people, they're the people that think about it. They have nothing better to think about!

As Mac Laughlin has written:

Old localisms of the past were based on the principle of exclusion and insulation. They tended to minimise contact with the foreign world and maintained strong, closed and prophylactic boundaries between that which was "inside" and that which was "outside." The localisms which are now emerging in Ireland are of a quite different nature and are far more extrovert. (1997: 13)

Joining the European Union was not just a socio-political act. It was also a cultural shift, a departure from a simple identity-opposition to the English and an entrance as a "modern Ireland" into the global community. The desire to embrace the global world more generally cannot be underrated, especially among younger generations. While some young people in the village are quite reflexive and proud of their localness, many cannot wait to become worldly cosmopolitans. Localness is not abhorred, it is simply not as important. Like today's generation of anthropologists who have sometimes shied away from "the very notion of boundaries" because of the "unasked-for legacies from the past" that they imply (Bashkow 2004: 444), younger people in Doolin sometimes feel that these finer distinctions are exclusive, provincial, and antiquated.

All of this reckoning over who is or is not a local occurs in the context of a heavily toured village, complicating the matter. When one is speaking to a tourist, whose knowledge of the community is limited, and for whom these distinctions are complicated, the local moniker is used more liberally. Anyone who is Irish is generally labeled a "local." This is usually a matter of convenience due to the limited nature of conversations that residents commonly have with tourists. If a more in-depth conversation with a tourist emerges, and the conversation happens to light upon the topic, the distinctions might be explained. But generally, the Irish who live in the area but are not from there are labeled "locals." If a permanent resident is from another country, essentially if they have a non-Irish accent, their status is explained in more accurate detail: "He's American but he lives here." In other words, the term "local" is used much more loosely in discussions with tourists because it is easier and more convenient to do so.

Besides the obvious economic impacts that tourism brings, there is a more subtle cosmopolitan orientation that is imbued in the whole community. It is commonly said that "there's no need to go see the world because the world comes here." Still, many villagers have seen the world. For example, many Doolin residents have lived abroad and traveled widely. But in conversation with tourists, whose knowledge of the community is understandably limited, and for whom these boundaries are needlessly complicated, local identities are sometimes played up. Locals actively participate in playing up their Irishness, becoming characters in what Bruner would call the "experience theater" of tourist interactions with the Other (2005: 48–49). For foreign tourists, it is an important part of their holiday experience to interact with the "Irish people," and since tourists often equate Irishness with localness, the broader equation between the Irish accent and localness makes sense to them. So, even Irish incomers might be introduced to tourists as "locals" to spread out the responsibility of these interactions. For example, if a group of permanent residents is sitting at the pub having a morning coffee, and a group of tourists engages this group in conversation (or the other way around), it is in the interest of the "true" locals to not dwell too much on distinctions between local and blow-in categories so that the focus of the tourists' attention is spread evenly.

This broader characterization of localness is also used for convenience in other situations, even among permanent residents. When I worked in the village as a bartender, I was always told to "mind the locals" or to "see if the locals want anything else" before closing time. In these cases and situations like them, all permanent residents are considered locals. This is understandable since blow-ins are neighbors too, regardless of their origins. Local or not, all permanent residents must be treated well to maintain good social relations in the village, and a special, local level of service must be provided.

Blow-ins

Sitting with Tim in his cottage that cold afternoon, we finished our glasses of whisky and rolled cigarettes. I was fascinated by his strict delineation around the local population, so I asked him about people who lived in Doolin but who were not born there. There were certainly plenty of them around, young people working furiously in the tourist service industry as well as others who had come to the village decades ago, started businesses and married into local families. Tim got up to fill the kettle and set it on his black cast iron stove to make tea. He said:

> People then, who come and live here, and marry here, and stay here, are called "blow-ins." That's what we call them: blow-ins. Like, they can be blowing out as fast as they blow in. Because they have no roots here—nothing to hold them here.

All international members of the community are called blow-ins, and so are Irish incomers from other locales.[2] For the incomer, the status of the blow-in is as much as they can achieve in their lifetime. Even when a blow-in is introduced to a tourist as a local, or is accorded "local service" by a barman, the incomer knows that this does not allow him to label himself this way in front of his local neighbors. One villager put it in more colorfully once: they "could live here until the day they grow daisies," he said, "and the day they grow daisies, they'd still be a blow-in. They'd never become a local." Strathern documented a similarly strict sense of localness in the English village of Elmdon where an incomer who'd lived there for "only forty odd years" was still considered a "newcomer" (1981: 6).

Rarely, an incomer might assert that they have now become a local, but almost all permanent residents—locals and other blow-ins—thoroughly quell such claims. Individuals who would be so cavalier would not do so very often for fear of swift recrimination. One would be seen as extremely presumptuous and pretentious, and if one pursued such a claim, might even be labeled a "Plastic Paddy," the ultimate insult. The term implies that the incomer is a fake and puts on their localness or Irishness, when in fact they have no claim to it.

Importantly, the boundaries surrounding the incomers themselves are not fixed, and are perceived differently by different people. For example, two people in the village distinguished between different types of incomers, but for different reasons. Nora has a strict definition of localness, but she has another term that she considers more respectful for incomers whose native language is English: "visitors." Therefore, only those who live in the area but are not originally from there, and furthermore do not speak English as a first language, are blow-ins. Kieran on the other hand told me, "you have locals, you have blow-ins, and then you have foreigners." Importantly, Kieran told me, locals are people born in County Clare, not just Killilagh Parish. Blow-ins are Irish incomers from other counties in Ireland, and foreigners are non-Irish. It is not language but nationality that is the important marker of difference for him. And like Nora's opinion about the term "blow-in," he told me that international incomers would not actually be described with the term "foreigner" because it was distasteful. Like Nora, Kieran wanted to be sensitive to the feelings of friends that he considered foreigners by not actually using his own label. He stressed that, while there is a difference in classification, these incomers should be imbued with personality and a name out of simple respect.

Both of these definitions limit the extent to which outsiders may be included into a deeper level of belonging to the village. One is based on language while the other is based on nationality. Nora's and Kieran's own social positions in the village are revealing. Nora is local through and through. From her perspective, a more restrictive definition of localness relates to a more expansive and composite definition of belonging for outsiders. The social capital of her localness is unquestionable and she can afford to be more laissez-faire in her conceptualization of outsiders. For Kieran, an Irish incomer to the area, his definition of a local is far wider than Nora's, while his definition of a blow-in is more strict than definitions like Tim's, which would simply include all Irish and all international incomers. Keiran knows he is not local, and can be more liberal about who is, but he also limits conceptual access to his own social status. In other words, each of these people restrict entry into the group that they themselves belong to, while widening the adjacent categories. Both cases illustrate the ways in which one's own classification of people reflects one's own position in the classificatory system. Like any categorical label, internal diversity proliferates within its boundaries.

Like on the Scottish island of Lewis (Ennew 1980: 117), there is a qualitative difference between recent and more established incomers in Doolin. Largely, this simply results from the fact that more recent arrivals have not cultivated the consocate relations in the village. New incomers in Doolin tend to be younger, and with fewer local ties, they are more able to come and go as they please. Similar to the situation on Lewis, many of these new incomers in Doolin are "attempting to retreat from 'pressures' of modern urban existence" (ibid.). Some are on a larger project of exploring the world before eventually returning home and more accurately might be considered "working tourists." Again, there is no clear-cut distinction. Sara, from Australia, who we met in the previous chapter, arrived in Doolin around the same time as my wife and I in 2002. She told me about her motivations for traveling:

> I always wanted to go traveling, but I never got my ass into gear … . I just got my money together and a ticket and just came over here. No plans, nothing. Just take each day as it comes.

I asked her why she chose to come to Ireland. She explained:

> I think it was more because my brothers were over here [in Ireland] and it was about time—it was about time to go traveling … . That would be the main reason.

> The first place I wanted to go traveling was Africa, first. Yeah, I was all into Africa. I didn't really know all that much about Ireland when I first came over here so I didn't know what to expect or anything like that.

"Why come out to Doolin then?", I asked. "Why not stay in Dublin?" She told me:

> I've always been brought up in small little towns. I find that when you're living in a city, you don't really—you don't really experience or learn about Ireland 'cause it's just so international—or a multicultural place, in Dublin. And I'm here to travel in Ireland and not a big city. You don't really meet the Irish. It's good to meet different people from all different countries, but I'm here to learn about Ireland and um—.

> I was actually going down to Dingle, but I got the job at [the pub], and I decided to stay here. It's a lot more nice. It's a lot more laid back. And you get to meet people that grew up here since they were little. And it's good to listen to the stories of how the place has changed and what it was actually like to live here.

In some ways, Sara is typical of these younger incomers whose first intention is to travel rather than to resettle. Staying for a long period in one place is not unexpected, but it is also typically meant to be temporary. In fact, despite the fact that Sara stayed for nearly a year, she described herself as a "traveler," definitely not a tourist but also not an incomer or a blow-in. Other researchers on tourists have noted this distinction and have argued that these long-haul travelers "see tourists as people who go on holiday in hotels where they are separated from the 'real' locals. 'Collecting' … new experiences … means going to places which are not organized for tourists but for locals" (DesForges 1998: 181).

Most recent blow-ins do not stay in the area indefinitely. They eventually move on to other places and seek other opportunities after a year or two. The extremely quiet winter seasons are often cited as reasons for moving on. There is a real lack of employment opportunities, which can be severe for blow-ins who rely on service industry work. The constant stimulation of the ever-renewed tourist crowd is also absent in the winter months. Comments like "I can't take another winter in Doolin" are common, and are again comparable to other contexts like Lewis (Ennew 1980: 117). Certainly though, a failure to develop more extensive relationships in the village itself plays a large part.

Understandably, the level of involvement in the community that new incomers achieve is far less in-depth than those who might marry into the community, start a business, and get involved in local committees. In fact, single blow-ins who do not "marry into the village" or start a business but stay for a lifetime are not unknown but they are rare. Sara is representative. She made good friends there, but without stronger economic affairs or kin ties to keep her there, she eventually moved on. Sometimes though, these travelers stay or return again and again. Indeed, despite the semi-transient and carefree nature of some younger incomers, many of the older, permanent blow-ins told me this serendipitous wandering was exactly how they were first introduced to the community.

Negotiations of Belonging

As has been noted elsewhere, "such designations do not affect day-to-day interaction … people might be slow to accept a newcomer, but it does not really make any difference to their behavior" (Strathern 1981: 7). Similarly, someone said to me once:

> [Doolin]'s very different, and I would say it's why it's been so easy for so many quote-unquote "blow-ins" to live here and eventually get absorbed into the village. They're still blow-ins, but they're very much a part of the place.

Blow-ins are heavily involved in every aspect of the community but with different degrees of success. When conflicts erupt, the enunciation of a person's blow-in status can be used to create a sense of exclusion from the local community, no matter how long a person has resided in the locale. It is a term that reminds everyone involved that a blow-in is not, and never will become, a local. This has to do with individual behavior, and also the particular domain of social life one is working within. Kieran, a Dubliner, stressed that:

> I'm a blow-in, but like, I don't consider myself as a "blow-in".

I'm a person. And I'm a person of equal value to a local. So I don't consider myself of less value than a local, whereas, I suppose, locals do consider blow-ins as of less value than themselves.

Obviously, as a person who falls somewhere between the categories of "insider" and "outsider," Kieran is very aware of the value judgments placed on his Liminal status. However, he told me that he tries not to think about it too much because, to him, "there isn't much value in the value-system. You know, I don't pay much heed to it myself."

Any separation between locals and incomers in terms of praxis and social relations is a fluid one, as has been pointed out in other contexts (Kohn 2002b). Blow-ins in Doolin are heavily involved in the social life and politics of the community. Inclusion flows through different channels and achieves different degrees of success. Those who have established a clear economic role in the village are taken seriously, and incomers who do have economic or kin relations in the village often find themselves getting involved in local politics. I detail below just how influential this can be in terms of coming to "belong" in Doolin, but social inclusion will ultimately fall short if blow-ins fail to create and maintain good social relations with neighbors and friends. Even extremely successful business owners will effectively be ostracized if they are unwilling or unable to adapt to the social life of the village. This actually goes for locals as well, if they fail to engage with people socially. This means of inclusion is not overtly obvious, and is dependent on constant subtle interactions with friends and neighbors. Generalized reciprocity, for example, is a prerequisite for proper social behavior amongst consociates. A liberal willingness to assist others with even small tasks is simply "neighborly," but it is significant. On the other hand, in this historically agricultural social climate, independence and privacy are also highly regarded. Maintaining a balance then between "helping out" and "meddling" can be a trick, and sometimes the incomer stumbles along to find this delicate posture. Interestingly, in a few cases, urban Irish blow-ins fare worse than international blow-ins who originated in rural areas.

Contributing something to the community is seen as an important vehicle of acceptance. A half-Irish half-American blow-in, told me modestly:

I don't do much for the community, but every year, I—you know—like something I did last week, I donate my time. Like, every year, I cook for the kids. And shit like that—people notice that. And they go, "Why is he doing that?" The reason I do it is—ah—first of all, it's fun. And you always have to give back a little bit. And it's four or five hours of my time. But that four or five hours is fucking worth a lot of points around here.

Volunteering for a local committee, setting up a "quiz night" to raise money for a local cause, or conscientiously helping out one's neighbors are all examples of contributions that people notice. These activities earn blow-ins social and symbolic capital. Respect leads to acceptance.

Kinship ties through marriage (or more rarely through distant consanguinial relations) are an extremely compelling means of inclusion. Marriage to a local is by implication marriage to the locale, propelling the incomer into a more immediate suite of relationships and responsibilities with locals, and therefore into a deeper web of belonging. One blow-in who married a local man several decades ago talked about how establishing kin-relations in the village is a potent and immediate way to become accepted, but how acceptance is not dependent on it:

> [H]aving a connection to the community helps—if you're actually married to somebody who's a regular part of the community. But there are people who have not married into the community who are very much accepted, who do regular jobs around for other people, who kind of keep their noses out of other people's business, and yet show up for things that—say, the community is raising money for something. They make a point of coming to those things and they contribute and they help.

Economically, incomers have become a central driving force in the recent success of the village's tourist economy. In this sense, Doolin is not unique. The phenomenon of the "incomer as entrepreneur" has been noted in other contexts in the British Isles too (Ardener 1989: 219–220). Indeed, the local tourist industry was historically built-up by a kind of partnership between locals and blow-ins. For the most part, it has been a co-operative development, and has provided blow-ins with an important and influential economic role. It is becoming clearer though, that tourism is not an ever-expanding economic arena in Doolin, and as competition for scarcer resources increases, so do tensions.

In terms of the blow-in population in Doolin, women have been rather more successful than men in the development of tourist oriented businesses. The most ubiquitous type of tourist business in the village, though by no means the most profitable, are the bed and breakfasts (B&Bs) that dot the landscape. It is not unusual for husbands and sons to do B&B work, but, more often than not, women run these businesses. Many households maintain a mixed economy in which men do some farming and women run the B&B. This feeds into older gender patterns of working life in rural Ireland, and dichotomies between men/women and public/domestic work. In the current economy though, far from reducing women's economic power, running a B&B out of the home means that women provide a steady income for the household. This is significant for the present discussion because it means that women who marry local men and settle in Doolin find the path to inclusion somewhat easier than men because there is an inbuilt and powerful economic role for them to play.

Generally, male blow-ins, like male locals, tend to work in the public sphere. Some male incomers have opened successful gift shops or restaurants, but for the most part there is less opportunity to start new businesses. Farming is not much of an option for several reasons: the exponential increase in property values, the fact that it is a finite resource combined with the conservative nature of inheritance, and, I suspect, the less attractive nature of farm work for incomers. Interestingly though, a few male blow-ins have successfully entered the small fishing economy in Doolin. At one point during 2002–2003, until one man uprooted and left the village, half of the local fishing operations were run by blow-ins. The difference here may lie in the more fluid rules of inheritance of fishing grounds, the mobile nature of fishing resources, and probably more to the point, because fishing is no longer thriving in Doolin as it once was. Despite the fact that it is an older more "traditional" economic domain, one that continues to carry a great deal of symbolic capital for this "fishing village," there is simply less competition in this industry today.

It is worth mentioning here that the limited nature of rural resources extends to land generally. Land is a resource that is carefully guarded, and locals will not quickly sell tracts to outsiders unless they are known and respected. However, due to the appeal of the landscape, property prices in and around Killilagh parish have skyrocketed in recent years, and the temptation to sell tracts of land to outside property developers who are not residents has obviously increased. As a corollary, so have tensions. One case, in which a tract of land with a great view of the Aran Islands was sold to an outsider who built a series of holiday homes, was vociferously decried locally. It was often brought up during a series of planning meetings in 2003 regarding local development issues as an example of how not to foster tourism in the village. Much of the development that has occurred since has also been resisted, and while not all objections have been successful, the underlying value of "local land for locals only" remains strong. In County Clare, this conservative stance concerning the sale of land to outsiders even entered into the realm of official planning and development policy. In the late 1990s, the county council attempted to implement a policy whereby blow-ins would be ineligible to build homes in "vulnerable areas or in rural areas deemed to be under development pressure" (Deegan 1999: 18). These areas included a fifty-mile stretch of coastline that included all of Killilagh parish. The policy, which was eventually struck down in the courts, would have disallowed even long-time resident blow-ins from developing properties. It is far from uncommon for local people to sell properties to blow-ins, but these attempted policies reveal the kind of resistance that can emerge when a limited and valuable resource is sold to outsiders.

Those incomers who do have long-standing economic interests or kin relations in the village often find themselves getting involved in local politics, especially the ones who have lived in the village longest and have more of a vested interest in the place. That vested interest, social or economic or both, provides more gravitas to their opinions. There is no formal hierarchical structure to local politics. In other words, there is no mayor or even an official village council. Instead, village affairs are represented and run by around a dozen volunteer committees that have evolved over the years. Indicative of the economic dominance of tourism in the parish, in 2003 the Doolin Tourism Co-operative was by far and away the most powerful. Other village committees tend to be topical as well and range from a local branch of the Irish Farmer's Association to a Kid's Club.[3]

Notably, blow-ins are sometimes more outspoken in village committees than locals. There are several reasons for this. First, outsiders bring with them a different set of values that motivate their level of involvement. One American blow-in who married a local gave me an example of why this occurs:

> I think of a thing as simple as the Board of Management in a school. Now, there are quite a number of blow-ins on the Board of Management. And the reason for that is that we come from a different background as regards education, where we simply think it's really important for the parents to be concerned, and where it's important to have a "say." Whereas many of the local people, many have the idea that you were told what to do by the priest, by the teacher, by the lawyer, by the doctor. So you didn't speak up, and it's up to them to go in and have a say. That's fading but it's there still.

There are other reasons why blow-ins get heavily involved in local politics besides the importation of "outside" cultural values. A blow-in has far fewer kin relations, even if they have married in to a local family, and can more easily state their opinions publicly without offending a large proportion of the attendees. Or, more precisely, they can more safely offend a large portion of the attendees. Even so, blow-ins must tread carefully. One woman who has lived in Doolin for decades after marrying a local man, explained the level of incomers' involvement in local politics this way:

> If there's resistance, say, to planning permissions [for a new building] … if people get up in arms about it, you'll find that it's blow-ins that are making all the noise. Well, of course, there's good reasons for that. First of all, they come here and have chosen to be here because they like the place. And secondly, and perhaps more to the point, they do not suffer under obligation to anyone else, whereas a local person is probably related in some way, has some connection, to the person they'd be protesting against. So they would either feel disloyal, or as is often the case, that they'll pay for it—that that person will have a resentment for them and get them back, which has happened. So there might be even a tendency to agreeing with you and giving lip-service to something a blow-in is saying, but when it comes down to it you won't find them signing any paper and putting their names on it.

So, sometimes, blow-ins are more conservative than locals about development and also more open about making their case. This is the second reason that blow-ins are occasionally more outspoken than locals. It is often said that blow-ins have a very different kind of attachment to the landscape and the community, one that is far more romantic, than the locals do. In the passage above, my informant pointed out that blow-ins "have chosen to be here because they like the place." Although obvious, this is significant. For some, romance results in a strong preservation instinct, a reluctance to allow changes to any aspect of the village that would radically alter the way Doolin was when they first "fell in love with it." In other words, the intensity of "falling in love" leads some blow-ins to romanticize their moment of arrival. Changes that occur beyond that moment are to be lamented. From this point of view, some romantic incomers fail to recognize that their original impression of the place was more like a snapshot of something constantly dynamic and changing rather than an immersion into a static, calm, rural idyll which is only now being supposedly "ruined" by change. Conversely, for locals who have grown up with constant change, recent developments are not to be lamented because they do not interfere with their longer term, constantly evolving relationship with the place.

My own experiences with local politics may be illustrative of the barriers and stumbling blocks that an outsider can run into. During the spring of 2003, the local people submitted a voluntary village "development plan" to the county council as a supplement to a regional development plan that was being drafted by the county bureaucrats. I knew a few of the people who wanted to create the local submission, and I was asked to get involved in the process. In Frankenberg's well-known study of local Welsh politics, he encountered similar circumstances in which locals encouraged newcomers to take leading roles in village politics (1957: 18, 78–88). In his case, he found that locals would actually use incomers to shield themselves from controversial decisions by making the incomers take lead roles. Thankfully, this was clearly not the case in Doolin. Still, I was very hesitant to get involved at all because I felt strongly that as an incomer, and one who intended to leave, I was in no position to make my own suggestions about the future of the place. After some discussion though, I agreed to be the secretary for the committee assigned to create the plan. That way, I could contribute to the effort but simultaneously remain outside the decision-making processes. I thought this was quite clever at the time, but it clearly backfired.

As secretary, I attended a series of local and regional meetings—some informational, some "brainstorming sessions." I took minutes and typed up all of the reports, but made no substantive contributions myself. Most of these meetings were with a small committee of volunteers, but a few were attended by county councilors and two were large public meetings. The committee solicited and compiled ideas for developmental guidelines from members of the community, but since this volunteer committee was not elected to represent the village, deciding what should go in a final formal submission to the county council became problematic. There was a strong sense among committee members that a community consensus was required, and so one last public meeting was organized to finalize the decisions.

Despite the fact that I contributed nothing to the substance of the development plan, my very public position in these politically sensitive meetings caused some serious consternation among locals who did not know me well. Rumors began to spread about my motivations. The chairman of the committee had to actively bring the issue up with some of his friends and neighbors to allay their concerns about me—a kind of political damage control. One particularly successful local businessman even confronted me in the pub one day when I was working, shortly after the final public meeting. In loud angry tones meant for the rest of the pub to hear, he verbally berated me for "getting too involved." I had become a "meddling blow-in" who ought to be "run out of town." Some of my friends told me not to worry about this confrontation, but others warned me that I had "crossed the line." Tellingly, my local friends were the ones who told me not to worry (and even found it highly amusing), while my blow-in friends were the ones who quietly scolded me for getting too involved in local affairs.

Whether in the economic, social, or political domain of village life, locals can afford to find blow-ins' gaffs amusing, but blow-ins must be careful. For the blow-in, a social misstep can be extremely damaging. Their mutual biography with the local community is incomplete, extending only back to the moment that they arrived. As Schuetz put it, "[s]een from the point of view of the approached group, [the stranger] is a man without a history" (1944: 501). It is a given that inter-biographical, or consociate, relations (Schutz 1970: 170) carry a great deal of weight. The blow-in has a temporally limited inter-biographical reputation to rely on, and for that reason, it is much more tenuous. The local's reputation, too, might be reduced by inappropriate behavior, they might be the focus of negative gossip, or they might even be ostracized by other residents if they caused a serious breach, but their claim to belonging—in other words, their claim to being a local—would remain unquestioned. As a result, the local is sometimes excused more quickly because they were, are, and will continue to be, locals. Their "rootedness" implies that local consociate relationships with that individual or at least with their family will continue indefinitely. The blow-in never had a claim to belong in this way. The loss of one's reputation and/or one's friends through ostracism, would be much more damaging and more difficult to mend. (Thankfully, in my case the tensions aroused by my presence on the committee quickly dissipated).

Unfortunately, tensions between incomers and locals in Ireland can degenerate into more overt intolerance. I was never witness to situations where the strain between locals and blow-ins grew to levels that were overtly discriminatory. In fact, despite the exposition of the tensions and limitations to inclusion outlined in this chapter, Doolin and northwest Clare in general are known to be extremely welcoming places for blow-ins.[4] However, it is clear from incidents elsewhere that tension can escalate well beyond mild ostracism and verbal abuse to blatant intolerance. For the first time in Irish history, mass immigration has replaced mass emigration, and according to one report, it is estimated that there are people from almost 160 different nationalities currently living in Ireland ("Varieties of Irishness"). Some of them are economic migrants, some are asylum seekers, and others are simply hoping to make a home in Ireland. Immigrant-cum-blow-ins, while sincerely welcomed in many cases, have also run into the predictable xenophobia. Even in the early days of the Celtic Tiger, a letter to the editor in *The Irish Times* bemoans the "extraordinary" increase of "non-nationals who are now resident in West Cork" which has led to "an alarming imbalance ... reach[ing] frightening proportions" (Ní Chonaill 1994). The xenophobic rhetoric is undisguised. More recently, in North Leitrim, a German couple were "terrorized" by locals who were "trying to drive them away" (Managh 2002: 3). In cases where the blow-in population is made up of non-white incomers, intolerance can become couched in racism. A Dublin blow-in of African descent told a reporter, "Black immigrants simply stand out more ... and many Irish people aren't too fussy about their insults" (cited by Cullen 2002: 7). These cases are indicative of a serious problem that is beginning to emerge for modern Ireland.

Unlike long-term incomers in Doolin, more recently arrived blow-ins (who also tend to be younger people in their twenties) often do not care a great deal about local affairs or local politics. And they react to exclusive attitudes as simple provincialism. They chose to live in Doolin and committed to it to a certain extent, but tend to spend most of their time with other blow-ins. Getting involved with the intricate political life of the village is seen as pointless unless it directly concerns them, which is rare. Many younger blow-ins also rent accommodation instead of owning property, and work in the cash based service industry rather than owning businesses. They have no long-term capital investment in the locale and can live a life fairly unencumbered by nine-to-five workdays, monthly bills, and onerous social obligations. For some blow-ins, it is this fact, that one can reduce ones economic and social ties rather than building them up by "coming to belong" to the place, that is the attraction. The complexities of local kinship and social relations do not need to be learned in detail in order to have a cohesive social group of friends, especially amongst other like-minded blow-ins. For some, the "normative communitas" (Turner 1992: 44) experienced amongst blow-ins provides enough of a sense of belonging, and the vicarious relationships they make with locals are fine but are not necessarily sought out. In fact, a confrontation with a new cultural pattern means that international blow-ins often find solace in each others' company because each new incomer is facing a similar confrontation. Schuetz wrote that the stranger who confronts a new culture:

> cannot stop at approximate acquaintance with the new pattern, trusting in his vague knowledge about its general style and structure but needs explicit knowledge of its elements, inquiring not only into their that but into their why (1944: 506).

In other words, new blow-ins from South Africa, America, England, or elsewhere, despite the internationality of their own interactions, find each others' company refreshing because they often discuss the why of this new, Irish, cultural pattern that surrounds them. Jokes are told about the Irish and their ways. Longer-term blow-ins provide explanations to newer, less acquainted blow-ins about Irish rules of behavior and habits. Schuetz goes on to say that

> the cultural pattern of the approached group is to the stranger not a shelter but a field of adventure, not a matter of course but a questionable topic of investigation, not an instrument for disentangling problematic situations but a problematic situation itself and one hard to master (1944: 506).

Blow-ins find shelter in the mutuality of their discovery-adventure. I recall a young Irish blow-in friend of mine pointing out the physical separation between blow-ins and locals one night in the pub. As we looked across the room, there was a distinct "set" of blow-ins gathered together "having the *craic*", and nearby, clustered around on barstools, a fairly distinct "set" of locals. He also mentioned how locals tend to socialize in the pubs on weekends, whereas blow-ins can be found in the pub most nights whether they are drinking or not. It is certainly not a fixed pattern, but the arrangement he described is fairly consistent, and it is something I occasionally noted for the rest of my time in Doolin. This may be due to the fact that the pubs become the center of the social universe for new blow-ins who do not have access to, or the cultural knowledge about, the more intimate social rituals of visiting one's neighbors, often do not have young children, and do not have heavy daily work such as tending B&Bs or farms.

So, for blow-ins, the process of coming to belong in Doolin is not clear of pitfalls and barriers. There is one domain of village life that is different though, one that is not constrained by the same tensions and resistance. Unlike politics, economics, or kinship, coming to belong to the traditional Irish music scene in the village is limited only by one's ability to play traditional music in a local style. It is not unknown for blow-in musicians who have lived and played music in the village for many years to adopt the local style of playing completely and wholly. Most of the traditional musicians in the village are, in fact, blow-ins (a topic that is taken up in detail in Chapter 7). Given the overt tensions that can be created in the political and economic arenas in the village, one would expect that this appropriation of the local music scene by incomers, arguably the basis of the local tourist economy, would produce even more acute tension. However, what is noticeable is the lack of tension.

Conclusions

As Amit (2002: 21) points out, much recent thinking on global cultural flows tends to simplify the ease with which individuals can move from one cultural milieu to another. In reality, negotiations and resistance accompany movement into any community, imagined (Anderson 1983) or real, however cosmopolitan the individual or the community may be. The idea of community identifications embedded solely in physical places have become partially disaggregated in an age of local incorporation into the global, and the definitional diversity of the term "community" even threatens to "reduce the concept to banality" (Amit 2002: 14). In place of "community," some prefer to frame groups of people in terms of delocalized collective identities (ethnic, national, occupational, leisurely, etc.) because "the very notion of boundaries has become emblematic of … essentialis[m]" (Bashkow 2004: 444). Certainly, definitions of community and culture need retooling; however, to problemetize the conceptual boundaries that constitute locality does not mean that localness ceases to be important. "Community, one would have to assume, must still 'mean' something," writes Amit (2002: 14). I would argue that, in fact, it means rather a lot for those who still lay claim to notions of localness (and for those attempting to adopt it) against the rush of globalizing processes like tourism. Indeed, one of the contributions I hope this book makes is to demonstrate exactly how community relationships aggregate around varying notions like locality, the musical experience, and day-to-day sociality.

In Doolin, blow-ins are included in local life, but do not find the path to inclusion free of stumbling blocks and occasional resistance. In this chapter I have detailed some of the means by which blow-ins come to belong. Some of these ways and means are structural. Incomers have made significant contributions to the local economy, some have married into the local kin groups, and politically, many incomers are actively involved in local committees. For the most part, there is a correlation between the length of an incomer's residence in the locale and the level of an incomer's involvement into these structural domains, but not necessarily. Some long-term incomers have not got involved in local economics, politics or kinship, and some recent blow-ins enter into these realms quickly especially through marriage or business investments.

Integration, however, is not simply due to involvements into these structural domains. Rather, inclusion into the local culture has at least as much to do with, as Schuetz put it, the success of an incomers' "attempt to interpret the cultural pattern of a social group which he approaches and attempts to orient himself within" (1944: 499). This has more to do with building long-term consociate relations through daily praxis in the social world of the village.

This is not necessarily the same thing as the cosmopolitanism that Hannerz (1996), Rapport (2006), and others (Breckenridge et al. 2002) describe, although a cosmopolitan disposition seems to help incomers along in the process of belonging. So, on the one hand, while this chapter details a particular aspect of a particular classificatory system, on the other, it is about how individuals maneuver between categories, maneuvers that are negotiated, contested, stymied, and pushed beyond precedents.

In Chapter 7, these nuanced distinctions between insiders and outsiders become key for the analysis of how blow-ins have appropriated, and been adopted into, the local traditional music scene. But first, in Chapter 6, I take a deeper look at how the Celtic Tiger, and tourism in particular, have impacted the music in Doolin.

Notes

1. This literally translates to "blow inwards." According to one informant, the phrase was later transposed into the English-sounding "shadies" revealing the suspicion incomers garnered among their neighbors. The more accurately translated "blow-ins" is used commonly today.

2. In particular, Irish incomers from outside of County Clare are as easily recognized as "outsiders" because the borders of regional accents roughly fall along county borderlines. Speaking with a Dublin accent or Kerry accent or a "northern" accent clearly marks one as a blow-in. Technically though, if one's natal house lies on the other side of the parish lines, one is not "local."

3. In 2002–2003, the following committees and organizations were in operation in Doolin: the Doolin Tourism Cooperative, the Doolin Community Harbour Cooperative, Doolin Community Centre Committee, The Coast Guard, Kid's Club, Doolin School Board of Management, the Irish Farmer's Association, the Micho Russell Festival Committee, Alcoholics Anonymous, the Doolin Artist's Cooperative, the GAA Club, Burren United, Senior's Night, and the Sproai Arts School.

4. For the most part, the local population is in fact extremely intolerant of intolerance. One blow-in, a black man, was beloved in the community, and for example when two drunken tourists began hurling racial slurs at him one evening, he gladly helped the barmen throw them out on their ears minutes after their racial abuse began. They were

told in no uncertain terms that they were not welcome in Doolin again. It was a story that was proudly told for weeks. This acceptance and defense of "difference" extends to the arena of sexual orientation and religious affiliation as well. Many residents claimed that this is largely a result of Doolin's long historical encounter with bohemianism: the bawdy antics of the Macnamara family in the early twentieth century, and the wild invasion of hippies, revivalists, and "good-lifers" since the 1960s.

PART III

Change and Continuity

Chapter 6

Consolidation and Globalization

> [I]t is inherently no more reasonable to adopt the new than cleave to the
> old. What is stupid is doing anything without awareness.
>
> —Henry Glassie (1995[1982]: 491)

Finbar Furey, a "star" in traditional Irish music circles, used to play regularly in sessions at the Roadside Tavern in Lisdoonvarna, just up the road from Doolin. With the hint of a smile uncurling his mustache, the Roadside's publican, Peter Curtin, told me about it in his characteristically gravelly voice:

> He used to kick off the session in the pub, and he'd be tuning up the fiddle
> around the corner here, and—
>
> he'd be tuning up and he'd say—
>
> he might say to me, he'd say, "Open the cash register, Peter!"
>
> And I'd open the register. And when you opened the register a little bell
> would ring. And he says, "Tonight now, Peter, we won't be tuning up to C
> sharp", he says, "We'll be tuning up to the register!"

Certainly, commerce has changed traditional Irish music since the revival period. The fact that this has happened is not debated. What is debated, and quite heatedly by musicians and connoisseurs of the music especially, is exactly how commercialization has impacted the music. Some feel strongly that the music has been ruined by money, while others see positive new opportunities in its newfound popularity. Taking a longer historical look at social and musical change over the last century though allows a more circumspect view of things. Every new era of musical and social change resurrects a debate between traditionalists and innovators. This is common across art-forms and across cultures, and in Ireland every generation announces the death of traditional Irish music. The following chapter looks in detail at the increasing commercialism surrounding the music to see if "the tradition" is resilient enough to handle a new wave of change.

Tourism—the vehicle of globalization and commercialization in Doolin—consolidates musical performances. By "consolidation," I mean several things. First, increased commercial gain from the music creates stronger social relations between certain actors, for example publicans and musicians, while simultaneously professionalizing some roles, like that of musicians. This chapter explores several examples of how this has happened. Second, the music industry at large has consolidated traditional music in the same way that it has done so for other musics: by creating "products" like records and stage shows, and creating markets for their consumption. This consolidates the very notion of what traditional Irish music is "about" by changing, or more often by creating, a public understanding of it. At the same time, these processes diffuse the music globally, and in fact that is part of the point of consolidation. Consolidation and diffusion are not opposing processes in other words; they are complementary. They are similar to what Lakoff has called "commensurability" and "liquidity" (2008: 277–278), but given their broader impact in this context I think it is useful to employ more general, rather than solely economic, terminology.

As Feld points out (2001: 190), globalization in general and the globalization of music in particular are parallel processes that occur at the local, national, and international levels. However, they are not always instantiated in the same ways everywhere. Developments that arise out of local particularities distinguish one music scene from another. In Doolin for example, the burgeoning tourist industry and the influx of blow-ins has had far greater impact than other international influences. Paying musicians to "seed" sessions, a national trend, creates specific local and regional interdependencies between musicians and publicans as well. Likewise, the influx of tourists every summer creates a very local need for amplification, and providing an environment in which traditional Irish music "bands" can flourish.

In this chapter and in the next, these issues of commercialization, consolidation, globalization, and what the music means to various actors will be teased apart as the ethnographic detail unfolds. Before focusing in on their impacts in Doolin specifically, it is worth examining a few broader influences: the worldwide spectacle called *Riverdance*, the explosion of music festivals, the institutionalization of the music by CCE and the Irish Music Rights Organization, and the widespread impact of the internet. These changes have been so dramatic that some writers have even gone so far as to make a distinction between traditional Irish music and "'new traditional' Irish music" (Quinn 1996: 386).

Traditional Music of the Celtic Tiger

Allen claims that the Celtic Tiger was "baptised" in 1994 (2000: 9), and in that same year a "Celtic" spectacle was born. During an intermission in the Eurovision Song Contest, a short piece called *Riverdance* was performed (Cinnéide 1996: 148, Wulff 2003: 197). Bill Whelan arranged the music while Michael Flatley and Jean Butler choreographed the step dancing (Ó hAllmhuráin 1998: 149). The performance created a sensation (Cinnéide 1996: 148), leading its creators to produce numerous full-scale theatrical shows to worldwide popular acclaim (ibid.: 150). Part of the success of these shows is the combination of dance, music, visual spectacle, and thematic Broadway-style theatricality (ibid.). As pointed out in Part One, traditional music and traditional dance were once corollary parts of a larger whole, but one result of the Revival and of competitions was that dancing and music-making began to separate (O'Connor 1998: 58). Competition and separation sped up the tempo of both the music and the dance leading to an emphasis on individual virtuosity. O'Connor has argued that *Riverdance* has taken this process full circle, rejoining the music and dance but at a higher skill level (ibid.).

Riverdance speaks to a wide variety of audiences, and it is intended to do so. The shows have traveled the world over and made its creators enormous sums of money. At the height of its popularity, multiple production companies traveled to different parts of the world and played in arenas that could hold audiences of up to 6,000 people at once (McCaughren 2003: 13). It intersected with a growing love of Irishness in the 1990s in the United States in particular (Casey 2002: 13), which helped launch its success. In the 2000 U.S. Census, 39 million U.S. citizens declared that they were "Irish-American", and according to Casey, this identification has increasingly become a point of pride (ibid.: 16) associated with a romantic vision of, and nostalgia for, so-called "folk" culture (ibid.: 19). Irish music, she argues, is:

> a means of connecting with the past, the authentic and the folk and, for many Americans, this is a fetish that requires little encouragement. The consumption of dance by paying audience members and buyers of compact discs and videos must be considered an extension of this presumed access to and desire for authentic folk culture (ibid.: 23).

I would suggest, and I am not alone in doing so (cf. Sommers Smith 2001: 124, Rapuano 2001, Williams 2006), that spectacles like *Riverdance* which tapped into this growing nostalgia are a starting point for many individuals who then become tourists attempting to seek out the "real thing" in Ireland itself, or even go on to learn how to play traditional Irish music. At the same time, writes Helena Wulff, "*Riverdance* became a symbol for Irish modernity" (2003: 197). In other words, *Riverdance* became a vehicle for exacerbating one of the central tensions about Ireland, between nostalgia for a supposedly "traditional" past and a surge forward into a modern future. In fact, if one were to buy into such simplistic dichotomies, the artistic spectacle of *Riverdance* is arguably far more "modern" than it is "traditional" (Wulff 2008: 93). What fans of *Riverdance* find when they go on holiday to Ireland is typically quite different than the polished concert performance, but this does not prevent them from seeking it out.

There's no doubt that the *Riverdance* phenomenon has left a significant mark on Irish music and dance (in general and also at the local scale), but there are other means by which traditional Irish music has become institutionalized. In addition to helping prompt the Revival of traditional Irish music, *Comhaltas Ceoltóirí Éireann*

(CCE) has subsequently had a great deal to do with its diffusion and consolidation. CCE's constitutional remit is to "promote Irish traditional music in all forms"[1] and "to establish branches throughout the country and abroad" (Henry 1989: 69). In this effort, it has been extremely successful over the past fifty years if one considers that branches now thrive in places as far flung as California and Japan. There are two very public activities. First, CCE runs education programs led by certified teachers, and now one can even earn a diploma in traditional music (McCarthy 1999: 168). Second, CCE hosts annual competitions at the local level which then lead to the "All-Irelands."

Now, in no small part due to the activities of CCE, people of very diverse backgrounds are committing themselves to learning Irish music (Fairbairn 1994: 597). There has been a concentration of power, though, in CCE since its inception by means of evaluating what is "good" traditional Irish music through its system of competition adjudication (Henry 1989: 91), and more recently, by even declaring what is or is not a "traditional" instrument (Commins 2004a). This is an attempt in a very real sense to consolidate an official traditional Irish music aesthetic. Promoting the diffusion of the music and sequestering it in the hands of "experts" and "professionals" are simultaneous processes. Musicians and dancers can use the symbolic capital of certified professionalism to join touring companies like *Riverdance*, or to jump-start a recording career (Larson Sky 1997: 114). What this means is that there is now a powerful economic incentive (not to mention the fame involved) for younger musicians to become professional virtuosos. Unsurprisingly, developments like these have been controversial. While recognizing the important role that CCE has played in ensuring the survival and promotion of traditional music, many musicians remain skeptical about its "authority."

As mentioned in Chapter 3, the biggest event organized by CCE is an annual series of competitions leading up to the "All-Ireland," known simply as the *fleadh*. Other, more localized annual festivals deemphasize competition. The Willy Clancy Summer School in Miltown Malbay is one example, independently organized by locals back in 1973. Harry Hughes, a local man who knew the celebrated *uilleann* piper Willy Clancy, told me that he and the other organizers originally thought about erecting a monument in his memory after Mr. Clancy's death, but they decided that a greater long-term impact could be made by teaching students of Irish music. The school started out very small, but has grown to international status. During the festival, the town explodes with visiting musicians from all over the globe. Today, there are so many new traditional music festivals like the Willie Clancy Week, also often in honor of a late local musicians, that one could easily go a festival every weekend in the summer.

Whether festivals foster a sense of competition or not, there is an inherent tension in all of them between economic and musical motivations. It takes a lot of resources to run festivals even if they are weekend affairs, and festival committees regularly turn to corporate sponsorship in order to fund them. The formal concerts can be expensive, especially if the musicians and groups hired are well-known and travel a concert circuit regularly. Sometimes, musicians must be hired to teach courses too. All of these events must be advertised to bring in the crowds, and it all costs money.

Doolin has its own annual festival that honors the Russell Brothers, and Micho Russell in particular. In 2003, it was sponsored by Smithwick's beer. Smithwick's posters and banners were draped across the interior surfaces of all of the pubs, and pubs that normally do not serve the beer put it on tap for the event. The beer's logo adorned all of the event's literature. This kind of corporate sponsorship and piggyback advertisement is typical. But feelings of discord began to emerge between the festival organizers and resident musicians during the weeks prior to the festival. Significantly, the festival committee was made up mostly of local businessmen. This fact caused some musicians and locals to suspect that the primary motivation for hosting the festival was to make money. Money-making and memorializing Micho were seen as opposing motivations. One person put it to me this way:

> I'm just disgusted with the whole lot of it … . The people who were closest to him have nothing to do with The Weekend, you know? So it's a money-making thing.

Several musicians refused to participate "on principle." The businessmen on the committee had a much more pragmatic attitude though. They felt that the musicians who complained or refused to get involved in what the organizers saw as an opportunity to promote Doolin and its traditional music were "prima donnas." One committee organizer simply laughed when we talked about the tensions that had arisen and asked me, "Who do they think they are? Bono or something?"

Tensions between music-making and profit-making are not just social tensions. They have recently expanded into the arena of copyright law and thus have become political and legal tensions (Stokes 1999: 147). "Ownership" in the commensurable light that copyright law throws it into can be held by an individual or a record company for lengthy periods, spanning decades, before it enters into the public domain. Recent incursions of this industry-generated view of musical "rights" are attempting to include traditional Irish music, which is considered by most to already be in the public domain. The growth of recordings of traditional Irish music though creates an extremely complex negotiation between two understandings of ownership. The first is that traditional music, by definition, cannot be individually owned. The second, more modern notion is that an individual's arrangement of particular tunes or sets can now be owned.

All of this has now entered into a highly bureaucratic domain. In 1999, after a long period of antagonism, the Irish Music Rights Organisation, a non-profit organization whose remit it is to "collect and distribute royalties arising from the public performance of copyright works" ("Mission Statement" 2003: 1), reached a contractual agreement with CCE which stated that "traditional music in its original form" was free from the strictures of copyright (as cited in McCann 2002: 70). However, according to McCann, despite their agreement with CCE, IMRO has begun to seek royalties from publicans who host live sessions in which copyrighted arrangements are being played

(McCann 2002: i, 76). Of course, this has been met with antagonism and incredulity (ibid.: 76–82). To say the least, individual ownership is a radical, modernizing shift in meaning. It is an attempt to literally commodify this music. This is extremely ironic given the supposedly publicly owned nature of folk traditions such as Irish dance music, but it is not unknown for traditional musics elsewhere either (Seeger 1996: 90, Scherzinger 1999). It is another extreme example of the consolidation of traditional music(s) in the modern world of expanding neoliberal capitalism.

To varying degrees, all of these things affect the way traditional music is understood in local places. In Doolin they contribute a powerful subtext to what goes on, but they may not always be central issues. *Riverdance* may have brought more tourists. The increasing influence of CCE and IMRO are also important, but they have peripheral, indirect effects. Other changes at the local level have been more influential during this same period.

Doolin's Celtic Music Industry

In 1994, the same year that witnessed the emergence of *Riverdance* and the "baptism" of the Celtic Tiger (Allen 2000: 9), Doolin's most famous musician, Micho Russell, was killed in a car accident. Exactly when one wishes to mark "the beginning of the end" of the Revival or the emergence of the Celtic Tiger on a broader scale, 1994 will remain in the lived memories of Doolin people as "the end of an era."[2] Two other changes began much earlier however. First, traditional music has been heavily influenced by the larger music industry. This involves performative and musical changes, but also a change in meaning. The second change results from, not the music or its performance, but the relationships between the people who find themselves at the nexus between traditional music and the tourist industry. This change revolves around the complex issue of paying musicians to play in sessions.

During the summer when hundreds of tourists pack Doolin's three pubs, the physicality of the situation and the volume of noise causes a practical problem (as it no doubt did even during the early Revival sessions): tourists have traveled great distances to hear a bit of this Irish music but cannot all squeeze into the space immediately surrounding the musicians' table. The answer to the problem is amplification. All three of Doolin's pubs have wired their session spaces for sound. The amplification takes two forms. Two pubs have a system whereby microphones hang down by wires over the musicians' table about five feet off the floor. They are connected by a metal "arm" that swings out from the wall. The microphones are connected into a PA system that is controlled from behind the bar, and from there, the music is sent out to speakers positioned throughout the pub. Usually, when musicians are seated, huddled around the table, leaning forward into the music, these hanging microphones are relatively unnoticeable. This system allows the musicians to sit around the table in a circular formation as they would in any pub without microphones. Musicians can come and go. Visiting musicians can join in and be heard equally well as anyone else. In other words, this system does not significantly alter the way in which a session normally works.

Figure 6.1 A Session with Hanging Microphones

The third pub in Doolin is different. There, microphones are set up on stands and placed in front of each musicians' instrument. Alternatively, some musicians have clip-on microphones that can be attached to the instrument and fed directly into the PA system. In that instance, the PA is controlled by the musicians themselves. This system of direct and individual amplification is simply a result of the particular space where the musicians sit. There is a small riser along one wall of the pub with three disconnected sets of railing in front of it, which creates a natural kind of "stage" for the musicians to sit on. Because this "stage" area is in a linear formation, there is no table and the musicians do not sit in a circle. They sit side by side along a bench against the wall. I was told that this used to be the "set dancing pub" in the old days, and for that reason, it was necessary to have the musicians sitting off to one side in this fashion. Today, the physical space lends itself to microphone stands and a linear concert-like physical orientation for the musicians. An interesting result is that it becomes, at the least, very difficult for visiting musicians to join the sessions there. Visiting musicians must step up onto the "stage" and then, to be heard above the amplified instruments, find their own microphones. When someone is invited up to play a few tunes, usually the other musicians are forced to step aside and let the visitor play a few sets or sing a song into the microphone they were just using.

Regardless of the variations, these amplificatory solutions allow tourists to choose whether or not they want to watch the session directly or simply listen to it where they can also find a place to sit and talk, even in another room where the music is piped in. On the other hand, it causes a change in the way the music is performed. Microphones, noticeable or not, also amplify the chat in between sets of tunes, an important social element of a session. In the pubs where the microphones are less noticeable, musicians sometimes forget that the microphones are there at all and that their conversations in between sets of music can be heard throughout the pub. Christy Barry told me how, once, he began to complain during a session about how there was "something wrong with my fucking flute." Another musician, having overheard him through the speakers as he returned from the toilets, sat down and teased him, saying, "Hey Christy! What's fucking wrong with your fucking flute!?"

Figure 6.2 A Session on Stage

More tourists get to hear the music as a result of the amplification, but sometimes they are disappointed by it. Although necessary in Doolin in the summertime due to the large crowds, microphones and amplification are markers for some tourists that the music has become overly commercialized. Musicians have differing opinions about the use of microphones and "stages." One musician, experienced at playing in both session settings and formal concert-halls, told me that at first he did not like it because it was "sort of like a concert venue, but not enough like a concert venue." The problem, he told me, was that it felt in between a concert set up and a session space. In pubs immediately outside of Doolin, amplification is rarely used if ever, even during the summertime. In other towns, the amplification of Doolin sessions is often cited as the most important indicator of how "commercial" and tourist-oriented Doolin has become. When I asked an Ennistymon publican to describe the differences between a session in his pub and Doolin sessions, he immediately responded, "Well, first of all, there's no amplification."

One result from the intensified interaction between sessions and tourism is strictly musicological. Hazel Fairbairn has shown that session music in Doolin has sped up and that musicians use more ornamentation since the 1950s (1994: 574). According to Fairbairn, these changes result from the widespread influence of early recordings of Sligo musicians, whose style is faster and more ornamented, and from the initial separation of the music from the dancing (ibid.: 577). More importantly, she maintains that two later changes in the music were caused by the influx of visiting musicians and large audiences. Firstly, she notes that sessions in Doolin tend to have a stronger, more consistent rhythm than in other places she observed which is a direct result of the long historical exposure to visiting musicians in sessions there (1992: 299). Secondly, Fairbairn argues that heterophonous playing is now reduced in Doolin in favor of a more homophonous, group "sound" (ibid.: 306). This has an important repercussion. It shows that tourism and the influx of visiting musicians over many years have in fact changed the music at its core in a few small but not insignificant ways.

Seasonal variability undercuts everything in Doolin though, including the music. Amplification is only used seasonally because the one factor that dictates its usage is crowd noise. In the winter, when the tourist crowds diminish, amplification is unnecessary. In that respect, it is a direct result of tourism. At O'Connor's Pub, since the microphones are fixed onto the wall in a large central room (what's often called the "main bar"), amplified sessions are located there. Starting sometime in October though, amplification becomes unnecessary except on the weekends when lots of locals come out to socialize. Instead, the musicians hold sessions in what's often called the "front room," which is the oldest room in the pub. It is a lovely space with the original fireplace built with flagstones that Packie Russell himself cut from Doolin's Doonagore quarry. Sessions there invoke the accumulation of Doolin's musical history. In a physical and emotive sense, pubs in northwest Clare such as O'Connor's revert to a seemingly "older" context during the wintertime as the more recent expansions of the buildings are closed off. The whole feel of sessions changes in the winter, transforming them into pre-Celtic Tiger performances.

After the massive summertime crowds have dissipated, the music is played largely amongst close consociate relations. As a result, the interaction between the audience and the musicians is much more interactive and porous. The musicians feel far less constrained to "perform" for the tourists, and it is altogether a more intimate environment. Their playing is also much softer in volume and more subtly decorated as well. In other words, even the sound of a summer session and a winter session are radically different.

Bands and Sessions, Performing and Playing

Traditional Irish music "bands" are one emergent adaptation to the modern music industry. Recording and selling records became an important avenue for making a living for musicians during the Revival. Bands like the Chieftains, Sweeny's Men,

Planxty, and the Bothy Band started this trend as early as the 1960s, and today, hundreds of bands record albums of dance music and songs, selling them to a worldwide market. It is worth recalling the example from Chapter 3 of the kind of language used to discuss bands, which imitates that of popular music magazines.

In Doolin, being in a band does not preclude participation in a regular schedule of sessions. It often complements a musician's musical experience. Bands are inherently different from sessions though, in that membership in a band is consciously exclusive. Either one is in a band or not. Bands will also create and rehearse various arrangements of tunes and sets of tunes. By contrast, a session is inclusive rather than exclusive, and membership can vary nightly. This is not to say that a band, playing in a pub session environment remains exclusive. Other musicians can easily join in these sessions as with any other session, but they would not suddenly be considered members *of* the band. They'd be playing *with* the band.

Bands play more formal concert settings as well as sessions. These are fundamentally different contexts. Concerts are normally scheduled far in advance, usually one of many on a tour. Unlike session musicians who must remain in a relatively small regional area to play at their regular weekly scheduled sessions, a band on tour travels widely, sometimes internationally, to perform in concerts, formal events set in large concert halls, or pubs with stages. Like any other concert, the audience pays for tickets taken at the door. Interestingly, one musician who plays regularly with a band and in sessions told me that often "people appreciate you more if they have to pay to hear you." He said that when he goes out on tour with his band, it is common to get a great reception at a concert one night, but get a poor response the next during a free pub session. This is despite the fact that the same musicians play the same sets of tunes. The act of paying to hear a band imbues the performance with an air of professionalism that a session purposefully downplays.

The bands in Doolin are also generally much better at marketing themselves than individual musicians who might only play in sessions. Many individual musicians will, for example, have their own CDs for sale in shops, but bands are often more conscious of selling them during sessions in pubs and performances at concert halls. It is not unusual for an announcement to be made about CDs for sale and where the band might be playing next. Overt marketing is acceptable for bands, but this is unusual for individual musicians at sessions because it would be considered shameless self-promotion in an egalitarian social context. But by joining a band, one has already entered the realm of the music industry, and self-promotion becomes an accepted and expected practice.

In certain instances, the differences between bands and sessions are not apparent and hardly matter to most audiences. Many tourists, lacking the receptive competence to distinguish between a concert and a session, often do not notice or mind either way. Other times, the concert-like atmosphere sets up the expectation for the audience of a "show," a professional performance. Arranging harmonic parts within predetermined tunes, interspersing ballads with instrumental tunes, transitioning from a jig to a reel (i.e., from a 6/8 to a 4/4 time-signature) in the same set, or increasing tempos all can be used to "work up" the audience by creating "participatory discrepancies" (Kiel 1994:

96). Inexperienced listeners are largely unaware of how these small, predetermined moments of what Kiel has called "out of syncness" (ibid.) are consciously used by bands to emotionally charge the listening experience. Likewise, some bands make use of amplification and staging expertly. For example, one band that regularly played in Doolin in 2003 was known for creating an intense performative aura. They bobbed their heads like rock stars when they flew through sets of reels at high speed. They often did encores at the end of their show, strolling back on stage waving at the crowd. One night, they even used the melody from Lynyrd Skynyrd's southern American rock anthem "Sweet Home Alabama" before launching into a set of traditional reels. They knew how to "perform" and were excellent at working the audience up into frenzied excitement. Audiences responded to their sets appropriately: they shouted and whooped for more as they would at a rock concert.

It is useful at this point to highlight the difference between "performing" traditional Irish music and "playing" it. Generally, the term "performance" is antithetical to the session context. It implies that musicians are not playing for their own benefit, but rather for the demands of the audience. It goes against one of the underlying principles of the session: the notion that it is a reciprocal social event for both the audience and the musicians (Kneafsey 2003: 33). The audience in that sense is just as responsible for creating a social environment as the players. This relationship is derived from the one that musicians used to have with set dancers, complementary parts of a single whole. As the music became its own distinct folk-art-form during the Revival, separating itself from the dance, that reciprocally inclusive principle remained. Also, the value on spontaneity prohibited any kind of performative structure. Finally, since sessions are played in pubs around tables, on the same physical level as the audience, there is no physical elevation of the music above the audience. So, musicians discuss "playing" in sessions where this reciprocal, spontaneous relationship occurs in amongst an interactive audience. "Performances" are different. They occur in formal concert settings and sometimes in partially staged settings in pubs as described above. There can be a conscious intent to please the audience, to put on a good show. In concert halls, where the music is most consciously performed, there is even a physical elevation of the musicians onto a stage above the audience.

As with most things relating to traditional Irish music today, there are extreme examples, but most situations lie somewhere in between, and this is the case with the notions of "performance" and "playing." Some circumstances may make musicians feel like they are performing for the audience even if the physical location is a typical session space. It is therefore also a subjective determination. The behavior of the audience, for example, can easily change a session into a performance despite the behavior of the musicians. One musician described the difference between the two this way:

> I always found a fairly grey line between a session and a performance … .
> You'd like it probably to be a session, but some nights it's inevitable that it's
> going to go the [other] way. And most of the people, a lot of the tourists who

come in, view it as a performance. They sit down, waiting for it all to start, and it probably isn't as interactive as it could be … .

If someone doesn't know the music, then a session is just music in the corner. Maybe for a musician, a session is sitting down, having a chat, a bit of *craic*, meeting new people, having fun, not having to play every two minutes … . It's not like a performance on a stage where you're knocking it out. It's more a social thing.

In a session then, the musicians are socializing too. They are not working for the audience. They are playing for the audience. In that sense, a session is at least as much for the benefit of the players as it is for the audience. When a session is turned into a performance by the tourists' gaze, it becomes work for the musicians, a job, because it is no longer for them. It is for the audience to consume.

Tourist audiences especially seem to have an embedded expectation to see "a good show." Bands have tapped into that expectation by producing a varied night of music. The owner of a Doolin B&B once told me that her patrons often find the partially staged performances of bands that tend to consciously utilize more musical variety more palatable than a session. It is a musical environment that they are used to:

A lot of people who aren't into traditional Irish music, it all sounds the same … but it's nice to do the slow ballad and then the "diddle-dee-i-dee-dee," and whatever—someone singing. They like the variety.

And in that respect it's more like a concert: always changing to get their attention back.

The result is that some audiences appreciate this kind of performance atmosphere more than sessions where "musicians seem to talk a lot" and "the music all sounds the same"—common refrains from tourists.

The use of microphones and stages, concert settings and tours, pre-arranged musical performances in which musicians work for the benefit of the audience, the marketing and selling of CDs, and audience expectations of a good show are all in the direction of the way in which popular music is created, performed, and consumed.

Paying to Play

Many popular myths surround traditional Irish music. One of the more pervasive ones is that traditional musicians were never paid in the past. How could a thing be traditional, the logic begs, if it is not freely given? Furthermore, if musicians get paid today, it must mean that the music has been transformed into a product, a souvenir, a commodity. However, this romantic and popular notion is unequivocally wrong. As I have written elsewhere, paying musicians is not new (Kaul 2007b: 707). In the "old days" they would be given a cut of the money collected at the door of a house dance for instance. Following the Dance Halls Act in 1935, *céilí* bands began to imitate big jazz bands, marketing themselves and the music at least as much as any modern band would do today. Gus O'Connor also told me how he would compensate musicians who played in his pub in the old days:

> I always gave 'em a few bob anyway, before anybody ever asked me for money. They'd get their food, three meals if they were there all day. And if they were going somewhere, then you'd give them a fiver or a tenner … anything they needed for a few pounds, you gave it to them. You didn't specify what amount, really.

At a *céilí* money was not involved in any way; instead, music was considered a gift in exchange for a story, some gossip, some tea and bread, and good company. As Glassie illustrates in rich detail in his book *Passing the Time in Ballymenone* (1995[1982]), this is a classic case of generalized reciprocity in which musicians were respected as skilled craftsmen of music, able and obliged to provide their services in exchange for other gifts and services. In fact, this understanding of the musician's role in society is embedded in the colloquial term that I described in Chapter 2: "musicianer." On par with other skilled trades, one might learn carpentry, farming, or musicianing. In this understanding, compensation for one's services is only natural and in no way impedes on notions of "traditionality."

Since the revival, the music began to be played primarily in a public arena, the pub, because it was the most accessible context for the strangers who began to arrive in larger and larger numbers. As the crowds swelled though, it became more difficult to play. Musicians began to look for quieter venues. This presented a real problem for publicans who wanted to maintain the larger crowds. Gradually, a codependent relationship between the music and tourism developed as publicans began to pay several musicians to "seed" or "anchor" daily sessions. A kind of "symbiotic relationship" emerged (Kneafsey 2003: 35). Inevitably, visiting musicians would join in, and at the baseline, it was simply their responsibility to start the session off (Kaul 2007b: 708). This ought to be seen as an extension of, rather than a radical shift from, earlier systems of reciprocation.

Today, a small number of musicians, typically two to four, are paid to arrive at a prearranged time (normally around 9:30 at night) to play on a given night each week. Typically, a publican asks one musician to find one or two others to join them. Beyond this arrangement, not much discussion needs to occur between musicians and publicans, unless there is some obvious problem. Musicians know to show up by 9:30 on their given evening every week to play, and they are paid at the end of the night. It is a fairly regular and self-regulating system such that one who is familiar with a local music scene will know that particular musicians will play particular nights in particular pubs. It is informal though, in the sense that no contract of employment exists, and either party can discontinue the relationship without much notice.

This system of paid-for sessions is clearly a move towards what Bohlman calls the "professionalization" of traditional music (1988: 85–86). As others have noted in the

Irish context, some musicians even get possessive of "their" sessions (Larson Sky 1997: 126), discouraging others from joining. However, even given this move towards a market mentality, the payments are not wages in the strict sense of that word. Rather, musicians are given the status of "desirable clients" (Fairbairn 1992: 159). Moreover, publicans are to some extent always concerned with the quality of the music, if only to attract a thirsty audience. Many, though, see themselves as patrons of the music. Some are even musicians themselves. Peter Curtin told me:

> You have to be careful, if people come playing music for money, that they don't just go through the mechanical act of playing the music for money for the sake of entertaining people, rather than them enjoying music for themselves … .
>
> If it becomes a "job," if it becomes a function of business, then that's— y'know—not the ideal scenario.

Essentially, Peter is contrasting between musicians he hires whose motivation is to play the music (and pay is secondary) and musicians whose first motivation is to get paid to perform. Again, there are extremes. Some musicians play only because they want the money or just to perform. There are also some musicians who, on principle, refuse to become paid musicians at all. More commonly, musicians avoid depending on paid sessions for their livelihood, thus preventing an erosion of their enjoyment of playing even while getting paid.

One might conclude that the system of paid-for sessions—and especially the fact that one musician is often chosen as the leader of a session—introduces a new social hierarchy out of a purely egalitarian context. This too would be romanticizing the past, and it would wrongly presume that no hierarchies exist in egalitarian contexts. In fact, this practice only institutionalizes a traditional pattern (Kaul 2007b: 708). Typically, one or two "alpha" musicians (Foy 1999: 85) lead any session, paid or not. Recognizing that some musicians are simply better than others in no way contradicts notions of egalitarianism. In fact, it also requires leadership and responsibility. Alpha musicians are expected to bring other players into the session circle, and for instance, often ask novices to take the lead for a set of tunes. Of course, there are virtuosos and bands that choose to use their paid session as a platform for their own agenda, to show off their skills, or sell CDs. This can become exclusive, and I have heard complaints about exclusivity from musicians who traveled to play in Doolin sessions. However, for the most part, paid musicians in Doolin strongly emphasize inclusive egalitarianism.

The very fact that some sessions are paid for at all, creates a new kind of hierarchy. Now there are semi-professional musicians, and what we might call "amateur" musicians (in the sense that they are not paid, not because they are lesser talents). There are various reasons why a musician might remain outside the system of paid sessions. One reason might be that a musician is still in a learning stage and does not have enough tunes or the confidence to "hold their own" in a session. Novices are encouraged to join sessions though because they are seen as the best venues to learn. Some weekly sessions can even turn into a "master class" on the particular instrument of the alpha musician. Another reason might be that they are fairly new to the community and have fewer connections than more established musicians. Weekly paid positions are valued, and rarely can a person simply get hired without having something of a reputation in the area, musically as well as personally.

So some musicians are not paid, and not all sessions in Doolin are paid for. The paid sessions almost always occur at 9:30 at night, the exception being the Sunday afternoon session, a traditional family outing day. For the rest of the week, afternoon sessions are always unpaid, spontaneous and irregular. Afternoon sessions occur at all three of Doolin's pubs, but most often at O'Connor's Pub for two reasons. First, the pub is most associated with the Russell Brothers and the early history of music in Doolin and therefore, many visiting tourist musicians like to make it a point to have a tune or two there. In fact, there is a balance between visitors and resident musicians starting off these unpaid sessions. Secondly, in the deepest of the winter months, O'Connor's is the only pub of the three in the village that opens before 6:00 p.m.

Informal sessions start at any time of the day that a musician decides to unpack an instrument. Often, they do not start until later afternoon or into the evening. If they go well, if there's good *craic* and an attentive, interactive audience, they can last for many hours. Anything goes during these sessions, and long periods of chat between friends and witty banter between locals and tourists might ensue. Typically, local paid or unpaid musicians will start these informal sessions, and oftentimes, they consist of only one or two players. When locals start afternoon sessions, they tend to be dominated by ballad singing. The songs are just as often cover versions of songs by the Eagles, John Denver, the Beatles, and Van Morrison as much as they are traditional Irish Ballads. Among the latter, songs about the region are common: *My Lovely Rose of Clare*, *From Clare to Here*, and *Freemantle Bay*, for example. There is no cognitive dissonance between the popular music and Irish ballads. The general philosophy is that "a good song is a good song." Somewhat less frequently, visiting tourist-musicians start afternoon sessions. These sessions tend to consist more of the instrumental dance music: jigs, reels, and hornpipes, because visiting tourist-musicians have come to play the instrumental dance music that made Doolin famous. Locals on the other hand can hear "traditional" sessions every night of the week and twice on Sundays, so the Eagles covers and ballads are refreshing.

The quality of unpaid, afternoon sessions varies from being nearly unbearable to being "great *craic*," but no matter how good an afternoon session might be, by 9:30 at night when the paid musicians come into the pub, they are forced to finish. Numerous times I witnessed strong unpaid sessions that led right up to 9:30 when the paid musicians came into the pub. Occasionally, the paid musicians would politely wait to start until the informal session wound down. On a few occasions in the wintertime, the paid musicians simply joined the unpaid players. But most often, the paid musicians—although not with any intended rudeness—simply sit down, tune up, and start their session. It is after all what they are getting paid to do. At O'Connor's pub, afternoon sessions almost always occur in the Front Room, the older part of the pub. However, in the summer, the official musicians' table is in the next room, in the Main Bar. In theory, the two sessions could occur simultaneously, but only if the speakers, projecting the paid session's music throughout the pub, are disengaged in the Front Room. But this only occurred on very rare occasions. Instead, the paid session is amplified as usual, and the unpaid session in the Front Room is forced to quit. It is the clearest moment of demarcation that occurs between paid and unpaid musicians.

Again, there is a marked seasonality to the sessions in Doolin. In the summer, at the height of the tourist season, publicans pay for nightly sessions and twice on Sundays. Visiting tourist-musicians arrive and set up additional spontaneous sessions. There is no end to the music. The crowds begin to thin out in the autumn though, and publicans pay for fewer sessions during the week. By November, they only pay for weekend sessions when the locals fill the pubs. In the depths of winter, business slows considerably and only two of the pubs even pay for these weekend sessions. After St. Bridget's Day, things begin to pick up again, and by March a regular set of sessions is reestablished.

In some ways, everyone benefits from the symbiosis between tourism and music. Publicans obviously benefit economically from attracting large crowds. Audience members, who are by sheer numbers overwhelmingly tourists especially in the summer, spend money at the pub on food and drinks and get to consume one of the more classic markers of Irishness—traditional music. Musicians are guaranteed a payment and an audience that is usually attentive and appreciative. The benefits are very different for the different parties though. Publicans obviously gain the most economic capital, but tourists often find the experience of a session impossible (and undesirable) to measure in monetary terms. For the musicians' part, it is clear that without tourism, there would be far fewer opportunities to play to large, appreciative audiences, and little or no money to be made (Kaul 2007b: 709–710). This has been noted in other contexts too in which music is promoted to tourists (cf. Atkinson 2004).

There are certainly drawbacks as well. Indeed, this relationship causes regular low-level tension between musicians, tourists, and publicans. That tension is defused to a large extent by two things though. The first is the general concern that everyone has to one degree or another about the dangers of over-commercializing the music. Second, musicians tend to maintain relationships with several publicans at once.

To over-commercialize the session would, as many stakeholders told me, "kill the goose that laid the golden egg." For that reason musicians maintain near total freedom over what occurs during a session. Publicans or tourists rarely try to (or want to) impose an agenda on sessions, and such attempts are forcefully repelled. For instance, one musician who was scolded by a publican for singing one too many traditional English ballads one night famously burned his gig money after the session. The publican was deeply embarrassed. In a similar situation, another publican complained that several regular musicians played too many traditional American and continental European dance tunes, which also led to a long-standing row. Musicians, no doubt, feel somewhat compelled to stick to "traditional" Irish dance music because it is what audiences expect. This is generally unproblematic though since this is what the musicians themselves typically prefer. More importantly, these kinds of critiques about the content of a session by the publican are rare, and also deemed inappropriate (Kaul 2007b: 714). More often than not, complaints from publicans center on basic violations of the arrangement: not showing up on time, drinking too much alcohol during a session, or talking too much in between sets of music.

Despite the symbiosis between tourism and the music, and despite the fact that the borders between a session and the audience are porous, audience members do not have any substantive control over the session either. Tourists sometimes ask to hear popular ballads like *Danny Boy*, but musicians typically deflect such requests by pretending not to know it and then teasingly encourage them to get up and sing it. Audiences impose themselves more forcefully by sheer volume and by using bright flashes when taking pictures. Almost universally, once the session starts, it is the musicians who control its content, choosing which tunes to play and who will lead the sets. They encourage local singers and tourists to join the session if they want to "give a song." They can even potentially relinquish their "alpha" role by letting non-paid musicians lead most of the sets. Musicians are required to start sessions off but they are not required to carry the night. Even though tension can potentially emerge over the content of sessions, almost everyone wants the musicians to maintain a large degree of creative freedom. Anything else would smack of "commodification."

The notion of commodification is a powerful one in the public discourse, but we should be careful when using the concept. One might conclude that at the nexus between the music and commercial gain the music becomes nothing more than a commodified souvenir for tourists. This plunges us into the overheated and muddied waters of "authenticity" that have flooded the literature on tourism for the last several decades. I argue elsewhere in more detail (Kaul 2007b) that the discourse surrounding "authenticity" and "commodification" glosses over several thorny problems. The first is that the notion of "authenticity" is too wieldy a concept to deal with most situations surrounding tourism. This is certainly the case in Doolin, and will be dealt with in more detail in the final chapter. The second problem is that we too readily label any increase in commercial activity "commodification" (Kaul 2007b: 706–707). The attempts by copyright organizations to turn particular arrangements of tunes into royalty-generating, legally commensurable, individually owned products with a predetermined market value, is an example of commodification. But not all commercial activities are so extreme. Most people involved in this symbiotic relationship that has developed in Doolin do not feel that making money in and of itself is the problem. Instead, problems arise either when the money becomes the sole motivation for people's behavior, or if musicians were to lose all control over the production of the music. It is certainly the case that music-making in Doolin is not completely controlled by the musicians as it is elsewhere in quiet pubs where musicians do not get paid. There are many of these types of sessions around County Clare. But at the same time, paid musicians in Doolin do not experience the kind of loss of control that occurs in more highly produced scenarios. Here I am thinking of stage-shows like *Riverdance* or staged dinner-theater productions, which are tightly controlled by musical directors, and which do have commensurable exchange values (i.e. ticket prices) attributed to them.

Again, Doolin exhibits a symbiosis, a compromise, between the commercial gain of the tourist industry and the production of music. And it is not alone in finding its sessions somewhat surrounded by commercializing processes. Musicians are paid in quiet little sessions in neighboring towns and villages too, although there, microphones and amplification are rarely seen. Ennistymon and Lisdoonvarna, for example, are not exactly on the "tourist trail" in the same way that Doolin is, and as a result, the sessions there tend to be more intimate affairs even at the height of the tourist season. Occasionally the locals might even clear away some tables and get up to dance a few sets just like in the "old days." But even these sessions have paid musicians.

Most musicians also support themselves with waged day jobs, and importantly, musicians also tend to maintain patron-client relationships with several publicans at once. This ability to move from one pub to another, which, in this rural part of Ireland, typically means playing in several different towns in different nights, reduces a dependence on a single patron.

One element that made the revival period exciting for local musicians was the fact that people were traveling around, sharing tunes from different regions within Ireland. Intensified mobility spurred on explosive creativity and a widening of musical horizons. Suddenly, the repertoire of tunes (and different versions of tunes) one might learn expanded quite a bit. Plus, if the session in one pub was going a bit "flat," one was free to simply head to the next pub in search of the *craic*. The system of paid-for sessions that followed this period limited that sense of freedom to some extent. Now, because of the verbal contractual arrangements that publicans and musicians make, paid musicians are more constrained. But it also allows for a certain amount of (limited) mobility in case the tension at a particular pub becomes unbearable. This affects a musicians' experience of a session in two important ways.

Firstly, a paid musician is required by their verbal contract with a publican to not only show up at a given time to start off a session, but also to sit the night out. In other words, they are paid to show up and to stay. This is important because in many musicians' estimations most sessions are simply mediocre or even worse. I was often told that only rare sessions are mighty or great *craic* anyway.[3] However, the paid musician cannot get up and leave a mediocre session and find a better one as they would have done during the Revival (and what some musicians still do on nights that they are not paid). The worst scenario for a paid musician is when a session goes truly bad. A terrible visiting musician might join the session and ruin the flow. An arrogant virtuoso might also join and attempt to dominate it. The crowd, for whatever reason, might be particularly unresponsive or too loud. A fellow musician might be drunk or in a sour mood. Regardless, the paid musician has to stay.

This is particularly evident on Bank Holiday weekends and in the summertime when the crowds swell and the noise becomes deafening. Musicians complain that on these particularly bad nights they cannot even hear themselves playing much less attempt to have a good session. One musician, a local banjo player, told me, "That's what we call a 'Put Your Head Down Night'." In other words, all you can do as a paid musician is put your head down, ignore the crowd as best you can, and get through the night. The natural porosity between the musicians and the audience gets clogged. Adam, a fiddler originally from South Africa, explains:

> The reasons for having a kind of "closed session" can be that the people there [the audience] don't understand what's going on. And that's the only way you can have a decent session, is by kind of insulating it, and just tearing into some tunes and listening to each other, and not caring what's going on outside you … .

> They want to keep it going and it's hard when there are too many distractions … and it can disjoint the whole thing.

Limited mobility impacts musicians in a second way. It disallows a regular paid musician from traveling great distances for sessions, travel that would require an overnight stay or longer. One musician went so far as to argue that this limited mobility, merely a result of the paid session system, has negatively influenced traditional Irish music more than anything else in recent years. The pay itself had no real influence, he argued, and tourism, the recording industry, and all of the other "modern" pressures on the music were secondary as well. Others felt differently for sure, but the fact is that paid musicians are less free to travel far afield, and this has no doubt changed the practice of session attendance.

Musicians do in fact travel regularly for their sessions though—just not as far. It is an important way not only to keep the performances fresh, but also to maintain control by playing gigs for several publicans at once. Many musicians have a standard weekly circuit that they have created for themselves, playing different nights in different towns. Below are examples of the weekly routes that two different musicians who play in Doolin regularly traveled in order to get to their paid sessions during the winter of 2002–2003. Both musicians played more than one night a week in some of these locations. In the first example, the musician played in Doolin two nights a week, and once a week in the other locations. The second musician played twice a week in Ennis, twice in Doolin and once in Killaloe.

This kind of regional travel for gigs is typical. Variety keeps performances fresh. The mania of the tourist season in Doolin can be taxing, and musicians often advise each other to maintain gigs outside of Doolin too. Quieter nights in other, neighboring towns can alleviate the stress caused if one were to play to large crowds every night over the summer. Sometimes, if two musicians play regularly with each other, they might travel and play along the same route for part of the week. But more often than not, different nights in different pubs in different towns means meeting up with different musicians. In other words, various combinations of musicians will meet weekly in different venues.

This pattern of traveling along a weekly route to specific sessions is not unique to paid musicians. Unpaid musicians also commonly travel for a particular weekly

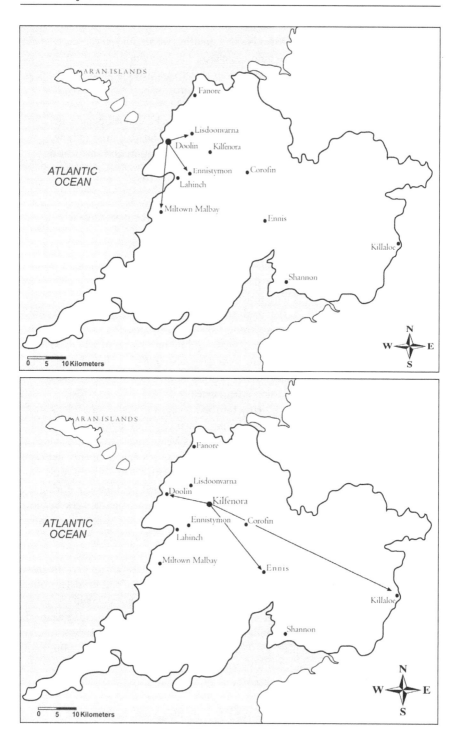

Figures 6.3 and 6.4 Musician's Routes

session in a particular pub. What is more, since most musicians do not play for paid gigs every night of the week, they are free to play as unpaid musicians on other nights. The result is that many musicians come and go on a weekly basis, they shift from venue to venue, and the attendance on any given night varies substantially. The only thing one can be relatively sure of is who the paid musicians will be at a gig. Of course, one might also arrive at a pub to hear a particular musician and find that someone else is sitting in for him or her.

Seasonality affects the transient membership of weekly sessions, and musicians' routes, in several ways as well. Firstly, since only a handful of weekend sessions are paid for in the wintertime, some musicians agree to play weekend sessions throughout the year. The weekends tend to be the busiest days of the week year round, so during the summer they often bear the brunt of the most disruptive crowd noise. But these musicians cope with it for the summer in order to ensure a steady (and quieter) gig in the wintertime. Secondly, as the seasons change, sessions are dropped from the weeknight schedules. In the spring, they are added back on, and this gives musicians the opportunity to form new combinations of players. Many musicians form good relationships with each other and with publicans along their session routes, and continue playing a particular night in a particular place for many years. Others like the variety, and set up new gigs more regularly. Season by season and year by year, paid musicians' session routes change as they set up new gigs for the new season, possibly with new musicians. Sometimes new musicians move into the area and enter into the system of paid sessions while others leave. Unpaid musicians, visiting musicians, or paid musicians with a night off from playing their own gigs, are free to join any session. On the surface, the weekly schedule of gigs is fairly regular and self-regulating, but upon closer scrutiny, it is a system that allows for a great deal of shifting, movement, and interchangeability.

Importantly, all of this movement from gig to gig from season to season is at the discretion of individual musicians. There are no formal contracts of any sort that bind musicians to particular gigs. The verbal agreements that paid musicians make with publicans are provisional enough that they must be renewed seasonally. It is a relationship built on reputation and trust. And despite the bad nights in which musicians are compelled by this arrangement to play what they consider to be mediocre sessions for overbearing crowds, the choice to become a paid musician is a personal one. Musicians are obliged by personal relationships and reputation to honor their verbal agreements to play, but without formal contracts they are free agents.

Conclusions

Social change, globalization, and commercialization inevitably alarm some and excite others. This is no less true in tourist settings, as has been exhibited in the ongoing debate between Bruner (cf. 1994) and Gable and Handler (cf. 2003). When considering the societal and musical changes I have described in Doolin, I prefer a circumspect approach to avoid simple alarmism or celebration. The long view of social change taken in this book reveals a history of adaptation, ebbs and flows, and shifts in meaning. The Dance Halls Act, poverty, and emigration supposedly "ruined" traditional music as it was played in the "old days" in contexts like Country House Dances. But this is only part of the story. The music also successfully adapted to changing pressures by imitating big band orchestras and moving into the dance halls themselves. There it thrived in a different form. During the Revival period, "guitar-toting balladeers" with rock-and-roll or folkie sensibilities packed the pubs, driving away dancers. This too supposedly killed the tradition. For many though, this was when the music came into its own. Now, some feel that tourism, commercialism, and global popularity are ruining the music. My contention is that adaptation doesn't necessarily mean ruination. Ends and beginnings exist in every shift in style, in every shift in meaning, every shift in which aspect of the tradition reaches new heights of popularity, and in every shift in audiences. It is nothing new, and if anything, the growing commercial success of traditional Irish music means that it reaches far wider audiences. Certainly, new opportunities are also fraught with danger, and a blind celebration of new eras of change is no less simplistic than melodramatic cynicism. A circumspect historical approach is useful, too, when discussing the fact that musicians get paid. "The question of how music is to be converted into hard cash," Stokes wrote, "and (not necessarily the same thing) how musicians get paid is, in many societies, a thorny matter at best" (1999: 146). True enough. This case illustrates some of the complex tensions that arise when music and tourism collide and collude. Still, it also illustrates the historicity of paying for music.

Today, attempts to commodify the music, for example the attempt to place copyright restrictions on particular tunes, are so antithetical to one of the central features of traditional art-forms—i.e., that it is a publicly owned resource—that they do indeed threaten the traditional performances of the music by forcing it wholly into the marketplace. On a practical level, it would mean that session musicians would need to obtain permission to perform particular traditional tunes. This may sound ridiculous, but McCann (2002: i, 76) reports that such accusations of "copyright violation" are not unknown. It is a classic example of neoliberal capitalism attempting to sequester the previously unquantifiable into statistical commensuration and the formerly communal into commodities. Such moves ought to be resisted. On the other hand, the intensification of commercial activity surrounding traditional performances need not worry us so much if musicians are allowed to maintain control over the music. This is, I believe, the case in Doolin's sessions. Likewise, the creation of commodified forms of something like traditional Irish music that complement rather than compete with other forms should not be seen as problematic. Here, I am thinking again of the highly commodified performances of traditional music for tourists at dinner theaters in Ireland or touring stage shows like *Riverdance*. Creating a commodified performance for new audiences does not necessarily detract from other, more "traditional" performances.

The globalization of traditional Irish music—its increased diffusion and popularity across the world, a process Lakoff calls "liquidity" (2008: 277)—cannot be separated from local processes of commercialization. For instance, since the revival the tourist interest in sessions prompted musicians and publicans to commercialize performances, which in turn solidified the semi-professional status of musicians. Likewise, *Riverdance* might not have had significant direct impacts on the way in which the music is played locally, but indirectly, there is no doubt that it continues to feed a local tourist industry which does have significant commercializing effects on musical performances. Together these two processes of globalization and commercialization consolidate the social role that traditional music performances have in Doolin.

Notes

1. I find this ironic in light of the recent public declarations by the current CCE chief, Seamus Duffy, that guitar and bodhran players are "destroying" traditional Irish music (Commins 2004a). The debate resulting from his comments reveal the partial disconnect between CCE's competitive performance oriented standards and those that exist *in situ* in sessions. Some musicians agree with Duffy's comments, while others have responded with vitriol (Commins 2004b). It is certainly the case that many people in Doolin are—to say the least—wary of bodhran players in particular (a common joke is that the only proper way to play a bodhran is with a very, very, large knife) and also sometimes tourists who break out guitars. But the main issue had less to do with the instruments themselves than with the unfortunately common presumptive attitudes of their owners. Many guitar and bodhran players are unfortunately unsubtle, showy, and obnoxious, throwing off the rhythm of the other musicians. Bodhrans are a particular target because of their ubiquity in tourist shops and because sometimes visitors assume that it is an acceptable means for them to join in a session even if they know little to nothing about the tradition. I witnessed several incidents in which either a musician or an audience member outright asked a bodhran player to leave, and during a festival once, a publican jokingly stood by the front entrance asking people coming in to "check your bodhrans at the door, please!" On the other hand, bodhran players who are deemed to be "good" (and there were several local players who were well respected) clearly know the tunes just as well as the other musicians at the table, and play complex rhythmic structures that enhance the tunes' melodies. They are greatly admired in part because they are so rare.

2. Again, I will leave the tributes to this local icon to those who knew him in life. I can only speak about the loss that the community feels in the years since Micho Russell's death. A constant refrain was "It's too bad you never met Micho." The gentle strength of the man's personality is present and palpable today in the area. Sadly, Gussie Russell, the third and last of the Russell brothers, died in 2004 almost exactly ten years after his brother Micho passed.

3. The social scientist in me always asked for figures, but most musicians notoriously hate quantifying things like "quality." They would often vaguely tell me that "one-in-fifty" or "one-in-a-hundred" sessions were "truly great."

Chapter 7

Adoption and Appropriation

> Meeting another musician for the first time is an elaborate encounter:
> a cat-and-mouse game, a courting ritual, or an exchange of phatic gifts.
> Ground rules are drawn up. It's a kind of poker, trying to suss out the
> other's hand, and whether he has any wild cards up his sleeve. We work out
> suits or suites or sets of tunes.
>
> —Ciaran Carson (1996: 75)

In the previous chapters, I described the historical circumstances that led, first, to the revival of the music, second, the movement of people through and into Doolin, and then thirdly, to the music's subsequent commercialization and consolidation. I described in detail some of the actors involved in those dramas—the locals, the blow-ins, and the tourists—and we have heard their voices. We have also seen how these actors interact, and in particular how blow-ins integrate into the local lifeworld (but within limits and not without negotiation). In the final chapters of the book, these three threads—the music, the tourism, and social change—become inseparable. The task so far has been to answer two questions: "what has happened?" and "what caused what happened?" For the remainder of this book, I will answer two slightly different questions; namely, "how is it possible that this has happened?" and "what might it mean?"

To answer the latter two questions we must first recognize what Anderson (1983) pointed out over twenty years ago in *Imagined Communities*: that the idea of the "nation" develops from ideas and ideologies rather than territorial boundaries or "cultures." "No less at issue," Hannerz argued over a decade later (1996: 22), "is the assumption that the carrier of 'a culture' is 'a people'." In the first part of this chapter, I take Hannerz's point that in the globalized and globalizing world—what he calls the "global ecumene" (ibid.: 7)—it is increasingly difficult to draw lines around people, places, and traditions. In the case study presented in this book, it is clear that incomers can successfully appropriate a particular local cultural tradition, which is often mistakenly assumed to have visceral, geographic, or genetic (one might even read this as "racial") connections to local people and local places (cf. Tansey 1999:

211, Rapuano 2001). In fact however, the "traditional Irish music community" is fluid, translocal, and transnational. It has become a global "public" (Warner 2002: 62). Like the practice of paying for music and like the music's history of incredible adaptability, this too is nothing new. Even a century ago, traditional Irish music existed quite prominently in Australia and North America for example (Curtis 1994: 51–53). At the same time, the way this music is played in sessions and passed down through consociate relations tends to simultaneously embed it in local places. These notions do not simply apply to performances of traditional Irish music outside of Ireland. Rather, the local and the global are intimately connected in, for example, Doolin's music scene. But even to say that they are "connected" is misleading, as if they were two separate entities. We need to be clear, although it might sound obvious enough: the local and the global are simply two scalar foci, part of the same whole. While some events (wars, shifts in economic policy, refugee crises) certainly have impacts across broader scales than others (personal dramas, local political battles, or the performance of community rituals and traditions), they are all part of the same milieu. In part, the goal of the following chapter is to illustrate exactly how the local and global are related to one another.

Appropriation

In 2003, during Doolin's annual music festival honoring Micho Russell, the first act of concert series in the Community Centre was a popular Doolin band that has recorded several albums and regularly tours. After playing their first set, one of the musicians introduced her fellow band members one by one. When she introduced one particular man, she smiled and said, "He's really the only true local among us!" A thunderclap of laughter rumbled through the crowd as people got the joke. Here was a local band playing at a local festival in honor of a local musician, and only one band member was apparently a "true" local. Many of the audience members who had come to the village for the festival may not have been aware of just how accurate her joke was. By the stricter definitions of local affiliation that she was clearly using to make her joke, the man she pointed out that day was one of the only "truly" local musicians who plays traditional Irish music in Doolin in general. Indeed, nearly all of Doolin's paid session musicians are blow-ins from other parts of Ireland or other countries. The reality of Doolin's traditional music scene is deeply ironic then: audiences made up primarily of tourists (especially in the summer) listen to a local style of traditional Irish music played primarily by an international population of blow-ins. One would presume that this appropriation of the crown jewel in the local tourist industry by outsiders would cause a great deal of acrimony. But it does not. In fact if anything it is noticeably unproblematic. There are several reasons why this is the case.

Firstly, music is not a finite resource like economic capital or property. It does not fall under the rules of a zero-sum game. The more music played in the village the better. Most musicians actually wished more visiting musicians came to play in Doolin like they did during the Revival. A livelier music scene would theoretically attract more tourists, so local stakeholders are also happy to see more rather than fewer musicians playing in village sessions.

Second, there are two distinct types of musical knowledge that blow-ins can adopt, an "oral tradition" and an "aural tradition" (Kaul 2007a). The oral tradition consists of the collective narrative about the local music scene. Of course, Doolin's musical domain has its own localized history. Some of this has been written down but much of it remains in the collective memory of villagers. There are local characters and musical "stars." Particularly famous (or infamous) events are often recalled, and as these stories are told and retold, embellished and re-embellished, they begin to take on some of the characteristics of legends. Tunes sometimes also have their own histories. In addition to this learnable history about the local traditional music scene, there is a unique aural character to the local style of playing that can be learned over time by an incoming musician if they listen carefully. Most noticeably, blow-in musicians can learn the local versions of tunes, but they can also learn the more subtle and unique "west Clare style" of playing by using particular decorations in particular places between the notes of tunes, or by developing the regional style's distinctive rhythmic sense of "lift." This west Clare style can be embodied in the incomer's playing and in turn passed on to others.

Thirdly, the way traditional Irish music is discussed reveals that there are two different understandings of the relationship between the music and musicians. The first understanding conceptualizes the music in terms of locality, embedding it within certain places. Natural features in the local landscape or the character of local people are even sometimes perceived to cause the variation in local styles of playing. In its most extreme form, this is a discourse of exclusivity. On the other hand, another discourse recognizes that traditional Irish music is a global phenomenon and has been so for quite some time. This understanding of the music, often referred to simply as "the Tradition," includes all of the variant local styles of playing as well as adjacent traditions (which we might refer to as "little traditions") like the music of Scotland, Britanny, or America (sometimes called "Old Timey" music). Occasionally, people also use the term to discuss the dance traditions associated with these musics. This is an inclusive conceptualization that recognizes its global, transportable, adaptable fluidity across national, linguistic, and cultural boundaries. As I have argued elsewhere (Kaul 2007a), it is the inherent connection between these two discourses that allows the incomer to move from the global "Tradition" into a local music scene with little cognitive dissonance on the part of blow-ins or locals.

Fourth, musicians from all backgrounds seek out moments of what the psychologist Csikszentmihalyi calls "flow" (1990), or more specifically related to music, what Feld calls "getting into the groove" or "feelingful participation" (1994: 111). In Ireland, these rare but much sought after moments are described as "great craic." "The craic" is a multifaceted, complex concept that describes diverse things: high quality social interactions and conversations, an entertaining night out, or the character of a witty person. In relation to traditional music, people use the term to describe particularly good sessions when the audience, the musicians, and the tunes all seem to come together in one harmonious "flow." It is a kind of enchantment, maybe the closest state of collective ecstasy that a group of people can achieve outside of religious rituals. I am not alone in discussing the intense, emotionally transformative power of music in this manner (Racy 2003: 6). Musicians in Doolin talk about it as a heightened state of embodiment when they "lose themselves" and the music itself seems to take control over the playing of it. Given the primacy of "great *craic*," it is little wonder that strict definitions of social status or a musician's country of origin matter far less than one's ability to play good music with and for others. When the bow strikes the fiddle, the quality of the music trumps any consideration of social status or role.

All of these factors are inherently intertwined in the direct experience of musical performance. None of them can really be extrapolated from the other when musicians sit down to play a few tunes. Therefore, much of the following discussion circles around itself and travels over the same terrain, but we should not falsify reality by making a complex social situation sound simple, or as Henry Glassie wrote, "have the culture reduced to formula" (1995[1982]: 14).

Adoption

In a concert setting, the line of demarcation between the performers and the audience is clear-cut. Elevated stages, theater seating, microphones, and the linear orientation of the musicians police the border between them. A duality of attention is clearly split along this border as well. The musicians' focus is on the audience, and the audience's focus is on the musicians. Likewise, the sonic experience of a concert is tightly controlled. Conversation between sets of music is kept to a minimum and generally has a subdued, functional role.

Sessions are different affairs altogether. They are inherently musical events of course, but to the same extent they are social events. In a session, musicians sit in a circle around a designated table facing one another. In other words, the musicians actually have their backs to the audience. The musicians are physically oriented towards the other musicians. Their attention focuses inward. This is not to say that the audience is unnecessary or unimportant; to the contrary. In a pub, many musicians told me, a session is not a proper session without an audience of some sort. Good sessions require interaction between the musicians and the audience. Unlike a concert however, this is not a one-way interaction from stage to audience. It is porous. While there is a clear physical borderland between the session and the audience—i.e., the musicians' backs—the social border is much less patrolled. The musicians and audience perform to each other across it. Conversation and jokes are passed back and forth from musician to listener and from listener to musician in between sets. Occasionally audience members come up to join the session to sing a song, and musicians may drop out of the session circle, perhaps even mid-tune, in order to have a conversation with someone in the audience. On quiet nights with a small crowd of known friends and few or no strangers around, the border between the audience and the musicians is very porous indeed.

Long periods of chat ensue after a set of tunes is played. Rounds of drinks are bought during these interludes, cigarettes are smoked, and chat bubbles to the surface. Unknown musicians might be introduced to each other. It is not uncommon for periods of conversation to be just as long as the actual sets of music, and indeed, these conversational interludes are integral and expected. Like the unfolding nature of the session itself, there is no clear-cut pattern of conversational ritual that occurs. They are often about the musicians' personal lives, but importantly, it is also during these breaks that musicians talk about the music, about playing, techniques and instruments, about the audiences, about decorations, about the history of tunes, where they first heard them, and from whom they "got" their tunes. Not surprisingly, these are particularly important opportunities for novice musicians to learn about the oral tradition surrounding the music from more established players.

In one recording of a session I made in 2003, Kieran, the Irish blow-in who we met in Chapter 5, asks if he could sit down to play a set of tunes on the tin whistle he brought with him to the pub that night. The other musicians tell him to "fire away!", so he sits down and launches into a set. The paid musicians take his lead every time he changes to a new tune. Afterward, everyone follows good session etiquette and thanks him for the tunes with a "Good man, Kieran" and a "Lovely, Kieran." Then, the following conversation ensues.

One of the paid musicians leans in towards him and says over the crowd noise, "Those second two tunes, we used to play here every night in this pub."

"Did you, yeah?", Kieran shouts back across the table.

"Every night with Micho," the paid musician tells him, "Every Sunday night." He pauses. "And in that order—the second two, the last two."

Because Micho Russell is an important local figure, Kieran greatly admires Micho's playing. In Schutz's terminology, Micho is a key "predecessor" in Keiran's lifeworld, one whom he can inherit tunes from secondhand through other musicians who knew him as a consociate. For the incoming musician, conversations like these during sessions provide ample opportunity to gain access to the oral tradition surrounding the music. It also provides them with a somewhat privileged inclusion into the social domain of the musical life of the village.

The story of Stephan, a Frenchman who became a good friend of mine during fieldwork provides another case in point. His progression from a tourist interested in learning a few tunes, to a blow-in, and more recently, to a paid session musician in the village was aided and abetted in no small part by his participation in this oral tradition.

As a flute-player interested in Irish music, he first traveled to Doolin with the intention of "learning how to play a few tunes" before returning to France. Over the course of two summer months in 2002 he took a few lessons from Christy Barry and picked up several tunes. He practiced them dutifully when he was not working as a cook in one of the local pubs. He played with other learning musicians (including myself) whenever he could, usually in someone's kitchen or yard. He attended a session every single night as an audience member over those two months that he stayed in the village, "absorbing" as much music as he could. But his skill as a player was still very preliminary. In August he returned to France.

Over the subsequent months, he found himself drawn to the idea of returning to Doolin. The feeling became more and more compelling, and in December of that same year he moved back. He rented more permanent accommodation in an old, damp cottage in Doolin. He began to fix it up. He brightened the walls with fresh paint and he bought supplies to make the cottage his home. He got his job back as a cook in the pub and made just enough money to live on. Again, he devoted himself to learning new tunes, and he practiced his flute for many hours each day in front of the coal-fired stove in the cottage to keep his fingers warm. Every night, he attended sessions and observed the musicians closely. Stephan and I would often meet at the pub to sip pints of Guinness or cups of tea and watch the sessions together. We would talk about the tunes, the musicians, the aural character of the local west Clare style, and various other aspects of the music. During the day, we would often play tunes together too. Even though his skills were improving rapidly (well beyond my stumbling attempts), he never joined a session. He admittedly lacked the confidence to sit down with the more seasoned musicians at the session table.

When the annual Micho Russell Festival took place in Doolin during the last weekend of February, musicians from all over the world poured into the village to play in swollen pub sessions, and in this context, made up of strangers of varying skill, Stephan suddenly found the confidence to join in. He told me later,

> I don't know, I just had to play. I just understand that I can play now. Like this (He snaps his fingers).

> I don't know—there was just lots of musicians. I just feel better. More comfortable with the music … . Something changed. Like you switch on a button inside you.

This experience clearly electrified him. He started to devote even more time practicing in front of his coal fire. After the festival weekend was over, Stephan started sitting in on sessions on a regular basis. He would not play very much because he only knew a small number of the tunes that the other musicians played. This was a frustrating period for him even though he felt a compulsion to keep learning. He would record sessions and practice along with the recordings at home. Eventually this meant that his ability to play along with particular musicians on particular nights of the week improved. More importantly perhaps, he was now publicly recognized as a novice, learning musician. This allowed him to get to know the regular session musicians very rapidly. He told me:

> I started to know the musicians around here, so it [became] much more easy for me to sit down with them. Sometime, if they saw me in the pub they [would] ask me if I [brought] the flute and, "Come sit with us."

> Do you know?

As expected, he was included in the chat during sessions. He also naturally began to enter into general conversations with the resident musicians outside of the musical context in the day-to-day ebb and flow of village life. Whether conscious of it or not, he began to learn the largely unspoken internal rules of session social behavior and etiquette as well—things like who the alpha musicians were in various sessions, when it was or was not appropriate to join in, and what subtle influences lead to a good session or ruin one. Eventually, he was even asked to start off a set of tunes now and again.

Stephan began to be recognized and discussed as a novice with considerable talent and drive who needed instruction and encouragement. Some established musicians are particularly keen to get learning musicians participating in the sessions, and are willing to teach eager learners whatever they want to know. During sessions, Stephan learned very quickly from them. Sometimes, I would see him at the periphery of the session circle, deep in conversation with another flute player who was instructing him on particular decorative techniques. Sometimes, these instructive conversations would go on for an hour after the session finished up. For Stephan the session chat was just as educational as playing along during the sets themselves.

After he started to sit in on sessions, Stephan's skill improved exponentially. As his confidence increased, he participated more until he had become a regular face at the musicians' table. This inclusion greatly enriched his playing, not only because he was listening more intently and playing along with the musicians in the actual context of a session (instead of playing to a recording of one), but also because of the session chat. Stephan now shared a common language, a common discourse, with other Doolin musicians. As the spring weather turned milder, Stephan also began "busking" at the Cliffs of Moher for tips. He made such good money that he cut down on his hours and eventually quit his pub job.

Only four months after the Micho Russell Festival, he was approached by the owner of a local restaurant[1] and asked if he would like to have a gig there once a week. For a standard fee, he started playing there every Monday night with another blow-in who he asked to accompany him on guitar. Initially, he was nervous about taking on a lead role, but within a month he confidently stormed through his weekly session. Other musicians (including occasionally me and my wife Rebecca) would join him to play along or to sing a few songs.

Stephan's entrance into the local music scene was perhaps more rapid than some, but his case is not at all unusual. Within almost exactly one year, he had moved from a tourist to a blow-in musician with his own paid gig. Without entering into the sessions as a more or less full participant, Stephan would never have been able to increase his skills so rapidly. The discourse that surrounds the music during sessions, the oral tradition, greatly accelerated his learning process. What is more, the conversation that goes on during sessions is a domain of discourse that the incoming musician can enter into, and even pass on. Some of the musicians that Stephan learned from during these chats were themselves blow-ins, and were in fact, passing along the oral tradition about the music that they had inherited from others.

When people claim in conversation or in print that traditional Irish music is "essentially oral in character" (Ó hAllmhuráin 1998: 6) even in the modern world of mass-produced recordings and concert performances, they are not wrong. I prefer to call the sonic aspect of the music that is transferred from one musician to another the "aural tradition" in order to distinguish it from the inheritable narratives, the "oral tradition," surrounding the music described above. Regardless of the label, the aural tradition refers to the important way in which the subtleties of the music must be heard *in situ* in order to be learned properly. The decorations and general "sound" of a regional style must be heard, listened to, and absorbed over a long period of contact with local musical performance. One must gain what folklorists call "receptive competence" in the local style in order to become what Feld calls a "socialized listener" (1994: 111). It is an aural distinction that can be learned by devoted listeners and certainly by devoted musicians.

Adam Shapiro, the South African fiddler we met earlier, described how this aural learning became embodied in his own playing style after years of intense listening to the musicians in northwest Clare. We were leaning into a coal fire one bitter winter afternoon, talking about the various places that he plays music. At one time, he told me, he did a lot of busking at the Cliffs of Moher. I asked him how this context was different from playing in a session. Interestingly, he responded by discussing the social importance, and the aural embodiment, of the music.

Well, I think of it as practice. I never practice. I get bored just practicing at home, especially with this music. I don't know why I can't do it. I can work on technique, but I find that boring too. And ah, I think once I got to a certain level, once I got a few of the "rolls" down and a bit of the technique, I just enjoyed listening and playing, playing along with other people. And I think personally, the best way to do it is—yes, you can practice, but I don't see the need. I don't know if it's just me, but I personally learn more by just being around the music, just living here. Hearing it. It doesn't even have to be the fiddle. You know, it can be any instrument. You just pick up things, not consciously even.

I find that I'm doing stuff now that I've never practiced, I've never worked on, and I can't recall hearing. (Laughs). I mean, yeah, obviously I've heard it in other people['s playing], but I've never consciously learnt it. And I'm doing it, and I think, "Huh? Is this me doing it?"

Because the more I've been here, the more I've learnt that it is an oral tradition. And the only way to learn it is by ear.

You have to learn the basics obviously … . When you're learning the basics, you have to go through some kind of, I think, structured learning. You have to practice. You have work on techniques, and work on your bowing, and work on everything about it. That's just getting the instrument out of the way, as such. But when it gets down to the music, you have to learn it by ear. You have to pick it up [from] whoever you're playing with.

"Getting the instrument out of the way" sums up just how embodied the aural tradition is in this music. What he calls "structured learning" is the kind of musical education that occurs in classroom settings, private lessons, or the less formal instruction on techniques that Stephan sometimes received during and after sessions. This knowledge is consciously taught and practiced. To couch it in the phraseology of the fiddler above, this is "working on the instrument." Adam distinguishes this from what he calls "working on the music." In other words, the musician should not have to think about where the fingers need to be on the fret-board or which hole to cover on the whistle. The fingers simply go there. Notes do not have to be recalled. One simply follows the other. Decorations unconsciously find their own place in between notes, and one tune follows the next without thought. This is something that Charles Keil might call the "kinesic" aspect of musical performance as opposed to the structure of the tune, which he might call its "syntax" (1994a: 72). The tune and the techniques are memorized but only then can one can start to truly embody "the music."

Playing a tune perfectly does not constitute "music" in this sense unless an emotive, expressive, embodied quality is present. In conversation, the music is often distinguished from what the fiddler here calls the "structure" of traditional Irish music. In fact, saying that a musician "is simply a good technician, but there's no music in that music" is the worst critique a musician might receive. This insult reveals this distinction between simply playing all of the notes correctly and fully expressing oneself in a truly embodied performance. This, it seems to me, is the point Charles Keil was making in his essay "Motion and Feeling through Music" (1994a): structure or syntax is only part of what goes on in the musical experience. Musicians in Doolin would certainly agree. The ways in which the musician utilizes decorations—rolls, cuts, and so forth, enhancing the standard notes of the tune, are a part of one's music; so are the very subtle variations of rhythm that Irish musicians call "lift." Furthermore, there is an important social element involved in music. This goes back to the distinction between "playing" and "performing." One "plays" to express oneself and to communicate that expression to others. Playing is therefore about building and maintaining relationships between people through music. If a musician does this well, and embodies it into their playing, someone might compliment them by saying that he or she "has lovely music."

Others have attempted to describe this emotive element in Irish music, which is sometimes called the nya[2] (Larson Sky 1997: 120–122). Adam ironically described the nya as "indescribable." Instead he emphasized the social aspects of the nya:

It's not a solo thing.

Um, You can't play this music solo … what it's about, for me, is playing with other people, being part of a group … . That's what people love about it: getting together with friends, chatting, drinking, watching a game of whatever on the telly, and playing music. It's all part of it. It's life. It's all part of your friends and people. That's the most important aspect of it. And that's what makes it, and that's why people from anywhere can play it, just as long as there's an understanding there. It's not the music. The music isn't important. It's sitting around having a conversation, and yeah, having a few tunes … . It's a context of people … . Anyone can learn it, but they have to be part of the group.

For me, that's why it is "folk" music. You have to have the "folk" in there!

Similarly, in an interview with Christy Barry, he argued that without passion, a player was simply a technician, not a musician. Christy argued that this passion, this *nya* that Adam Shapiro talks about, cannot be taught. It must be heard, listened to and passed down:

The players are exceptionally talented today. They're exceptionally skilled and all that because they have access to all that: colleges and schools of music. There's all kinds of things going on, but it still doesn't matter. Our music, the music for what it was, is still not there.

You can't teach it, you see.

It has to be handed down. You can do your best to teach it. One young lad might pick it up. Everyone will play it, but they won't have it, d'y'know? The one young fellow might have it. They might "get it" alright. Some young lad with enough passion might. He'd be into it, d'y'know? And he'd be as close as you'd get to it, d'y'know?

I said:

So, let me ask then what the difference is between someone who can play all the notes and play all the tunes, but they "don't get it." I mean, what is it they "don't get?"

He responded:

I just listen to their skills or whatever, and I say, "OK, fine. That's nice," you know? But I still say, "Well, where's the *tune?*", d'y'know?

"Which tune are you playing, really? Because I can't relate to your tune. Is it the same tune we're thinking about?", d'y'know! (Laughs).

The aesthetics of traditional Irish music, then, include much more than the notes of tunes and the techniques of filling those notes with decorations. At this level, the inculcation of the "music" is more dependent on an individual's personality and ability to express the *nya* than their social status as a local, a blow-in, or as a visiting tourist-musician. Local players certainly have an advantage since they have a lifetime's experience building up consociate relations with other resident musicians and becoming socialized listeners. But that does not necessarily mean that they will have the interest or the skills to play the music well, or that they will have qualitatively good social relations with other resident musicians. Understanding the *nya* and learning to play "lovely music" can obviously be difficult, but it is not uncommon for blow-ins to enter in to local social relations, adopt the local style of playing, and come to an understanding of, in the Adam's words, "what it's really about."

There is an unfortunate but popular notion that only native-born Irish have this ability to hear the finer distinctions between local styles and adopt a "true" traditional Irish music aesthetic sensibility. This conflation of culture, genetics, nationalism, and musical ability is romantically simplistic at best. At worst, it is elitist and dangerously exclusive. Rapuano for example reports that the traditional Irish musicians that she interviewed in the midwest of the United States believe that "an Irish-born or an Irish-American musician has an inherent ability to play the music due to their Irish 'roots'" (2001: 108)[3]. This is a silly but not uncommon claim, and I suspect that ethnic or genetic identifications with Irishness are far more important for musicians outside of Ireland who may feel a need to validate their interest in traditional Irish music. Unfortunately, however, this rhetoric can quickly descend into balkanized (and racialized) boundary-making. I found no sense of self-consciousness about playing traditional Irish music in Doolin, and in fact, given the egalitarian ethos of the session context, I found the opposite: a very liberal willingness to accept newcomers (regardless of their origins) with a sincere interest in learning how to play the music.

I am not alone in arguing that local styles, local techniques, and a local understanding of "the music" in this deeper sense, is something that can be learnt by the devoted blow-in musician. In a personal communication, ethnomusicologist and fiddler, Hazel Fairbairn, who herself spent some time playing in and analyzing Doolin's sessions in the early 1990s, concurred with this assessment. She wrote to me:

> My friend … who is a real old style Clare musician … also agrees that it is possible for incomers to pick up the style, in fact she says it would be almost impossible not to if you absorbed yourself and lived there for any length of time as the west Clare style is such a strong one.

Embodying the music at this level places a local style into what the philosopher John Searle would call a musician's "Local Background," the learnable motor-neural skills, abilities, and understandings specific to particular social settings (1983: 150–151). That is to say that the musician who fully immerses him/herself into a local style and becomes competent enough to hear it and even embody it in their own playing has absorbed the local musical habitus into the realm of the unconscious.

Complementary Discourses

Different styles of playing relate to geographic areas of Ireland. Typically, these styles are drawn up along county borders, although it is common to have several styles within a single county. In fact, as I describe above, musicians in Doolin play a "west Clare style." Like the strict notion of who is or is not a local, there is a discourse about local styles that conceptually embeds it in the very landscape of a locale. It is a discourse of "rootedness." Although it may seem contradictory, this conceptualization of the music in fact coexists symbiotically with a widely inclusive discourse of what is often simply called the "Tradition." The Tradition is a global phenomenon shared and transmitted by a worldwide Irish music public. In part, this coexistence explains the lack of tension over the appropriation of the music scene in Doolin (Kaul 2007a).

The idea that traditional Irish music is rooted in the landscape is succinctly summed up by the title of a paper given at a conference on traditional music in Dublin in 1996: "Irish Traditional Music—the melody of Ireland's soul; it's evolution from the environment, land and people" (Tansey 1996: 211). It is also seen by some as part of a larger, localized, social landscape:

> local styles of housebuilding were handed on, [as were] ways of farming, cures for ailments, accents, and dialects … . Local styles of singing and playing music are essentially part of the same vernacular tradition (de Grae 1999: 389).

In Doolin, musicians sometimes talk about how their style of playing emerges out of the unique landscape of Killilagh parish, which lies at the convergence of the turbulent Atlantic Ocean to the west, the stony mountains of the Burren to the north, the sharp shale Cliffs of Moher to the south, and the rolling green pastures to the east. This discourse carries with it an extremely potent mix of images, and often leads people to conceptualize traditional music as a natural resource. Significantly though, the metaphor of rootedness does not create a social barrier for non-locals. If anything, local people and the few local musicians that get paid to play in the sessions in Doolin are more likely to be impressed with a blow-in musicians' dedication and their ability to take on the local west Clare style of playing. Again, they often wish that more people would come to Doolin and play, like they did during the Revival.

Traditional Irish music, as it is played in miscellaneous local places the world over, is not isolated either. There have been global interdigitations in the Irish music "public" for a long time, and local music is influenced by the global, Tradition. Perhaps the best example of the historicity and influence of the global aspect of traditional Irish music is the fact that the most influential collector of traditional Irish tunes in the "old days" was not based in Ireland at all. The Irish-born Chicago police chief, Francis O'Neill published two volumes of 1,850 and 1,001 tunes in 1903 and 1907 respectively. These collections have now come to be so influential for traditional musicians all over the world that people might say they first got a tune from "The

One-Thousand-and-One." In any case, it is illustrative that places like Chicago with vibrant traditional Irish music scenes were not unusual even in the "old days."

The inclusive and expansive understanding of the discourse of the global Tradition emerges regularly in conversation amongst musicians when they discuss the history of the music, its sonic colonization of other parts of the world, and even adjacent art-forms like traditional set dancing or step dancing. This global discourse includes the instrumental dance music, the ballad tradition, and even includes other intimately related "little traditions" of music, for example, in Scotland and America. At this broad conceptual level, it may be more useful to think of the global Tradition more as a phylogenetic tree of art-forms which are constantly contested, stretched, cross-pollinated, and revived than as distinct "canons" of tunes, repertoires and styles, or a simple delineation of instruments or contexts. It is all part of the Tradition, and its bearers are a perfect example of a global public with a shared language and knowledge base. In the terminology of the music industry, traditional Irish music has become one genre of "world music" (Quinn 1996: 386).

Due to the Revival and more recently to *Riverdance*, popular interest grew enormously in the late twentieth century. CCE branches and local Irish music scenes now thrive not only in the English-speaking world to where the Diaspora relocated in the highest numbers over the last century and a half, but also to places like Tokyo, Japan (Williams 2006). Likewise, my informants in County Clare often told me that some of the best traditional sessions they ever played in were not in Ireland, but in Boston or New York. Influences from abroad return to Ireland, too. An obvious example of this global flow is the Revival itself, which had roots elsewhere before it impacted the music in Ireland. The historical trajectory of the banjo from Africa to America through the slave-trade and then relatively recently over to Ireland via the Tradition is another commonly-cited example. In that sense, the Tradition is far greater than any local or national place including Ireland. However, this is not to say that a connection to Ireland is unimportant for traditional musicians in other places (again, see Rapuano 2001).

In practice, the discourse of "rootedness" and the discourse of the Tradition are not normally conceptually distinguished from one another the way that I have done here. Instead, they are complementary rather than contradictory. The way that they are discussed reveals that locally rooted music feeds into the larger Tradition. I am not alone in suggesting that metaphors of fluidity and geography[4] are probably the most effective way of describing traditional Irish music in the modern world. Local music scenes might be considered "rivers" of sound that feed a larger "ocean of music"(Kaul 2007a). For incomers, this fluid conceptualization of Irish music aids their movement into local music scenes like Doolin. An understanding of these discourses can even enhance one's playing, imbuing a performance with deeper meaning. One becomes part of a larger musical history, and the responsibility of carrying the local and global tradition can give purpose to the notes.

Phenomenology of the Session

During the phenomenological, emotional, existential moment of performance, when one carries and becomes the bearer of the weight of The Tradition, one's status, social role or any other sort of identity is secondary at best. Music certainly can be used as a vehicle for the creation of group identities (cf. Austerlitz 1997, Reily 2000, Kruger 2001, Toner 2003) but when a session reaches the heights of intensity in moments of perfect "great *craic*," all identifications dissipate completely. This is what all musicians hope to attain when they sit down at the session table. The music takes over, and it seems that the instruments play themselves, or perhaps better put, the musician becomes the instrument for the music. This is what Turner meant when he described the state of flow: a "centering of attention on a limited stimulus field" in which "the 'self' that normally acts as broker between ego and alter becomes irrelevant" (1992: 54–55). These moments are rare in a session, but according to musicians and listening connoisseurs, the satisfaction of that one good session is always worth "slogging through" forty-nine mediocre or bad ones.

Before discussing what these moments of great *craic* are, why they are important to musicians, and how they can inculcate blow-in musicians into the musical domain, it is worth spending some time first exploring the interplay between the structure of the music and various phenomenological aspects of its performance.

Premeditated Spontaneity

Tunes are specific pieces of music, and although they may or may not be written down or learned from written sources, they are collections of specific notes and played in fairly specific ways. One can, in other words, play a tune wrong. Most tunes have a specific name, or more commonly, several names (Carson 1996: 7–10). A basic melody, a series of specific pitches played at specific intervals, lies at the heart of each tune. Micheál Ó Súilleabháin has called these the "set notes," or a tune's "setting" (1990: 119).[5]

Gussie O'Connor expressed how important it was to play the tunes properly by telling me the following story:

> I used to see old men crying down there,
> playing the music,
> absolutely crying.
>
> And I remember there was two old fellows down there … .
>
> And they were both great concertina players. But whatever mistake [the one] made, [the other] got up and threw the concertina down on the chair, and when he walked back in, he was crying. (He chuckles).

I asked, just to be sure, "What, because he was hurt that there was a mistake made?" He replied:

> There was a mistake made.

Oh, they were really sincere … . Music was played very seriously. And there wouldn't be a wrong note.

D'y'know?

Christy Barry explained how sacred a tune's setting is as well when he sardonically criticized the younger generations' playing today and also what he hears on a lot of modern recordings:

The whole thing has been just put away [so] that it fits in a minute on a tape or something. Cut out all the angles. Cut out all the corners.

What we want here is speed. What we want now is speed. The world is going fast now, so we got to play fast. So, we have to cut pieces of the tune out so that we can *cope*. D'y'know!

And these people like to go mad. They're on drugs! They really like to make sure that nothing gets in our way. They like to go mad-fast.

Just add a treble here and there. (He imitates the sound). Just frighten the people a bit more and get 'em to take more drugs! D'y'know?! (He Laughs).

The tune's "set notes" must be played at the correct moment in other words. But the tunes, in the assessment of some musicians like Christy, are nowadays lost in favor of the performance. Carson summed it up this way: "while there is no ultimate correctness in traditional music, there is wrong" (1996: 11).

Having said all that, musicians constantly vary the way tunes are played. The setting only provides a basic skeleton around which the musician is able to—indeed expected to—weave his or her music. In fact, variation is an essential part of the traditional aesthetic. Tunes are typically repeated three or four times in a row, and musicians decorate the basic melody differently each time with rolls, cuts, triplets, slurs, etc. A musician might also drop one part of a phrase down an octave, or play a short phrase in counterpoint to the melody. The collective spontaneity of all the musicians at the table results in an infinite amount of polyphonic variation within the conservative structure of the tune's setting.

So any particular performance is much more than simply the aural manifestation of a musical score. What's more, this means that the scores published in tune-books are not the same as the tune. During actual performances, tunes are spontaneous, creative, ever-becoming "ideas of music," instead of just collections of notes to be literally read from a page or figuratively read from a memory bank. The notated tunes in tune books refer to something that can be heard during a performance, but the performed tune cannot, by nature, be encapsulated in a *single* written version or recording. A setting, whether learned from a score or by ear, is something more akin to a mnemonic device for playing a single version of a tune.

Decorations around the basic notes of a tune are improvisational in that the musician can choose where, when, and what type of decoration is used at any given moment. However, even the type of decorations and their placement are somewhat controlled by conservative aesthetic standards. Too much decoration, misplaced decoration, or the "wrong kind" of decoration is discouraged. Moreover, decorations are dependent on the instrument that one plays (Ó Súilleabháin 1990: 122). The basic physical differences between instruments disallow certain decorations for certain instruments. In combination, the impromptu usage of this arsenal of decorative techniques, variations in octave usage, and even the variation created by breathing patterns or tonguing techniques for whistle and flute players, picking styles for plectrum instruments, and subtle bowing techniques for fiddle players, leads to a near infinity of subtle modification each time a tune is played. This leads to an infinite variety in what Keil has called "participatory discrepancy," the subtle "semiconscious or unconscious … out of syncness" in music (1994: 96) that leads to a powerful creative tension. Often it is so subtle that it is unnoticeable except as a "good feeling." It can occur with the texture of the tones of notes that are momentarily dissonant. When it occurs rhythmically, Keil calls this tension "groove," but in Ireland it is called "lift." It seems to compel listeners to tap their feet and bounce their heads and shoulders. Ó Súilleabháin puts it nicely when he calls lift "an invitation to dance" (1990: 123).

Furthermore, musical works are always "'riddled with … places of indeterminacy" (Benson 2003: 81). Traditional Irish music, I would contend, gives this empty space of indeterminancy a central place. Indeed, the simple structure of a tunes' setting is simple precisely because there is such an emphasis on decorating the spaces between the notes. The point is that there really is no one single version of any tune because the notes-in-between-the-notes so to speak, are infinitely variable. As Ó Súilleabháin wrote, it is "music-making of an informal and spontaneous kind" (1990: 118). This is a difficult concept for many learning musicians to contemplate, especially if they have classical training. The emphasis in traditional Irish music playing is not on the score as such. It is on playing with the score. This is an inherently live music, a music firmly embedded in the spontaneous chaos of the social context.

Even the names of tunes vary a great deal. Much of the time, no one playing a tune will know its name, or other times different musicians might know the tune under different names. Names of tunes, like the notes in a setting, are mnemonic devices rather than official. As Carson puts it:

[T]he tune is not a story, but stories might lie behind the tune … the names summon up a tangled web of circumstances; they not only help to summon the tune into being, but recall other times and other places where the tune was played, and the company there might have been (1996: 8).

So tunes often end up with different names, and often none of them are authoritative. I recall one quiet winter's afternoon when several musicians gathered at O'Connor's Pub to play some tunes. After a set, a visiting New Yorker asked the musicians what the names of the tunes were. Christy Barry cracked back, "If we start naming things around here, there could be a *row*!"

The ways in which tunes are put together in a set is often spontaneous as well, creating another level of variety. During a performance, there may be a free-associational relationship between tunes as they are played. Mental images, personal memories of past musical contexts, or a spontaneous sense of the flavor of the current set might inspire the next tune. Often, particular tunes fit well together, but this is a loose and subjective determination. And this fitness is toyed with. Different combinations of tunes within a set are often agreed upon and tried out before the musicians launch into performance. Sometimes, even if the order of tunes is not predetermined beforehand, musicians who know each other may know exactly which tune will typically come next in a set because they know the musical preferences of their fellow players. Other times, when a strong alpha-musician leads a session, he or she will make immediate and spur-of-the-moment choices about which tune will come next. There is a small pause in playing as the other musicians wait to hear the first line of the new tune as it is played by the alpha-musician. Then, everyone joins in as soon as possible. In a concert performance, this kind of spontaneity is avoided at all cost—it is perceived to be unpolished and unprofessional, but in a session the risk is exciting and essential.

All of these levels of spontaneity in Irish music are different from the improvisation of jazz solos. In jazz, there are predetermined moments in an arranged piece of music for on-the-spot melodic improvisation, what Benson calls "premeditated spontaneity" (2003: 133). Instead, this is a very different version of the same idea. The tunes and the basic melodies are known beforehand, as are the techniques to create decorations, but the order itself—in other words their arrangement—and the variation on the basic structure of notes of each tune are improvised.

Music as a Conversation

Meeting a new musician presents a challenge. Common musical territory must be mapped out, tunes known to all parties must be determined, and a kind of dance ensues as the points on the map are plotted out. Whole towns and cities of commonly known tunes emerge from the landscape, and roads between them are drawn up. The relationships between tunes can be made by their names, or they might be freely associated in sets by the old musicians that made them famous. They might be paired off because of the similar "feel" of them, or they might be paired up because of their lack of similarity, to create contrast.

In that sense, traditional Irish music played in a session context is very much like a dialogic narrative instead of a rehearsed performance. The notes of tunes might be metaphorically compared to grammatical structure, tunes form words and sentences, and a session as a whole conversation.[6] Not every conversation we have is a particularly good one of course. Many of them, in fact, are rather routine, matter-of-fact, or even painfully boring. Occasionally however, we have those rare conversations that build from a strong premise and grow into a discussion that enlightens, entertains, or teaches us something new. We walk away stimulated and maybe even tell other people about it. Good sessions, like good conversations, momentarily connect us with others around a particular topic, using a common language. The topic can build and grow and evolve, and although we might have different viewpoints or different rhetorical styles, we can possibly learn something new, or entertainingly pass the time. The metaphor of music as a kind of language is, in this sense, apt, one often used by the musicians I interviewed. Adam Shapiro used this analogy extensively when we were talking about the unspoken rules of session behavior:

> For good music, it's as important to listen as it is to express yourself. It's the same as a conversation, really. It's common courtesy not to speak over someone and not to interrupt, or barge in with your point.

> It's the same with the music. You don't just arrive at a session and tear into your own tunes. You listen to what they're doing, and play along with what they're doing. And if they ask you, then you express yourself. And most the time, they will [ask]. If you're sensitive and, um, a good listener as well as a good player, you will get asked: "give us a few reels" or "give us some tunes there," you know. And they want to hear you because you've been courteous to them.

> It's all intertwined. It's, it's like I said, it's like a language. It's a conversation.

> And that's what is fun about a session. It is music, but it's just like talking. Like, you know, different styles, different accents, but you can still understand each other, and still have a good conversation if you're willing to listen and not tread on people's toes.

Traditional Irish music in this case is the *lingua franca* of a session. The tunes can be introduced as topics and paired with other tunes to create a challenge to the other musicians. One might react to such a challenge by presenting another point of view in the next set of tunes. Or, the pairing of tunes can create a kind of musical joke. A purely musical banter can evolve between musicians in a session. Actual language is not necessary for this kind of communication to occur, and it is a conversation that the listening audience may be unaware.

Herein lies one of the more important reasons for understanding the embodiment of traditional Irish music, the yin-yang relationship between the global and local discourses about it, and the premeditated spontaneity of performances. A musician's linguistic or cultural background is not directly related to one's communicative ability as a musician in the session context. Instead, if a musician can creatively engage with the unfolding musical "conversation" and embody the music by using spontaneous innovation in the form of varying decorations and the occasional polyphonous line while not extending the melody too far from its setting, then their performance of the music is deemed "traditional" and "authentic" even if they cannot speak the same language as the other players. There is also no need to dwell on ethnic, genetic, national, or cultural identities either.

Perfect Embodiment and Good Craic

Taking into account all of the ways in which the music becomes embodied in the musician, and the deeper understanding of the notion of what the music is "really about," it is necessary to briefly discuss the notion of "good *craic*" in more depth. Culture-bound terms are almost by definition untranslatable, and as Racy points out in the context of the Tarab musical tradition (2003: 5–7), this is perhaps even more the case when the term relates to an emotional state caused by a socio-musical environment. Still, *craic* is often loosely rendered to mean "entertainment," "fun," or simply "having a good time" (McManus 2000). Carson simply defines it as "social exchange" (1996: 71). Later, he relates it to the term "crack" as it is commonly used in English, as in, "cracking a joke," or "cracking up" (ibid.: 83–84). Glassie describes "the crack" as a moment of witty "engagement and excitement" in conversation (1995[1982]: 36). Adrian Peace probably gets closest when he describes it as "an intensity of shared emotion and well-being ... generated in specific places already endowed with a strong sense of belonging" (2001: 98). It is a highly polysemous term, and arrives in conversation at many points. When meeting someone on the street, one is commonly greeted with, "What's the *craic*?" (i.e., "what's going on?"). Alternatively, one might ask, "Is there any *craic*?" One also "has the *craic*" with others when there is good conversation. A person's character might also be assessed in terms of the *craic* as well. "She's great *craic* altogether" is a high complement indeed. There really is no such thing as "bad *craic*." By the nature of the term, it is either present or absent. However, there is a distinction between merely "having the *craic*" and "great *craic*." When the evening's conversation in the pub is good and the music is even better, when the drinks are flowing, and when friendly teasing and bursts of laughter permeate the night, one might be able to say "the *craic* was mighty!"[7] These uncommonly good nights are the ones that people talk about for weeks afterwards.

So, the *craic* is by no means just applicable to the music. In fact, at its core, it describes the quality of general social relations. The distinction between the *craic* and the music is furthered by assessments of a night in the pub, like "There was loads of music, but no *craic*." Fairbairn makes this distinction as well. She writes that it is "not restricted to describing musical events but it is a general term for any form of enjoyable discourse" (1992: 30) but since it is often applied to the music, it "indicates the importance of the social aspect of music-making" (ibid.).

Peace describes the energetic and inchoate social nature of *craic*:

> The *craic* is unpredictable, though, in that it is difficult to anticipate why certain events generate this pronounced sense of collective well-being when others do not ... . At the end of the evening, the *craic* has been enjoyed by all, but no one can say precisely why in this particular bar on this particular night. There is always a measure of the inestimable which inheres in the *craic*,

and that is its attraction. What remains incontestable is that the performance is collectively produced (Peace 2001: 98).

Since the *craic* is a qualitative assessment of a social environment, and since sessions are inherently social, sessions also exude good *craic*. Good rapport between musicians is a baseline for a good session. This may or may not mean that they play regularly together. It simply means that the musicians have a "good feeling" from one another, musically and socially. Beyond that, it becomes difficult to determine why one particular session in fifty is good whereas the next forty-nine nights are mediocre or bad. Even in Doolin, with its consolidated socio-economic structure of weekly paid sessions and the teeming crowds of tourists in the summertime, once sitting at the musicians' table, anything could happen. Others have discussed these moments of piercing awareness in other contexts. Turner describes them as imbued with a "sense of harmony with the universe ... and the whole planet is felt to be in communitas" (1986: 43). Unusual, challenging situations present us with risk. Risk makes us take chances, and sometimes, the more risk that is involved, the more exciting the outcome becomes when it is successfully taken on. Musicians are led into a liminally creative state which, given the right mood in the room on the right day, potentially results in a genuine sense of communitas and an exceptional performance.

During a performance that is great *craic*, music can consume the musician. When the final goal of musical production—this perfect liminality—is reached, one loses a sense of oneself as a separate being. Emotion and physical sensuality briefly but totally consume reason and thought. When these rare moments of "good *craic*" take over, history becomes meaningless, and identity labels become pointless distinctions. Amplification, tourists with flashing cameras, microphones, and all other signs of commercialization become moot. Even the notes of the tunes, and all other technical aspects of the music itself, to recall the quote from Adam Shapiro, just "get in the way." Individuality dissolves into the sheer energy of the moment. Instruments and their musicians become extensions of each other during performance. A flute is no longer a tool. It is a physical extension of breath. Fingers are conjoined with fretboards and dance along the strings. One's arm and one's bow collectively saw out the notes on the fiddle. The musician does not control the instrument, the tune does, and the musician becomes the instrument of the tune. Tunes become real, visceral, actual, and felt, not just heard. It is one reason why musicians in many contexts close their eyes: they want the social-musical collectivity, the phenomenological moment of physical and aural connection to consume them whole, without distraction. It is a meditative musical moment, one that is shared, collective, and difficult to describe.

The risky, unpredictable nature of "good *craic*" is part of its allure. Some sessions which promise to be great, for whatever reason turn out to be awful. Others that one might initially presume will turn out terribly end up sweeping everyone along into its powerful tide. One example highlighting these characteristics of risk and unpredictability is worth exploring here. In late January of 2003, only a small handful of tourists visited the village each day and the weather was poor. Sessions only occurred at the weekend. Generally, things were very subdued. Amongst the thin crowd of tourists was a professional photographer from the U.S. passing through Doolin on holiday with his wife. He happened to be in O'Connor's Pub one night when Christy Barry led off the session. The photographer was so impressed with the music that he asked Christy if he would organize another session later that week. He wanted to photograph it. Christy agreed and handpicked several well respected musicians from the area, some who had never played together before. Since January is such a quiet month, the musicians that Christy asked to join him for this one time, unpaid session needed little prompting. It was a unique musical opportunity, and word spread throughout the village.

The photographer and his wife arranged the tables for the specific "look" they wanted for their photographs. They set lit lamps on each table for more subtle lighting and when everyone arrived, they ordered extra pints of Guinness to dot the tables despite the fact that most of the musicians did not drink Guinness. While the musicians played sets, the photographer moved around them with multiple cameras, shooting the scene. In between sets he reloaded and "directed" the scene in various ways. For instance, he asked one musician about half-an-hour into the session to pretend to be talking on his mobile phone to, presumably, juxtapose the "traditional" and the "modern." The musician was embarrassed but after some prompting from the photographer, he reluctantly complied. The musicians found this amusing because in reality it would be extremely rude behavior to talk on a phone during a session.[8] For a few shots, he asked a number of audience members to sit around the musicians' table, creating a staged "audience" for the camera. Later, he photographed the scene with no alcohol at all in it, and then again with just pints of Guinness. In other words, it was a visually contrived scene. The extra pints of Guinness, the lamps and the various roles

Figure 7.1 Photographing the Session

he compelled people to play existed solely for the camera. This constructed scene may be a perfect example of the kind of paradoxical situation that Bruner has called an "authentic reproduction" (1994).

Despite the consciously contrived nature of this session, and its "production" on the part of the photographer, a good crowd of villagers attended. It was a nice way to pass such a cold, rainy, winter's day. There was a good atmosphere in the room as well. Jokes and conversation peppered the afternoon. The musicians, not having played with each other in this combination before, were highly energized after only a few sets. In fact, the session went on for hours, set after set, and the intensity only increased. Finally, late into the afternoon hours, the musicians began to tire and the session eventually wound down. During the weeks that followed every one of them described it independently as a "good session," or a "mighty session," or "great *craic*." Indeed, despite the irony of it all, this completely manufactured session, created for the sole purpose of *visually* consuming it, was full of great music. Once in the room and tuned up, the reasons for coming together mattered less than the tunes themselves. Another part of the explanation that people gave me for why it was so good on that particular day was that the environment, although a complete set up, was so nice. The photographer was professional, and yet warm and friendly. He put everyone at ease, and even his attempts at directing the scene did not get in the way of the music. So, it was risky and exciting, unusual and unpredictable. It was also comfortable and fun.

The point is that good *craic*, while elusive, momentary, and created by unknown ingredients, emerges from the risk of spontaneity and indeterminacy. Unique situations, like festivals with one time combinations of musicians, or rare performances, or the cross-fertilization between traditions, provide social environments in which musicians can take risks, sometimes with exciting results. Since achieving "good *craic*" is so central to music making, it is no wonder that one's social status as a blow-in, or a local, or a tourist, matters far less in the musical domain that it does in, for example, the economic realm.

Conclusions

The nature of traditional Irish music allows for its appropriation by non-locals in various, built-in ways. Firstly, the music is adoptable. This is possible because a keen outsider can, over time, enter into the oral tradition of a local music, and after listening intently to a local style for many years, they can also begin to hear its aural tradition. Both the oral and aural traditions can be embodied and passed on by the blow-in.

Secondly, there are two types of imagined musical communities at work. There are local music "scenes," and out of this understanding of the music stems the discourse that the music is rooted in local places, emergent from the very landscape, and played amongst consociate relations. This understanding of an Irish music community sometimes leads to a sense of exclusivity in the same way as the strict definitions of "locals" and "blow-ins." At the other extreme, there is also a global traditional musical community that is expansive and inclusive. This understanding of the musical community accommodates the fact that traditional Irish music has not been coterminous with Ireland or "the Irish people" (however defined) despite the exclusive rhetoric that sometimes emerges. If Irish music is a "river of sound," then it broke its geographic banks long ago and flooded into many different parts of the world where it is listened to and played by people of very diverse cultural backgrounds. Today, those floodwaters have also allowed other entities including people and other musical influences to flow back to the sonic river itself to become part of its current at its very core. These two communities and discourses are complementary rather than contradictory, and it is the connection between them that allows incomers to make a relatively smooth transition into a local music scene.

Finally, in the embodied performative moment of musical practice, one's identity in the village as a local, a blow-in, or a musician-tourist, matters far less than one's ability to contribute a voice to the conversation of a session. Put simply, the music takes precedence over the musician. With the phenomenological understanding of the music comes the realization that the musical domain of the village does not play by the rules of a zero-sum game. Economic competition may detract from others' success and political ambition may be construed as "meddling," but more musicians playing more music does no harm. Indeed, it adds to the cultural capital of the village. The lack of tension caused by the local music scene's almost complete appropriation by blow-ins then is not so surprising.

I am reminded on Moya Kneafsey's comments about a session in Country Mayo with a crowd well-populated with tourists. She wrote:

> I wonder if the visitors knew that some of the musicians were also visitors? Or, did they think it was all local people playing, in some time-honoured ancient way? … It struck me that most of the musicians tonight were from other places - I think only Seamus was actually born in the county. Yet this has nothing to do with its authenticity — it's easy to fall into the trap of thinking that if it's not being played by the local-born Irish, then it's fake. Ultimately, whether authenticity is endowed on an event depends on the meanings that musicians and listeners attach to it. (2002: 256)

This question of "authenticity" is complicated and will be dealt with in some detail in the final chapter of this book. As Kneafsey points out, it is a misleading concept, but it deserves special attention not least because it is important to musicians and listeners alike.

Notes

1. This was an entirely new "gig" because restaurateurs do not normally host sessions. In fact, this session was held several hours earlier than the pub sessions so as not to compete with them.
2. According to Cowdery, this culture-specific term may go back to the nasal qualities of *sean-nos* singing (1990: 39).

3. Rapuano seems to fall into this rhetorical trap herself, claiming that non-Irish musicians "can only become a peripheral part of the Irish music culture" (2001: 107).

4. For example, Michael O'Suilleabhain produced a television series in the mid-1990s on RTE about traditional Irish music called "A River of Sound." Moya Kneafsey has called it an "ever-becoming geography of music" (2002: 358) while Reiss (2003: 161–162) and Taylor (2003: 280–281) both borrow Appadurai's metaphor of the landscape (1996: 33) to describe Irish music's modern flow across the globe.

5. The folk-terminology in traditional Irish music can sometimes be confusing. The "setting" or the "set notes" should not be confused with the term that is used to describe several tunes strung together, which is called a "set" of tunes.

6. I am aware of the debate about what exactly music "communicates." I am not concerned here with the idea that music may or may not communicate any particular semantic message or have a kind of meta-logic of its own; rather, in the case of traditional Irish music, the communication is primarily emotive and evocative not verbal, logical, or intellectual. There is, nonetheless, a great deal of communicative and meaningful dialog that goes on between musicians, and between the musicians and listeners.

7. Alternatively, some people substitute the word "ninety" for "mighty."

8. The photographer told me that he later sold this photo to a mobile phone company for an advertisement.

Chapter 8

Conclusions

Kneafsey depicts the interplay between traditional Irish music and tourism as "a kind of symbiosis" which is "complicated, messy, always shifting and changing" (2002: 358). She continues:

> perhaps the best way to describe it is as an "ever-becoming" geography of music, one which is constantly changing its contours as individuals' musical practices and performances are woven into its thick, rough texture (ibid.).

As the ethnographic material in this book shows, this "musical geography" shifts and changes historically and seasonally, and the people who occupy that geography or move through it also change. Using a geographic metaphor, some might read this book in light of what ethnomusicologists like Solomon (2000) would call the "musical construction of place," or perhaps more specifically, how music is used in service to the "tourist construction of place" (cf. Atkinson 2004). On one level, this book does document how music and tourism created the Doolin that exists today; however, I want to go beyond simply reinscribing the lines around Doolin or any other single location. At the least, it is essential to recognize the complex multidimensionality of "place-making" whether through music (cf. Rice 2003) or other means.

Of course, the place called Doolin is unique in many ways. It has its own undeniable historical particularities. For example, I think it is safe to argue that many of the trends towards cosmopolitanism and an intensification of social and economic globalization (via tourism for example or the influx of a relatively substantial immigrant population) began earlier there than in many other Irish towns and villages in the region. But what fascinates me is how just these kinds of particularities in the history of a place like Doolin also help redefine many of our preconceived notions about the relationships between place, community, traditions, social structures, and identities. The place described here cannot be detached from what might be called a "global geography" (Appadurai 1996) or cosmopolitan identity making. As Adrian Peace wrote, "an anthropology of Ireland may already be difficult to distinguish from an anthropology of the global system" (2001: 132). In Doolin, there is a constant movement of people, ideas, and practices, all of which converge here and initiate a constantly evolving performance of the local. It is an example of what has been called a "vernacular cosmopolitanism" (Werbner 2008: 14–16).

Additionally, while this is an ethnography about the complex construction of a particular *place* in time via tourism, music, immigration, and social change, it is also about the construction and performance of musical and social *spaces* in the present, and the diverse actors who occupy them. In this final chapter, I want to, first, very briefly reiterate what I think this case study contributes to some of the larger theoretical debates current in anthropology and adjacent disciplines. Second, I want to delve deeper into how those musical and social spaces are performed. In other words, I hope to answer one set of final questions: How does the musical experience *happen* in Doolin, or put another way, exactly how does the listener actively participate with the music? And, since this is a case in which a diverse body of actors inhabit and move through Doolin's musical spaces, how do various individuals perceive those musical experiences in light of that loaded notion of "authenticity?"

History, Globalization, and Tourism

It may be clichéd to say that knowing ones history is important for understanding modern circumstances, but it is worth reiterating in a discipline like anthropology that has a tendency to bury itself in the ethnographic present. In Ireland, where history is something of an obsession for scholars and the public alike, this is even more the case. Not only should history matter to us, but we ought to recognize its importance to our subjects even if—or perhaps especially because of—the way in which modern social relations increasingly occur across time and space in such a way as to occasionally disembed them from particular, local, consociate relations, a process that lies somewhere in between what Giddens has labeled the "distantiation" of the globalizing world and what Harvey has called its "space-time compression" (Inda and Rosaldo 2008: 8). Local people in Doolin are very conscious of their particular history, and they live that history in their modern social relations. It frames how they understand the present and their place within it. Even the local social structure is a living product of history. The broad historical picture I presented in the first chapters shows how individuals react to, and interact with, the structuring structures of history, tradition, and globalization.

The broad historical backdrop in the first chapters paints a localized picture of Ireland's transformation from a third-world country at the periphery of Europe to one of the wealthiest nations in the Eurozone. In the past, during eras of hyper-nationalism, being a peripheral nation on the edge of "the metropole" was debilitating to say the least. Now though, in an era of neoliberal economics, borders matter less, and indeed for awhile at least Ireland benefited greatly from the same geographic position, as did the "Asian tiger" economies situated near the Asian economic giants that the Celtic Tiger was named after. The huge economic transformation that occurred in Ireland in the 1990's and early 2000's, prior to the worldwide economic downturn, underwrote all other shifts during the era described in this book, and its influence cannot be understated.[1]

In regards to traditional Irish music, a broader historical perspective also reveals that what is often presented to be pure and whole in some distant past (and by implication, somehow impure and fractional in the present) is in actuality constantly evolving. The environmental pressures that cause this constant evolution in traditional Irish music, whether social, political, or economic, are not new either. The historical material in the previous pages presents examples from all three of these categories in fact. The pressures vary in kind and strength, but even under the more oppressive regimes of change—the Dance Halls Act for example—adaptive strategies emerged. The Dance Halls Act may have been a paranoid and cynical ploy aimed specifically to suppress traditional music-making, but most pressures have not been as targeted.

The session context itself is often assumed to be some "time-honoured ancient" ritual when in fact it is a relatively recent import to Ireland (Kneafsey 2002: 256). It might be considered a classic example of an "invented tradition" (Hobsbawm and Ranger 1983). Also, the revival of traditional music, described in Chapter 3, might represent a classic case of a "revitalized ritual" in Boissevain's understanding (1992a). But I want to go beyond these kinds of conclusions precisely because I believe they reify the modern expression of traditional Irish music. I even want to go beyond a conclusion that Doolin's sessions are simply a *re*invented tradition. Instead, I think that what has happened over and over again is the *reorientation* of a tradition. By taking a much broader view of developmental history, we can easily see how it has adapted to dramatic changes in the past while maintaining continuity. At Country House Dances and house *céilís*, this was music played for consociate relations. There was an orientation inward, towards one's face-to-face community. The Dance Halls Act effectively relegated the playing of traditional Irish music at Country House Dances and at Crossroads to the hinterlands, but it adapted and thrived in another context, the Dance Hall, and in a format appropriated from the big band scene, the *céilí* band. This was no longer music for oneself and one's consociates; rather, it was performed for the consumption of contemporaries who listened and danced to it. In other words, the orientation became, at least in part, extroverted. Radio, television, and popular music nearly wiped out this latter context in the 1950s and 1960s, but by the late 1960s a new context, the session, emerged and thrived. Once again, a shift in meaning and function occurred. The Revival sessions, though now increasingly detached from the dancing, were again played with an inward functional orientation in that the music was obsessively played for its own sake and only secondarily for the consumption of others. The Revival brought together musical contemporaries from all over the globe, so this was another inward reorientation but largely amongst "strangers" in the Irish music "public" with a common interest rather than amongst a close-knit community of mutual biographies. Today, the modern features of live performances in places like Doolin are simply another adaptation, this time to the pressure incurred by tourism. And again, the orientation, at least during the tourist season, is an outward one. In other words, the adaptation to or adoption of new contexts, formats, and venues is nothing new in Irish music.

Change may be constant and it is also tends to be Janus-faced. Despite the commodification of some forms of traditional Irish music today, it would be ridiculous to claim that modern pressures have been either entirely positive or negative. The modern popularization of the music, which is instantiated for example in the tourist consumption of sessions in places like Doolin, in the explosion of record sales in the last few decades, or in the global theatrical phenomenon of *Riverdance*, is perhaps the most dramatic example of the double-edged nature of change. Traditional music has benefited to some extent from modern pressures like tourism and the music industry, which have transformed it into a wildly popular global phenomenon enjoyed and performed by people from all over the world. On the one hand, the larger tradition's survival has been ensured. But on the other, the music has also been commodified in certain instances, or turned into an elite, almost classical art-form in other contexts. In some of the more popular expressions, Irish music (the appellation "traditional" is certainly arguable in these cases) has been streamlined into more globally palatable forms for broad consumption. An example of this might be the "Irishy-sounding" music embedded in so many Hollywood soundtracks in the past few years when a sense of The Ould Country is evoked. This is an extreme example of what I have called "consolidation" in this book, or what Lakoff has called the process of "commensuration"; once it occurs, it allows a culturally specific behavior, practice, or product become "liquid," and enter the global flow as a commodity (Lakoff 2008: 277–278). With this level of professionalization, enclosure, commodification, and commensuration, the loss affects the masses. Any gains have benefited the few. In these cases, the retooling and retailing of what Foster calls "The Irish Story" (2001)— in this case the story of Irish music—has streamlined its meaning to the point of meaninglessness. It is perhaps a form of what he describes as "remembering the future and imagining the past" (ibid.: 34).

Like others (Lewis 1993: 53, Tsing 2000) I am critical of historical or anthropological models of the new globalized world that neglect the specifics of individual lives, individual circumstances, particular contexts, or the ethnographic specificity of varying "global situations." Recent concentration on global flows (Appadurai 1996), or the "structuring structures" of the habitus (Bourdieu 1977), can too easily take precedence over the movement of particular people, or the agency and complex narratives of individual lives. While I find models like these "good to think with," we also must bear down on the lived experience of our subjects. I find phenomenological sociology of Alfred Schutz (1970) and Charles Keil's (1994) similarly phenomenological analysis of the musical experience quite useful in that regard. Likewise, in tourism studies, I find Ed Bruner's (2005) careful narrative analyses refreshing. Thankfully, more recent attention has been given to the people, the "cosmopolitans," who move in and out of culturally disjunctive social spaces (cf. Hannerz 1996, Rapport 2006, Werbner 2008). In the previous pages, I have made a concerted effort to allow the individuals who occupy the "shifting geographic" spaces of Doolin to present the ethnographic reality of globalization, cosmopolitanism, remembered history, and social change from their own perspective, and thereby connect structures with actors, history with lived experiences, and global flows to local circumstances. It is my hope that by doing so, I have not revived the false dichotomy between global flows and local places. To the contrary, it is my hope that this ethnography is an example of what Tsing meant when she called on ethnographers to more carefully analyze the particularities of singular "global situations."

Despite globalization, incomers, and mass tourism, it is clear that the value of some sort of community and face-to-face sociality is not disappearing, but instead adapting (albeit sometimes radically) to modern circumstances. Likewise, traditions remain healthy and have even been revitalized not in spite of globalization, tourism, commercialization, and appropriation by incomers, but rather partly because of these factors. This is not a terribly new conclusion, but it bears repeating. Sometimes, globalizing factors that are, in some circles, decried as supposedly consuming and "homogenizing" local cultures act, in fact, as tools for empowering, strengthening, and diffusing them (cf. Bilby 1999).

More generally, a globalized economic and social landscape orients us away from a focus on nations, ethnic enclaves, and localisms and more towards the new channels that are cut across these categories (Tsing 2008: 66–67) and the "awkward connections" (Inda and Rosaldo 2008: 33–35) that they create vis-à-vis the global movement of money, people, and traditions. But what is also clear from the ethnographic material presented here is that a complete rejection of the local and of notions like community and tradition for a concentration solely on the global is as shortsighted and wrong as it is to pretend that communities and "cultures" are somehow bounded entities unto themselves. For example, cosmopolitan incomers in this instance have adopted and been absorbed into local performative traditions and consociate relations. There is no either/or dichotomy here between the local and the global. It is both/and.

Ultimately, this is an ethnography that attempts to untangle the complicated web of social interactions that occur at the nexus of tourism and traditional Irish music sessions in one particular place. As I wrote in the beginning of this book, I would not go so far as to claim that one might see a whole culture in a traditional Irish music session. However, it would be disingenuous to assert that one could wholly tease apart economic processes of change in Doolin from changes in the music, or changes in the social structure from changes in the local tourism industry, or the complicated interactions between international tourists and the way local lives are lived. In the moment of performance, a session in Doolin reveals a great deal about historic, economic, social, and musical changes on local, national, and international scales.

Appropriation, Tradition, and Cosmopolitanism

The social structure of the village has been transformed as a direct result of the revival of traditional Irish music, the burgeoning tourism industry, and immigration in Doolin. Blow-ins are now a driving force in village affairs, and indeed, they have appropriated and been absorbed into the local traditional music scene. While tensions can arise in many arenas of village life particularly when it comes to politics and economics, the appropriation of local music does not arouse such tensions. Ability and praxis precede role and status in the musical domain. Also, during the rare moments of musical intensity during a pub session that emerge during the performance of the music in pub sessions, issues of identity, history and even one's subjectivity become moot. These are moments that all musicians strive for when playing and all audiences long for when listening. They are disembodying moments of "flow" (Czikszentmihalyi 1990) when people lose themselves in the music. In these moments, social status becomes—not just secondary—but meaningless. In fact, taken to the phenomenological level, the direct experience of live music—what Charles Keil calls "participation"—render such distinctions between insiders/outsiders, authentic/inauthentic, and even musician/ audience completely beside the point. Keil quotes Owen Barfield who writes that "[p]articipation begins by *being an activity*, and essentially a communal or social activity" (in Keil 1994b: 97, my italics). This is the moment of perfect embodiment called "great *craic*," or "flow," described in the previous chapter. It is, writes Keil, "the opposite of alienation" (ibid.: 98).

The inclusive and adoptable nature of traditional Irish music does not detract from its meaning. Too often, we conflate "traditions" with "people." This book provides a strong ethnographic case to the contrary. In fact, what all of this shows is that the notion of tradition is a much more pliable and adaptable concept than is typically thought. Living traditions are not representative of everything that is moribund, antiquated, balkanized, or conservatively "local." Instead of being conceptualized as being in opposition to globalization and cosmopolitanism as is usually done, traditions can clearly thrive in their midst. I would even go so far as to suggest that the notion of "tradition" is in fact an incredibly useful one for examining the complexity of modern cross-cultural and disjunctive circumstances.

Indeed this argument interdigitates once again with the emergent literature on cosmopolitanism. While Pollock et al. have made the case that defining cosmopolitanism as a "positively … uncosmopolitan thing to do" (2002: 2), they suggest that it is an identity in search of the imaginary, the possible, and "the Other" rather than the known, the extant, or the cognate (ibid.: 2). But if cosmopolitanism is a general reveling in, celebration of, and willingness to encounter what Appadurai calls the "cultural disjunctures" of the modern world, then is it not possible to suggest that one avenue towards cosmopolitanism is the search and exploration of an existing tradition, habit, custom, or experience that one is unfamiliar with? Is it not true that the adoption of the now global tradition of Irish music is one expression of cosmopolitan exploration? Instead of seeing globalization or cosmopolitanism as a force that consumes the local or the traditional, I agree with Diouf (2002: 112) who writes that:

> we must inquire into the modes on the basis of which native modernity relies on, confronts, and/or compromises an instrument and a modality of the incorporation of the local into the global.

Diouf borrows the label "vernacular modernity" as shorthand for this more nuanced stance about globalization and cosmopolitanism. It is one that seems appropriate when considering the way in which traditional Irish music—a music which has an imagined homeland but which is more or less "unbounded, unobstructed, unlocated" (Pollock 2002: 22)—has made a compromise with the modern world.

The Trope of Authenticity

There is one more theoretical point that is worth drawing out before closing: the highly loaded issue of "authenticity," which has more or less shackled tourism studies beginning with the seminal works by Cohen (1988), Smith (1989[1977]), Greenwood (1989[1977]) and MacCannell (1989[1976], 1992) among others. Still, the question of "authenticity" remains important if for no other reason than the fact that tourists in places like Doolin throw this powerful but simplistic word around quite a lot, and it is a concept that musicians discuss frequently as well. Scholars are not immune from the romantic power of the term either. Indeed, despite the fact that Lionel Trilling warned us years ago that it is one of those terms "like love, which are best not talked about if they are to retain any force of meaning" (1972: 120), it has become a staple concept in the diet of tourism studies, and an implied one in other disciplines like anthropology, ethnomusicology, and Irish studies. I take the lead from Bruner (2005) though: "authenticity" is an awkward concept worthy of considerable critique. Bruner, Wang (2000) and others have shown how this is a polysemous concept that means radically different things to different people in different contexts. Below, I hope to situate various actors' judgments of the quality of performances within the complexity of ethnographic reality to show how individual epistemologies of the same experience create differing assessments of it. This is a constructivist approach, because I also suggest that some individuals' assessments are more "credible" than others.

The notion of authenticity disguises a tangled discourse rife with personal agendas and political undertones. It does not mean one thing, although it is often presented as though it does. Wang, for example, distinguishes between various types of authenticity from an objectivist "museum approach" (2000: 47, 49) to the postmodern rejection of any sort of authenticity (ibid.: 54). In between these extremes lies an "existential authenticity" whereby subjective determinants create the standards by which experiences are assessed (ibid.: 56). Likewise, Bruner discusses several uses of the term. The first is used when something is "an original" rather than a reproduction (this is similar to Wang's objectivist "museum approach"). Second, when something is "mimetically credible," for example, a modern reproduction that accurately represents how a thing would have existed in the past, it might be deemed "genuine." Third, when a thing is "believable to the public," it achieves a notion of authenticity that he labels "verisimilitude." This may be closest to what Wang calls "existential authenticity." Finally, there are "official" versions of things sanctioned by powerful figures and/or institutions, which he calls authenticity by "authority" (2005: 149–151). "The problem with the term *authenticity*, in the literature and in fieldwork," writes Bruner, "is that one never knows except by analysis of the context which meaning is salient in any given instance" (ibid: 151). I agree. It is wholly dependent on context.

Let us begin an analysis of "authenticity" as it applies to traditional music in Doolin by recognizing two points of departure. Firstly, I agree with Bruner that a postmodern rejection of any version of "authenticity" is "narrow and distorted" and not a little bit "elitist" (2005: 168). In fact, what is ironic about the postmodern stance is not the rejection of "authenticity" altogether, but that in doing so it seems to focus on notions like "authenticity" so much. Secondly, "living traditions" are by definition constantly evolving and changing, so we must also reject the objectivist or "museum approach" to authenticity in our analysis. Since originals never truly existed, this definition of authenticity simply does not apply. Here, I will begin with the more relative existential notions of the term and build from there. What I hope to show is that we can take it further though.

Given an existential definition, must we necessarily preclude a novice listener's experiences from the realm of authenticity in this case? I should think not. An inexperienced listener can have an entirely authentic experience of a particular performance in Doolin even if a musician or an experienced connoisseur deems it inauthentic. This claim is plausible if we focus solely on the shared phenomenological experience of the performance itself, what Schutz has called the mutual "tuning in" (1970: 216–217) or what Keil calls being a "full participant" (1994b: 97–98) during a live performance, rather than focusing upon musical syntax, structures, or the assessments varying actors make about the performance afterwards. Keil suggests that this kind of "participation," this being in the music, is especially possible for musicians and audiences of musical styles that emphasize improvisation over composition (ibid.: 96). The successful use of slight rhythmic and melodic "discrepencies," in Keil's terminology, encourages creative tension during live performances. There is no doubt that this kind of articulation between performers and listeners via the music creates the potential for what Durkheim would have described as a moment of collective, emotional solidarity, or "great *craic.*"[2]

The inexperienced listener has little or no basis for determining whether or not a performance is authentic because they have nothing to compare it with. Conversely, an experienced listener or perhaps a musician, can only make determinations about the quality of a performance based on their in-depth experience of it. They can never (re)experience it as a novice. In other words, following the performance, everyone is constrained by his or her subjective knowledge about the music. It is precisely because of this variance that one person can experience existential authenticity in a performance determined to be inauthentic by others. Conscious assessments of performances occur only after the phenomenological experience of them (Keil 1994b: 97), but this does not mean that the concept of authenticity cannot be applied to both situations—the experience and the assessment of it. Again, Keil provides us yet another solution. Especially when applied to non-Western and non-classical musical forms, he is critical of the commonly made distinction between the intellectual understanding of music and the embodied emotion that musical performances evoke (1994a: 54–56). Quite rightly, he argues the goal of our analysis of music should not be a kind of musical syntax (a study of "the score" so to speak); instead, we must also include a fine grained kinesic analysis of musician's body language and gestural communication (ibid.: 72–73). In other words, we must collapse the false dualism between the score and the performance of the music as well as the intellectual understanding and the emotionally embodied understanding of the music. I would extend this one step further and suggest that the audience's embodiment into the performance, their "participation," must also be included. Even though a first-time tourist might not fully understand a tune's "syntax" or even some of the most basic aesthetic features of the genre, the total kinesic embodiment of being a participant-listener can lead to a rich, engaging, and "authentic" experience.

Benson argues "that an essential ingredient in having a genuine experience (*Erfahrung*) is the element of surprise: it is precisely when we do not expect something that it affects us most" (2003: 118). He goes on:

> [I]t is in the act of truly listening that we have a genuine experience in which we make contact with that which we hear. But, since a genuine experience is surprising and shocking, we cannot continue to experience a piece by having it performed repeatedly in the same way. It needs to be changed, not merely so that we can hear it anew but so that we can truly hear it at all (ibid.).

Listeners who are less familiar with the ways in which traditional Irish dance music is performed than others, might find an arranged, amplified performance inclusive even of World Music and rock-and-roll genre elements, a positively surprising experience, and therefore "genuine." But consciously produced performances (in terms of the way in which the music is somewhat prearranged by the musicians) cannot be repeated to the same audience members over and over. Over time, the repeated performances are likely to seem less and less spontaneous or genuine.

Many tourists and connoisseurs of traditional Irish music alike become familiar with the genre at the outset through strictly staged performances and spectacles. The music from *Riverdance* or a Christy Moore recording or a Waterboys record might be the extent of one's experience with Irish music prior to seeing it played live in a pub in Doolin.[3] This may be especially true for many of the North American tourists. Irish Festivals in the US are often highly staged affairs and heavy on balladeering. For many tourists, an amplified, staged performance with predetermined musical changes by a band will be even more palatable (i.e., "authentic") than an unarranged, unstaged session full of premeditated spontaneity and conversation. In other words, in an arranged performance the switch from jigs to reels, the pointed semi-arrangement of particularly placed tunes within a set, and the heavier and more conscious, punctuated use of ballads, keeps an audience without a deep receptive competence "listening." There is always something new and surprising. Since these kinds of determinations of authenticity are subjective at this broad level and are only later articulated, it is all too easy for us to discount others' less qualified experiences as superficial based on the subjective determinations we have formed through our own more extensive experiences.

Credibility

By no means do I want to simply argue that "it is all relative" though. We can be much more specific about the perceptions and assessments of performances than that. It is important to recognize the fact that individuals with a closer relationship to traditional Irish music (whether they themselves are musicians or not), and to northwest Clare and its permanent residents, possess a more authoritative expertise about the quality of performances there. The phrase "authoritative expertise" conjures up images of professional arbiters of artistic taste whose judgments are final though, and that is not what I am after here. Instead, as I have argued elsewhere (Kaul 2007b) it is important to recognize that some actors are "closer to the action" as it were. Local musicians, for example, "know better" than other actors with little or no experience of a place or the performances that occur there, and their assessments are therefore more sophisticated. In order to reflect reality, we also must leave significant room for discursive disagreement even amongst those whose intimate relationship to the music and the social context of performance means that their opinions about the music's quality deserve warranted respect.

In order to separate this approach from the overburdened (Bruner 2005: 209) and misleading term "authenticity" discussed above, we might use a different term altogether: "credibility."[4] This notion, in my thinking, leaves room for the existentially authentic experiences of any actor with any level of knowledge about a performance, and also for the fact that some actors have a deeper epistemological ability to assess a particular performance in relation to its quality and its historical continuity or discontinuity with what is largely considered to be traditional. In other words, it recognizes that some people have expert local knowledge while allowing for the fact that those local experts may not always agree in their assessments or even on the strict definition of terms like "quality" or "tradition." Importantly, credibility need not coincide with existentially authentic experiences of a given performance that some actors might have. In other words, some actors (e.g., the musicians) might not find a given performance credible, but this does not preclude another actor (e.g., a visitor to the village) from having an existentially authentic experience.

It is obvious at this point that in the present case study, the phenomenological perception of authenticity, or credibility, is dependent on a number of contextual and biographical factors including one's social status, one's subjective experiential history or what Schutz has called one's "previously constituted knowledge" (1970: 191), and the spatial and seasonal context of one's socio-musical interaction. How the musical experience *happens* is complex. The following relationships and contextual factors all contribute to an individual's immediate perception of the quality of the music in Doolin. Each one combines to create an overall complexity of individual perception.

One's Relationship to the Locale

This includes one's social status as a mass tourist, a returning visitor with friends in the village, a domestic tourist, or a permanent resident of the locale (either a local or a blow-in). Consociates who share an interbiographic local history with one another (Schutz 1970: 80) have historically different qualitative relationships with the locale and its residents (including the musicians) than strangers or even traditional Irish music contemporaries who are unfamiliar with the village.

One's Epistemological Relationship to the Music

This includes one's status as a paid session musician, an unpaid musician, a learning musician, a publican, a non-musician (who may have degrees of exposure to traditional Irish music on a spectrum from no exposure to being a connoisseur), a domestic tourist with relatively broad exposure to, but no interest in, Irish music, or any combination or gradation thereof. Epistemological variation is great. A first-time tourist may have only read about traditional Irish music (or that Doolin is the so-called "capital of traditional Irish music") but might never have actually heard it. Of course this reading also creates preconceived knowledge that might frame their perception of quality. Given the fact that traditional Irish music is a global phenomenon, a second first-time tourist with no consociate relations in the village may be a connoisseur and have a deeper relationship to the music than even a local who prefers country and western music. One's commercial relationship to the music is important as well. A person with a commercially vested interest in the music (a paid musician, or a local businessperson with an interest in promoting the locale's attractions, for example) may be more inclined to promote a more libertarian notion of authenticity to themselves and others.[5]

Immediate Context

Here, I am referring to the particular pub in which one might experience a session. Each pub has a different "character" dictated by the physicality of the building and its furnishings, by the personality of the publican and his or her employees, by the kind and quality of the drinks they provide, by the usage or non-usage of amplification, and the nature of the clientele. As subtle as some of these environmental characteristics may seem, they contribute to one's experience as a musician or an audience member.

Seasonality

The effect of seasonality in Doolin cannot be understated. Whether one is exposed to a session during the summer months (generally attended by more mass tourists than anyone else), during a festival (with their specialty tourists in large numbers), during a busy Bank Holiday weekend (dominated by large numbers of domestic tourists), or during a quieter winter session (largely amongst a small number of consociate relations) has a significant impact on anyone's experience of performances. Larger crowds, whether they are keen to hear the music (for example during the Micho Russell Festival weekend) or not (for example during a Bank Holiday weekend), can achieve a certain noise threshold whereby the musicians are forced to "close off" the session and end any social interaction with the crowd. This is cited as one of the major factors that typically ruins a session, and is directly related to these seasonal factors.

The Interaction of Personalities

This includes all of the actors involved in the session context: the musicians, the tourists, the permanent residents, the publicans, and the staff. The personality of an alpha musician, for example, may dictate the interaction between the session and the audience. Some musicians are keen to include the audience in performance while others simply prefer to "perform." One musician may play particularly poorly or particularly prodigiously and thereby ruin a session.[6] Likewise, particular audience members—regardless of their social status—may dictate the nature of the interaction. For example, even one disrespectful audience member has the ability to close off a session by talking too loudly near the musicians, or by trying to interact with the session too much (by talking to them too much or by attempting to play or sing inappropriately). Even more specifically, the mood of the individual musicians is often cited as a determining factor in the quality of the music, as is the overall collective "mood" of the crowd or the session musicians. A poor interaction between the musicians may create a bad feeling and thereby lead to a bad session. Sometimes, as I indicated above, a crowd can be too raucous and noisy, but interestingly, tourist audiences especially can actually be too quiet during sets of tunes as well, making the musicians feel like they are simply "performing."

All of these individually complicated factors are intimately interrelated. They combine to form an overall complexity that determines how different individuals perceive the quality of a particular performance. A simple spectrum or dichotomy of performances cannot be drawn up. It must also be recognized that a perception of quality and a perception of authenticity, while deeply interrelated, are not the same thing. The reason is that there are different determinants by which the quality of a performance is gauged and by which it is perceived to be authentic. In other words, a performance might be perceived to be high quality but inauthentic, or the other way around. For example, tourists often view a modern element of the music, like payment, as an indicator of "inauthenticity," whereas musicians tend to see payments as largely inconsequential. The conclusion that a performance is a *quality* performance merely informs but does demand that it is an *authentic* performance. One's receptive competence of the music changes the relationship between the two notions. For an inexperienced audience member, quality may have a one-to-one relationship with authenticity ("It's good music, therefore, it's 'real' music"), whereas someone with a great deal of receptive competence might make a distinction between the two in a given performance ("I heard a lot of notes, but there was no music"), for example in a high quality but inauthentic competitive or concert setting.

What makes all of this even more complicated is the fact that the scope of one's perception is inherently limited. Two people of similar taste and experience may perceive the same session differently given the circumstances of their interactions on any given evening. One musician might take a night off to socialize with friends while another plays in the session, and their two perceptions of the quality of that session, although both "credible," may be totally different simply due to their differing proximity to the music on that particular evening. In other words, we must also allow for discursive disagreement between individuals with relatively similar epistemological relationships to the music and the locale.

This is why "great *craic*" is so spontaneous, so rare, and so sacrosanct. Any number of complexly subtle influences can prevent or ruin it. Of course, great *craic* itself is a subjective determination of quality. However, there are sessions (or moments during particular session) when things are "flying" and it would be difficult to argue that the *craic* is only purely subjective. Indeed, definitions of *craic* usually include elements of "social exchange" (Carson 1996: 71), moments of "engagement and excitement" (Glassie 1995[1982]: 36), and "an intensity of shared emotion and well-being … generated in specific places already endowed with a strong sense of belonging" (Peace 2001: 98). This gets back to the collective nature of what Keil (1994) calls "participation" as well. Good *craic* is therefore dependent not only on the individual's relationship with the factors listed above but also on the interaction between various people in a given pub on a given night who bring their own subjective relationship with those factors into the mix.

Despite this complexity, an individual who has long-term exposure to sessions in Doolin can recognize rough patterns and make decisions about where one might, according to their own determinations of quality, have a higher chance of hearing a good session and "having the *craic*." In other words, they can come to a credible determination about the quality of a performance. Growing up in the locale grants an individual a lifetime of consociate relations and expert local knowledge. One's expertise as a traditional Irish musician imbues a person with another form of credibility. None of this is necessarily consciously explicated by anyone in this kind of detail. This knowledge is for the most part taken for granted, and when it is articulated, it is too easily condensed into simplified, romanticized caricatures. Riddled as this social situation is with inconsistencies, contradictions, paradoxes, and increasing cultural change, it is no wonder that the question of authenticity, once taken for granted, forms so easily on the lips of tourists, local stakeholders, and musicians.

It is intellectually easy—especially when the topic at hand is culture change, traditional music, and the impacts of commerce—to promulgate romantic stereotypes, but it only does a disservice to those we study. It is just as simplistic to maintain a cynical, disappointed detachment about modernity, although ironically this latter stance more often than not gets paraded around as intellectual sophistication. For me, the complex, contradictory, multivocal truth of the modern world, of situations like the traditional Irish music session in Doolin, is far more interesting and powerful than either romanticism or cynicism.

Good Man Yourself

During the Spring of 2003, friends of ours from the United States were visiting us in Doolin. Of course, in addition to touring the local sites, Rebecca and I also took them to several sessions where we introduced them around to our friends. They had been looking forward to experiencing a session since we had already told them so much about it. We tried to explain this elusive notion of "great *craic*" to them on the phone and in letters before their arrival, but our descriptions never seemed adequate. We always said, "But you'll see for yourselves. Hopefully, we'll have at least one really good night out while you're here." As it turns out, we happened to go to one particularly great session at O'Connor's Pub.

It was late spring, so the stillness of the long, lonely winters was fading as the small trickle of tourists grew incrementally day by day. The handful of tourists added some excitement to the sessions. If the crowds grew any larger though, the sessions would have to take place in the "big room" with the microphones turned on. But that night they played in the front room around the coal fire. As the music began, we knew it was going to be a good session. Set after set, Christy Barry and the other musicians present that evening played with an urgency perhaps sparked by the knowledge that the busy tourist season was upon them, and that this might last of the more intimate winter sessions that year. At times the music was buoyant and ebullient. The musicians gave the tunes a strong "lift," and as Christy later described it, "There was great music in that music." The crowd felt the excitement and it permeated the pub. The energy the tunes produced seemed to pass through the crowd like electricity and then soak into the walls. In between sets, there was a lot of laughter and convivial socializing with the crowd. At other times during the evening, like when Seamus McMahon sang a few *sean nós* songs, the air became thick with sombre (if not quite sober) silence. This was a great session, one that buzzed.

Finally, late into the night, Seamus was prompted by his friends to sing one last *sean nós* song. "Go on, Seamus, give us another song!", they shouted. He smiled slightly and nodded once, capitulating to the request. His eyes were squeezed tightly shut and his head turned at a slight angle as he lilted through the sad story of unrequited love and emigration. Even though Seamus was an imposing man, his voice shook with a gentle fragility. Besides the sad, soft song, the pub had gone nearly silent. Some watched him sing while others gazed glassy eyed at the floor or into the coal fire. As he came around to the end of the last line of the last verse he suddenly shouted out "Up the Banner, boys!" expressing his local pride in County Clare, the "Banner County." Everyone awoke back into the smoky present of the pub as Seamus broke into a broad smile. The crowd roared with laughter and cheers and orders for another round of drinks. "Good man yourself, Seamus!" one man shouted above the din of clinking glasses and nodding approval. My friend leaned over to me and said, "This is it, isn't it?" He didn't need to ask me. Anyone around us could have answered his question. I just smiled and nodded.

Notes

1. In 2005, a quality of life survey by *The Economist* even ranked Ireland the number one place to live out of 111 countries worldwide ("Quality of Life Index, 2005"). Of course, with the economic downturn, things are shifting once again.

2. Others, like Racy (2003: 5) in the context of Tarab music, have made the same point about the deep, highly charged emotional contact between listeners and performers.

3. The same is true for the recent flourishing of American traditional genres like "Sacred Harp Singing" following popular movies like *O, Brother Where Art Thou* and *Cold Mountain*.

4. I am not the first to use this term in relation to music and tourism. See for example Connell and Gibson's discussion regarding the "credibility" of musical innovators (2003: 44), Bruner's use of the term (2005: 132), and Gable and Handler's version in which they suggest that it is a kind of "vernacular authenticity" (2003: 372–376).

5. In my first interview with one local businessman, the rapport I gained throughout the first forty-five minutes or so was completely lost when I asked him if he felt that the music had changed as a result of tourism. He immediately became defensive and insisted that it had not changed at all. The nature of the question implied that there was a possibility that the

music was somehow less than "pure." It effectively ended the interview. Most people are a bit more circumspect, however. It was clear that his commercial relationship to the music through the promotion of the local tourist industry colored his perspective.

6. I have seen musicians shake their heads in disgust when one or two musicians dominate a session by being virtuosos. The performances themselves are impressive to listen to, but they can ruin the socially inclusive nature of the session.

Bibliography

"1901 Census of Clare – Killilagh DED" www.clarelibrary.ie/eolas/coclare/geneology/1901 census/killilagh. Clare County Library and Clare Local Studies Project: Ennis, County Clare, Ireland.

Adler, Judith. "Youth on the Road: Reflections on the History of Tramping." *Annals of Tourism Research* 12, no. 3 (1985): 335–354.

Ahmed, Akbar S. and James B. Mynors. "Fowlmere: Roundheads, Rambo and Rivalry in an English Village Today." *Anthropology Today* 10, no. 5 (1994): 3–8.

Allen, Kieran. *The Celtic Tiger: The Myth of Social Partnership in Ireland*. (Manchester, 2000).

Allen, R. Raymond. "Old-Time Music and the Urban Folk Revival". *New York Folklore* 7, (1981): 65–81.

Amit, Vered. "Anthropology and Community: Some Opening Notes". in Vered Amid and Nigel Rapport (eds), *The Trouble With Community: Anthropological Reflections on Movement, Identity and Collectivity*. (London, 2002), 13–25.

Anderson, Benedict. *Imagined Communities: Reflections on the Origin and Spread of Nationalism*. (London, 2002).

Appadurai, Arjun. *Modernity At Large: Cultural Dimensions of Globalisation*. (London, 1996).

Ardener, Edwin. *The Voice of Prophecy and Other Essays*. Malcolm Chapman (ed.). (Oxford and Cambridge, Massachusetts, 1989).

Arensberg, Conrad M. 1959(1937). *The Irish Countryman: An Anthropological Study*. (Gloucester, 1959 [1937]).

Arensberg, Conrad M. and Solon T. Kimball. *Family and Community in Ireland*. (Cambridge, 1968 [1940]).

Atkinson, Connie Z. "Whose New Orleans? Music's Place in the Packaging of New Orleans for Tourism." in Sharon B. Gmelch (ed.), *Tourists and Tourism: A Reader*. (Long Grove, 2004), 171–182.

Austerlitz, Paul. *Merengue: Dominican Music and Dominican Identity*. (Philadelphia, 1997).

Bashkow, Ira. "A Neo-Boasian Conception of Cultural Boundaries.", *American Anthropologist* 106, no. 3 (2004).

Benson, Bruce E. *The Improvisation of Musical Dialogue: A Phenomenology of Music*. (Cambridge, 2003).

Bilby, Kenneth. "'Roots Explosion': Indigenization and Cosmopolitanism in Contemporary Surinamese Popular Music." *Ethnomusicology* 43, no. 2(1999): 256–296.

Blaustein, Richard. "Rethinking Folk Revivalism." *Transforming Tradition: Folk Music Revivals Examined*, 258–274. in Neil V. Rosenberg (ed.),(Urbana and Chicago, 1993).

Bohlman, Philip V. *The Study of Folk Music in the Modern World*. (Bloomington and Indianapolis, 1988).

Boissevain, Jeremy. "Introduction: Revitalizing European Rituals." in Jeremy Boissevain (ed.), *Revitalizing European Rituals*,(London, 1992),1–19.

Bourdieu, Pierre. *Outline of a Theory of Practice*. (Cambridge,(2000[1972]).

Bourke, Angela. "Seamus Ennis in County Clare." *Dal gCais* 8 (1986): 53–56.

Breckenridge, Carol A., Sheldon Pollock, Homi K. Bhabha, and Dipesh Chakrabarty (eds),*Cosmopolitanism*. (Durham and London, 2002).

Brody, Hugh. *Inishkillane: Change and Decline in the West of Ireland*. (London, 1973).

Bruner, Edward. "Experience and Its Expressions." in Victor W. Turner and Edward M. Bruner (eds), *The Anthropology of Experience*. (Urbana and Chicago, 1986), 3–29.

———. "Abraham Lincoln as Authentic Reproduction: A Critique of Postmodernism." *American Anthropologist* 96 no. 2 (1994): 397–415.

———. *Culture on Tour: Ethnographies of Travel*. (Chicago and London, 2005).

Bryant, Beth (assisted by Susan Poole). *1979–80 Arthur Frommer's Guide to Ireland Dublin/ Shannon*. (New York, 1979[1977]).

Buchanan, Donna A. "Metaphors of Power, Metaphors of Truth: The Politics of Music Professionalism in Bulgarian Folk Orchestras." *Ethnomusicology* 39, no. 3(1995): 381–416.

Burke, Eimar. "'Customs Clearance': A Project to Achieve Better Cultural Understanding Between Immigrant and Native Populations in Ireland." Dublin: The Irish Committee of the European Cultural Foundation. Available at www.europeanmovement.ie/ ECFReport.htm. Accessed 5 May 2004.

Byrne, Anne, Ricca Edmondson, and Tony Varley. "Introduction to the Third Edition." in Conrad M. Arensberg and Solon T. Kimball (eds), *Family and Community in Ireland*, 3rd ed. (Ennis, 2001).

Caldwell, Melissa L. "Domesticating the French Fry: McDonald's and Consumerism in Moscow." *Journal of Consumer Culture* 4, no. 1(2004): 5–26.

Callan, Lou, Fionn Davenport, Patrick Horton, Oda O'Carroll, Tom Smallman, and David Wenk. *Lonely Planet: Ireland*. (London, 2002[1994]).

Cantwell, Robert. *When We Were Good: The Folk Revival*. (Cambridge Massachusetts and London, 1996).

Carson, Ciaran. *Last Night's Fun: In and Out of Time with Irish Music*. (New York, 1996).

Casey, Natasha. "Riverdance: The Importance of Being Irish American." *New Hibernia Review* 6, no. 4(2002): 9–25.

Casey, Ruth. "Defining the Local: The Development of an 'Environment Culture' in a Clare Village." in Michael Cronin and Barbara O'Connor (eds), *Irish Tourism: Image, Culture and Identity*, (Clevedon, Buffalo, Toronto, Sydney, 2003): 42–60.

Chaney, David. "The Power of Metaphors in Tourism Theory." in Simon Coleman and Mike Crang (eds), *Tourism: Between Place and Performance*, (Oxford, 2002):193–206.

Cinnéide, Ó Barra. "The Riverdance Phenomenon: Crosbhlealach an Damhsa." in Fintan Vallely, Hammy Hamilton, Eithne Vallely, and Liz Doherty (eds), *Crosbhealach An Cheoil: The Crossroads Conference 1996*. (Dublin, 1999):148–155.

Coady, Michael. 1996. *The Wellspring of Water: A Memoir of Packie and Micho Russell of Doolin County Clare*. (Carrick-on-Suir, Tipperary, 1996).

Cohen, Erik. "Authenticity and Commoditization in Tourism." *Annals of Tourism Research* 15 (1988): 371–386.

Coleman, Simon and Tamara Kohn (eds), *The Discipline of Leisure: Embodying Cultures of "Recreation"*. (New York and Oxford, 2007).

Collins, Liam. "Irish 'Cead Mile Failte' is Now Dispensed by Foreigners." *Sunday Irish Independent,* 4 August 2002: 4.

Commins, Michael. "Comhaltas Chief Blasts Guitar and Bodhran Players as Destroyers of Traditional Irish Music." *Western People,* 24 March 2004.

———. "Seamus Prompts a Right Auld Session in Irish Music Circles." *Western People,* 21 April 2004.

Connell, John and Chris Gibson. *Sound Tracks: Popular Music, Identity and Place.* (London, 2003).

Connerton, Paul. *How Societies Remember.* (Cambridge, 1989).

Cotter, Geraldine. 1989(1983). *Traditional Irish Tin Whistle Tutor.* (Cork, 1989[1983]).

Cowdery, James R. *The Melodic Tradition of Ireland.* (Kent and London, 1990).

Crawford, Caroline. "Happy Days Now the Great Boom is Over: the Celtic Tiger is Dead, but We're Still Smiling … ." *Irish Independent,* 12 March 2003: 3.

Cronin, Michael and Barbara O'Connor (eds), *Irish Tourism: Image, Culture and Identity.* (Clevendon, Buffalo, Toronto, Sydney, 2003).

Csikszentmihalyi, Mihalyi. *Flow: The Psychology of Optimal Experience.* (New York, 1991).

Cullen, Paul. "Vibrant Africans Overcome the Threat of Racism." *The Irish Times,* 30 July 2002: 7.

Curran, Catherine. "Changing Audiences for Traditional Irish Music." in Fintan Vallely, Hammy Hamilton, Eithne Vallely, and Liz Doherty (eds), *Crosbhealach An Cheoil: The Crossroads Conference 1996,* (Dublin, 1999): 57–63.

Curtin, Chris and Thomas M. Wilson (eds), *Ireland from Below.* (Galway, 1989).

Curtis, P.J. *Notes From the Heart: A Celebration of Traditional Irish Music.* (Dublin, 1994).

Danaher, Dan. "Tourism on the Net." *Clare Champion,* 10 May 2002: 22.

Davies, Norman. *The Isles: A History.* (London, 1999).

Dawson, Andrew. "Leisure and Change in a Post-mining Mining Town." in Nigel Rapport (ed.), *British Subjects: An Anthropology of Britain.* (Oxford, 2002): 107–120.

Deegan, Gordon. "Clare Wants to Impose No Go Building Zones for Blow Ins." *Irish Examiner,* 26 October 1999: 18.

Deegan, James and Donal Dineen. *Tourism Policy and Performance: The Irish Experience.* (London, 1997).

———. "Developments in Irish Tourism, 1980–96." *International Journal of Tourism Research* 2, (2002): 163–170.

de Grae, Paul. "Style and Authenticity." in Fintan Vallely (ed.), *The Companion to Irish Traditional Music,* (Cork, 1999).

Desforges, Luke. "'Checking Out the Planet': Global Representation/Local identities and Youth Travel." in Tracey Skelton and Gill Valentine (eds), *Cool Places: Geographies of Youth Cultures.* (London and New York, 1998), 175–192.

Devas, Nicolette. *Two Flamboyant Fathers.* (London, 1968).

Diouf, Mamadou. 2002. "The Senegalese Murid Trade Diaspora and the Making of a Vernacular Cosmopolitanism." in Carol A. Breckenridge, Sheldon Pollock, Homi K. Bhabha, and Dipesh Chakrabarty (eds), *Cosmopolitanism,* (Durham and London, 2002), 111–137.

Edensor, Tim. "Staging Tourism: Tourists as Performers." *Annals of Tourism Research* 27, no. 2 (2000): 322–344.

Ennew, Judith. *The Western Isles Today.* (Cambridge, 1980).

Eyerman, Ron and Andrew Jamison. *Music and Social Movements: Mobilizing Traditions in the Twentieth Century.* (Cambridge, 1998).

Fairbairn, Hazel. *Group Playing in Traditional Irish Music: Interaction and Heterophony in the session*. Ph.D. diss., Cambridge University, 1992.

————. "Changing Contexts for Traditional Dance Music in Ireland: the Rise of Group Performance Practice." *Folk Music Journal* 6, no. 5 (1994): 566–599.

Feld, Steven. "Aesthetics as Iconicity, or 'Lift-up-over Sounding': Getting into the Kaluli Groove." in Charles Keil and Steven Feld (eds), *Music Grooves: Essays and Dialogs*. (Chicago, 1994): 109–150.

————. "A Sweet Lullaby for World Music." in Arjun Appadurai (ed.), *Globalization*. (Durham and London, 2001): 189–216.

Foss, Daniel A. and Ralph W. Larkin. "From 'The Gates of Eden' to 'The Day of the Locust': An Analysis of the Dissident Youth Movement of the 1960s and Its Heirs of the Early 1970s — The Post-Movement Groups." *Theory and Society* 3, no. 1 (1976): 45–64.

Foster, Roy F. *The Irish Story: Telling Tales and Making it up in Ireland*. (New York, 2001).

————. *Luck and the Irish: A Brief History of Change from 1970*. (Oxford, 2008).

Foy, Barry. *Field Guide to the Irish Music Session: A Guide to Enjoying Irish Traditional Music in its Natural Habitat!*. (Boulder, 1999).

Frankenberg, Ronald. *Village on the Border: A Study of Religion, Politics and Football in a North Wales Community*. (Prospect Heights, 1957).

Gable, Eric and Richard Handler. "After Authenticity at an American Heritage Site." in Setha M. Low and Denise Lawrence-Zuniga (eds), *The Anthropology of Space and Place: Locating Culture*. (Oxford, 2003): 370–386.

Geertz, Clifford. *The Interpretation of Culture*. (New York, 1973).

Gefou-Madianou, Dimitra. "Cultural Polyphony and Identity Formation: Negotiating Tradition in Attica." *American Ethnologist* 26, no. 2 (1999): 412–439.

Glassie, Henry. *Passing the Time in Ballymenone: Culture and History of an Ulster Community*. (Bloomington and Indianapolis, 1995[1982]).

Gottheil, Fred. "Ireland: What's Celtic about the Celtic Tiger?" *The Quarterly Review of Economics and Finance,* 43 (2003): 720–737.

Graburn, Nelson H.H. "Tourism: the Sacred Journey." in Valene L. Smith (ed.), *Hosts and Guests: The Anthropology of Tourism*, 2nd ed. (Philadelphia, 1989[1977]): 21–36.

Graham, Brian. "Ireland and Irishness: Place, Culture and Identity." in Brian Graham (ed.), *In Search of Ireland: A Cultural Geography*. (London, 1997): 1–16.

Greenwood, Davydd J. "Culture by the Pound: An Anthropological Perspective on Tourism as Cultural Commoditization." in Smith, Valene L. *Hosts and Guests: The Anthropology of Tourism*, 2nd ed. (Philadelphia, 1989(1977)): 171–186.

Hall, Reg. "Heydays are Short lived: Change in Music Making Practice in Rural Ireland, 1850–1950." in Fintan Vallely, Hammy Hamilton, Eithne Vallely, and Liz Doherty (eds), *Crosbhealach An Cheoil: The Crossroads Conference 1996*. (Dublin, 1999): 77–81.

Hannerz, Ulf. *Transnational Connections: Culture, People, Places*. (London and New York, 1996).

Henry, Edward O. "Institutions for the Promotion of Indigenous Music: the Case for Ireland's Comhaltas Ceoltoiri Eireann." *Ethnomusicology* 33, no. 1 (1989): 67–95.

Hobsbawm, Eric and Terence Ranger (eds), *The Invention of Tradition*. (Cambridge, 1983).

Inda, Jonathan X. and Renato Rosaldo. "Tracking Global Flows." in Jonathan X. Inda and Renato Rosaldo (eds), *The Anthropology of Globalization: A Reader*, 2nd ed. (Malden, 2008): 3–46.

Jabbour, Alan. 1993. "Forward." In Neil V. Rosenberg (ed.), *Transforming Tradition: Folk Music Revivals Examined*, xi–xiii. (Urbana and Chicago, 1993).

Kaul, Adam R. "At Work in the Field: Problems and Opportunities Associated with Employment During Fieldwork." *Anthropology Matters* 6, no. 2 (2004): 1–9.

_____. "On 'Tradition': Between the Local and the Global in a Traditional Irish Music Scene." *Folk Life: The Journal of Ethnological Studies* 45 (2007a): 49–59.

_____. "The Limits of Commodification in Traditional Irish Music Sessions." *Journal of the Royal Anthropological Institute* 13, no. 3 (2007b): 703–719.

Keenan, Brendan. "Normality Required to Keep the Tired Kitty Purring Along." *Sunday Independent*, 7 December 2003: 19.

Keil, Charles. "Motion and Feeling Through Music." in Charles Keil and Steven Feld (eds), *Music Grooves: Essays and Dialogs*. (Chicago, 1994a): 53–76.

_____. "Participatory Discrepancies and the Power of Music." in Charles Keil and Steven Feld (eds.), *Music Grooves: Essays and Dialogs*. (Chicago, 1994b): 96–108.

Kelleher, Suzanne R. *Frommer's: Ireland 2003*. (New York, 2003).

Kiberd, Declan. *Inventing Ireland*. (London, 1995).

King, Tim. "Ireland Takes Second Place in Eurostat's Cost-of-Living Survey." *Business This Week*, a supplement to *The Irish Times*, 2 August 2002: 1.

Kneafsey, Moya. "Sessions and Gigs: Tourism and traditional Music in North Mayo, Ireland." *Cultural Geographies*, 9 (2002): 354–358.

_____. "'If It Wasn't for the Tourists We Wouldn't Have an Audience': The Case of Tourism and Traditional Music in North Mayo." in Michael Cronin and Barbara O'Connor (eds), *Irish Tourism: Image, Culture and Identity*. (Clevedon, Buffalo, Toronto, Sydney, 2003): 21–41.

Kockel, Ullrich and Joseph Ruane. "Different Irelands: The Problem of Context in Irish Ethnography." *The Anthropological Journal on European Cultures* 1, no. 2 (1992): 7–35.

Kohn, Tamara. "Incomers and Fieldworkers: A Comparative Study of Social Experience." in Kirsten Hastrup and Peter Hervik (eds), *Social Experience and Anthropological Knowledge*. (London, 1994): 13–27.

_____. "Island Involvement and the Evolving Tourist." in Simone Abram, Jacqueline Waldren, and Donald V.L. Macleod (eds), *Tourists and Tourism*. (Oxford, 1997): 1–28.

_____. "Becoming an Islander Through Action in the Scottish Hebrides." *Journal of the Royal Anthropological Institute* 8, no.1 (2002a): 143–158.

_____. "Imagining Islands." in William H. Waldren and Josep A. Ensenyat (eds), *World Islands in Prehistory: International Insular Investigations: V Deia Conference in Prehistory*. (Oxford, 2002b): 39–43.

Koning, Josef. "The Fieldworker as Performer: Fieldwork Objectives and Social Roles in County Clare, Ireland." *Ethnomusicology* 24, no. 3 (1980): 417–429.

Kruger, Jaco. "Playing in the Land of God: Performance and Social Resistance in South Africa." *British Journal of Ethnomusicology* 10, no. 2 (2001): 1–36.

Lakoff, Andrew. "Diagnostic Liquidity: Mental Illness and the Global trade in DNA." in Jonathan X. Inda and Renato Rosaldo (eds), *The Anthropology of Globalization: A Reader*, 2nd ed. (Malden, 2008): 277–300.

Larson Sky, Cathy. *"I'd Barter Them All": — Elements of Change in the Traditional Music of County Clare, Ireland*. MA. thesis, University of North Carolina, 1997.

Lele, Veerendra. "'Demographic Modernity' in Ireland: A Cultural Analysis of Citizenship, Migration, and Fertility." *Journal for the Society for the Anthropology of Europe* 8, no. 1 (2008): 5–17.

Lewis, Herbert S. "A New Look at Actor-Oriented Theory." *Political and Legal Anthropology Review* 16, no. 3 (1993): 49–56.

Lewis, Susan. "National Day: Achieving Collective Identity on the Isle of Man." in Nigel Rapport (ed.), *British Subjects: An Anthropology of Britain*. (Oxford, 2002): 49–66.

Livingston, Tamara E. "Music Revivals: Towards a General Theory." *Ethnomusicology* 43, no. 1 (1999): 66–85.

Loker-Murphy, Laurie and Phillip L. Pearce. "Young Budget Travelers: Backpackers in Australia." *Annals of Tourism Research* 22, no. 4 (1995): 819–843.

Lortat-Jacob, Bernard. "Community Music and the Rise of Professionalism: A Sardinian Example." *Ethnomusicology* 25, no. 2 (1981): 185–197.

McCann, Anthony. *Beyond the Commons: The Expansion of the Irish Music Rights Organisation, the Elimination of Uncertainty, and the Politics of Enclosure.* Ph.D. diss., University of Limerick, 2002.

McCann, May. "Music and Politics in Ireland: The Specificity of the Folk Revival in Belfast." *British Journal of Ethnomusicology* 4 (1995): 51–75.

MacCannell, Dean. *The Tourist: A New Theory of the Leisure Class.* (London, 1989[1976]).

———. *Empty Meeting Grounds.* (London, 1992).

McCarthy, Marie. *Passing It On: The Transmission of Music in Irish Culture.* (Cork, 1999).

McCaughren, Samantha. "Riverdance Downsizing to Smaller Venues". *Irish Independent*, 4 March 2003: 13.

Mac Laughlin, Jim. "Ireland in the Global Economy: An End to a Distinct Nation?" in Ethel Crowley and Jim Mac Laughlin (eds), *Under the Belly of the Tiger: Class, Race, Identity and Culture in the Global Ireland*, (Dublin, 1997): 1–19.

McManus, N. "Craíc." Local Ireland.www.local.ie/content/41090.shtml/arts_and_culture/ general. Accessed 9 April 2004.

McNally, Frank. "New Bard Opens a Window on World for Comhaltas" *Irish Times*. 21 August 2003: 12.

Maher, D.J. *The Tortuous Path: The Course of Ireland's Entry into the EEC 1948–73.* (Dublin, 1986).

Managh, Ray. "Couple 'Terrorised' after Opposing Development." *Irish Independent*, 15 August 2002: 3.

Messenger, John C. *Inis Beag: Isle of Ireland.* (New York, 1969).

"Mission Statement". Irish Music Rights Organisation Limited. http://www.imro.ie/about/ what_we_do.shtml. Accessed 31 May 2004.

Molony, Julia. "Halfway between Love and Contempt." *Sunday Irish Independent*, 4 May 2003: 16.

Munroe, Ailie. *The Folk Music Revival in Scotland.* (London, 1984).

Nadel-Klein, Jane. "Reweaving the Fringe: Localism, Tradition, and Representation in British Ethnography." *American Ethnologist* 18, no. 3 (1991): 500–517.

"National Tourism Policy Review: A Regional Perspective". Shannon Development Submission to the Tourism Policy Review Group. (Shannon, 2003).

Ní Chonaill, Áine. "Imbalance in West Cork." *Irish Times*, 20 September 1994.

O'Connor, Barbara. "Riverdance." in Michel Peillon and Eamonn Slater (eds), *Encounters With Modern Ireland: A Sociological Chronicle 1995–1996.* (Dublin, 1998).

O'Connor, Barbara and Michael Cronin (eds), *Tourism in Ireland: A Critical Analysis.* (Cork, 1993).

Ó Dálaigh, Brian. *The Strangers Gaze: Travels in County Clare 1534–1950.* (Ennis, 1998).

Ó Gráda, Cormac. *A Rocky Road: The Irish Economy Since the 1920s.* (Manchester, 1997).

O'Hagan, J.W. *The Economy of Ireland: Policy and Performance of a Small European Country.* (London, 1995).

Ó hAllmhuráin, Gearóid. *A Pocket History of Traditional Irish Music.* (Dublin, 1998).

Oliver, Tove M. "The Consumption of Tour Routes in Cultural Landscapes." in Geoffrey I. Crouch, J.A. Mazanec, J.R. Brent Ritchie, and A.G. Woodside (eds), *Consumer Psychology of Tourism, Hospitality and Leisure*, vol. 2, (Wallingford and New York, 2001): 273–284.

Ó Súilleabháin, Micheál. 1990. "The Creative Process in Irish Traditional Dance Music." in Gerard Gillen and Harry White (eds), *Irish Musical Studies: Musicology in Ireland*, volume 1, 117–130. Dublin: Irish Academic Press.

O'Toole, Fintan. "Pretending We're on Top of the World". *The Irish Times*, 13 August 2002: 12.

Peace, Adrian. *A World of Fine Difference: The Social Architecture of a Modern Irish Village.* (Dublin, 2001).

Phillips, Scott K. "Natives and Incomers: The Symbolism of Belonging in Muker Parish, North Yorkshire." in Anthony P. Cohen (ed.), *Symbolising Boundaries: Identity and Diversity in British Cultures.* (Manchester, 1986): 141–154.

Pollock, Sheldon. "Cosmopolitanism and Vernacular in History." in Carol A. Breckenridge, Sheldon Pollock, Homi K. Bhabha, and Dipesh Chakrabarty (eds), *Cosmopolitanism.* (Durham and London, 2002): 15–53.

Pollock, Sheldon, Homi K. Bhabha, Carol A. Breckenridge, and Dipesh Chakrabarty. "Cosmopolitanisms" in Breckenridge, Carol A., Sheldon Pollock, Homi K. Bhabha, and Dipesh Chakrabarty (eds), *Cosmopolitanism.* (Durham and London, 2002): 1–14.

"Quality-of-Life Index". *The World in 2005.* (London, 2005).

Quinn, Bernadette. "The Sounds of Tourism: Exploring Music as a Tourist Resource with Particular Reference to Music Festivals." in M. Robinson, N. Evans, and P. Callaghan (eds), *Tourism and Culture, Towards the 21ˢᵗ Century: Culture as the Tourist Product.* (Sunderland, 1996): 386–396.

Racy, A.J. *Making Music in the Arab World: The Culture and Artistry of Tarab.* (Cambridge, 2003).

Rappaport, Joanne. "History and Everyday Life in The Colombian Andes". *Man* (new series) 23, no. 4 (1988): 718–739.

Rapport, Nigel. "The Body of the Village Community: Between Reverend Parkington in Wanet and Mr Beebe in *A Room with a View.*" in Nigel Rapport (ed.), *British Subjects: An Anthropology of Britain.* (Oxford, 2002): 299–319.

———. "Anthropology as Cosmopolitan Study" *Anthropology Today* 22, no. 1 (2006): 23–24.

Rapuano, Deborah L. "Becoming Irish or Becoming Irish Music? Boundary Construction in Irish Music Communities." *Journal of American and Comparative Cultures* 24, nos. 1 and 2 (2001): 103–113.

Reily, Suzel Ana. "Introduction: Brazilian Musics, Brazilian Identities." *British Journal of Ethnomusicology* 9, no. 1 (2000): 1–10.

Reiss, Scott. "Tradition and Imaginary: Irish Traditional Music and the Celtic Phenomenon." in Martin Stokes and Phillip Bohlman (eds), *Celtic Modern: Music at the Global Fringe.* (Lanham and Oxford, 2003): 145–169.

Rice, Jeff. 1995. "Profile: Sweeney's Men." *Ceolas.* www.ceolas.org/artists/Sweeneys_Men. html.

Rice, Timothy. "Time, Place, and Metaphor in Musical Experience and Ethnography". *Ethnomusicology* 47, no. 2 (2003): 151–179.

Riley, Pamela J. "Road Culture of International Long-Term Budget Travelers." *Annals of Tourism Research* 15, no. 3 (1988): 313–328.

Sassen, Saskia. "Spatialities and Temporalities of the Global: Elements of a Theorisation." in Arjun Appadurai (ed.), *Globalization*. (Durham and London, 2001).

Scheper-Hughes, Nancy. *Saints, Scholars, and Schizophrenics: Mental Illness in Rural Ireland.* (Berkeley, Los Angeles and London, 1979).

Scherzinger, Martin Rudoy. "Music, Spirit Possession and the Copyright Law: Cross-Cultural Comparisons and Strategic Speculations." *Yearbook for Traditional Music* 31 (1999): 102–125.

Schuetz, Alfred. "The Stranger: An Essay in Social Psychology." *The American Journal of Sociology* 49, no. 6 (1944): 499–507.

Schutz, Alfred. *On Phenomenology and Social Relations: Selected Writings*. Helmut R. Wagner (ed.) (Chicago, 1970).

Searle, John. *Intentionality: An Essay in the Philosophy of Mind*. (Cambridge, 1983).

Seeger, Anthony. "Ethnomusicologists, Archives, Professional Organizations, and the Shifting Ethics of Intellectual Property." *Yearbook for Traditional Music* 28 (1999): 87–105.

Shandy, Dianna J. and David V. Power. "The African Irish" *Bulletin of the General Anthropology Division* 14, no. 1 (2007): 1, 7–8.

Shields, Hugh and Paulette Gershen. "Ireland." in Timothy Rice, James Porter, and Chris Goertzen (eds), *Europe: The Garland Encyclopedia of World Music*. (London, 2000).

Siggins, Lorna. "Call for Second 'Capital' to Aid Growth in West: East Absorbing 90 Per Cent of Public Investment, Says Economist". *The Irish Times*. 16 July 2003: 2.

Sillitoe, Paul. *Managing Animals in New Guinea: Preying the Game in the Highlands*. (London and New York, 2003).

Skinner Sawyers, June. *The Complete Guide to Celtic Music: From the Highland Bagpipe and Riverdance to U2 and Enya*. (London, 2000).

Smith, Valene (ed.). *Hosts and Guests: The Anthropology of Tourism*. (Philadelphia, 1989[1977]).

Solomon, Thomas. Dueling "Landscapes: Singing Places and Identities in Highland Bolivia." *Ethnomusicology* 44, no. 2 (2000): 257–280.

Sommers Smith, Sally K. "Irish Traditional Music in a Modern World." *New Hibernia Review* 5, no. 2 (2001): 111–125.

Stokes, Martin. "Music, Travel, and Tourism: An Afterward." *The World of Music* 41, no. 3 (1999): 141–155.

Strathern, Marilyn. *Kinship at the Core: An Anthropology of Elmdon, a Village in North-West Essex in the Nineteen-Sixties*. (Cambridge, 1981).

Tansey, Seamus. 1999. "Irish Traditional Music—The Melody of Ireland's Soul; Its Evolution from the Environment, Land and People." in Fintan Vallely, Hammy Hamilton, Eithne Vallely, and Liz Doherty (eds), *Crosbhealach An Cheoil: The Crossroads Conference 1996*. (Dublin, 1996): 211–213.

Tansey, Webster, Stewart and Company, Economic Consultants. "Executive Summary." in *The Impact of Tourism on the Irish Economy*. (Dublin, 2002).

Taylor, Timothy D. "Afterward: Gaelicer Than Thou." in Martin Stokes and Phillip V. Bohlman (eds), *Celtic Modern: Music at the Global Fringe*. (Oxford, 2003): 275–284.

Tonkin, Elizabeth. *Narrating Our Pasts: The Social Construction of Oral History*. (Cambridge, 1992).

Toner, P.G. "Melody and the Musical Articulation of Identities." *Yearbook for Traditional Music* 35 (2003): 69–95.

Trilling, Lionel. *Sincerity and Authenticity*. (Cambridge, Massachusetts and London, 1972).

Tsing, Anna. "The Global Situation." in Jonathan X.Inda and Renato Rosaldo (eds), *The Anthropology of Globalization: A Reader*, 2nd ed., (Malden, 2008).

Tucker, Hazel. "The Ideal Village: Interactions Through Tourism in Central Anatolia." in Simone Abram, Jacqueline Waldren, and Donald V.L. Macleod (eds), *Tourists and Tourism: Identifying with People and Places*. (Oxford, 1997): 107–128.

Turner, Victor. "Dewey, Dilthey, and Drama: An Essay in the Anthropology of Experience." in Victor W. Turner and Edward M. Bruner (eds), *The Anthropology of Experience*. (Chicago, 1986).

———. *The Anthropology of Performance*. (New York, 1992(1987)).

Uriely, Natan. "'Travelling Workers' and 'Working Tourists': Variations across the Interaction between Work and Tourism." *International Journal of Tourism Research*, 3 (2001): 1–8.

Urry, John. "Tourism, Europe, and Identity." in Sharon Bohn Gmelch (ed.), *Tourism and Tourists: A Reader*. (Long Grove, 2004): 433–442.

Vaillant, Emery. "Strawboys in West Clare." *Dal gCais* 7 (1984): 77–83

Vallely, Fintan. "Revival." in Fintan Vallely (ed.), *The Companion to Irish Traditional Music*. (Cork, 1999).

"Varieties of Irishness". *Irish Times*. 6 August 2002: 13.

Vogt, Jay W. "Wandering: Youth and Travel Behavior." *Annals of Tourism Research* 4, no. 1 (1976): 25–41.

Waldren, Jacqueline. *Insiders and Outsiders: Paradise and Reality in Mallorca*. (New York and Oxford, 1996).

———. "We are not Tourists – We Live Here." in Simone Abram, Jacqueline Waldren and Donald V.L. MacLeod (eds), *Tourists and Tourism: Identifying with People and Places*. (Oxford, 1997).

Walvin, James. *Beside the Seaside: A Social History of the Popular Seaside Holiday*. (London, 1978).

Wang, Ning. *Tourism and Modernity: A Sociological Analysis*. (Oxford, 2000).

Warner, Michael. "Publics and Counterpublics." *Public Culture* 14, no. 1 (2002): 49–90.

Werbner, Pnina. "Introduction." in Pnina Werbner (ed.), *Anthropology and the New Cosmopolitanism*. (New York, 2008): 1–32.

White, Harry. *The Keeper's Recital: Music and Cultural History in Ireland, 1770–1970*. (Cork, 1998).

Williams, Sean. "Irish Music and the Experience of Nostalgia in Japan." *Journal of the Society for Asian Music* 37, no. 1: 101–119.

Wilson, Thomas M. "From Clare to the Common Market: Perspectives in Irish Ethnography." *Anthropological Quarterly* 57 (1984): 1–15.

Wilson, Thomas and Hastings Donnan. *The Anthropology of Ireland*. (New York, 2006).

Winters, Dennis C. *The Piper's Chair No. 2: A Collection of Tunes, Songs and Folklore from Micho Russell*. Cottekill. (New York, 1997[1986]).

———. *Doolin's Micho Russell: A Portrait of the Whistler from Clare; His Brothers, Packie and Gussie; and Their Village*. (New York, 1990).

Wolf, Eric R. *Europe and the People Without History*. (Berkeley, Los Angeles and London, 1997[1982]).

Woods, Anthony. "The Myth of the Celtic Tiger." *Clare County Express*. September 2002: 15.

Wulff, Helena. *Dancing at the Crossroads: Memory and Mobility in Ireland.* (New York and Oxford, 2008).

————. "Steps on Screen: Technoscapes, Visualization and Globalization in Dance." in Christina Garsten and Helena Wulff (eds), *New Technologies at Work: People, Screens and Social Virtuality.* (Oxford, 2003): 187–204.

www.comhaltas-jp.com. The official CCE Tokyo Branch website with links to the active pub session scene in Japan.

www.lahinchgolf.com. The website for the Lahinch golf course established in 1892.

Index